D1391429

BLUNDELL AND DOBRY'S

PLANNING APPEALS
AND
INQUIRIES

AUSTRALIA
The Law Book Company Ltd.
Sydney : Brisbane : Melbourne : Perth

CANADA
The Carswell Company Ltd.
Agincourt, Ontario

INDIA
H.M. Tripathi Private Ltd.
Bombay
and
Eastern Law House Private Ltd.
Calcutta and Delhi

M.P.P. House
Bangalore
and
Universal Book Traders
New Delhi

ISRAEL
Steimatzky's Agency Ltd.
Jerusalem : Tel Aviv : Haifa

PAKISTAN
Pakistan Law House
Karachi

BLUNDELL AND DOBRY'S

PLANNING APPEALS
AND
INQUIRIES

FOURTH EDITION

By

ROBERT CARNWATH Q.C., M.A., LL.B.

GARRY HART LL.B., *solicitor*

ANNE WILLIAMS B.A., M.Phil., *Barrister*

CONSULTING EDITOR

His Honour

JUDGE GEORGE DOBRY Q.C., M.A., C.B.E.

LONDON
SWEET & MAXWELL
1990

First Edition   1962 By Lionel A. Blundell and George Dobry
Second Edition 1970 By Paul L. Rose and Michael Barnes
Third Edition   1982 By Robert Carnwath
Fourth Edition 1990 By Robert Carnwath, Judge George Dobry,
                           Garry Hart and Anne Williams

Published by
Sweet & Maxwell Limited of
183 Marsh Wall, London, E14 9FT
Computerset by
LBJ Enterprises Ltd., Chilcompton, Somerset
Printed in Great Britain by
Butler & Tanner Ltd.

British Library Cataloguing in Publication Data
Carnwath, Robert, Judge George Dobry, Hart, Garry,
   Williams, Anne
   Blundell and Dobry: planning appeals and
   inquiries.–4th ed.
   1. England. Environment planning. Decisions of local
   authorities. Appeals
   I. Title II. Blundell, Lionel A. (Lionel Alleyne).
   Blundell and Dobry's planning appeals and inquiries 711.1

   ISBN 0–421–39070–0

PREFACE

The first edition of this practice guide was written by me nearly 30 years ago. This fourth edition has the same objectives as the previous. It provides an up-to-date guide for those who practise regularly in the field of Town and Country Planning, including all planning authorities; and above all for all others who are not familiar with planning procedures, whether appellants or local objectors.

Some of the original text survived, because the system is basically the same. Yet there are far-reaching changes in procedures brought about by legislation—including, for example, the 1988 Inquiry Procedure Rules, and from changes in practice; much of it is derived from the Development Control Review Report of 1975.

In 1962 there was simply a procedure for holding a local public inquiry on an appeal to the Minister. Now there is complex sub-division into transferred appeals, and appeals which are not transferred and appeals "recovered" by the Secretary of State; and different types of Inquiries: (a) *standard* (b) *major* and, most importantly, (c) *informal hearings* (see para. 2.28). All these have been streamlined (see *e.g.* para. 2.30) and have a tight timetable. And there are also appeals in *writing* with their own code. In Appeals determined by the Secretary of State there are 12 procedural steps including provisions for service of outline statements by the local planning authority, the applicant and 'other persons'; and a "statement of relevant matters" by the Secretary of State defining issues of importance to him. All this resembles in spirit the modern approach to pre-trial procedures, sometimes referred to as the "cards on the table" principle. Most importantly, proofs of evidence must now be exchanged: this is similar to the modern practice in the High Court—(R.S.C. Order 38 R. (1)A). And where there are rules galore a welcome feature of this book is advice on *Procedural Pitfalls* see para. 2.20.

This forward is not intended as a review or synopsis of this new edition of the book; and I will say no more about it save to commend it to its old and new friends. At the same time I cannot resist looking forward to the future, if not as far ahead as the next 30 years. I have two observations to offer. First I feel that the practitioner would be misled if he placed too great a reliance on the presumption in favour of development (see para. 2.8 which corresponds to para. 23 of the 2nd Edition). This principle was first introduced into planning policy in 1948 and repeated in innumerable circulars, but never truly observed. When proceeding to an appeal the best policy is to present your case as best you can for or against development unencumbered by the chains of burden of proof; and to rely on what should be a truly judicial approach by the Inspector. The Inspectorate provided that 30 years ago, and can—and probably does—provide it now. Anyhow, the development of judicial review—secures a sanction, similar to appeals to the Court of Appeal in ordinary litigation. And there is no fundamental objection to a judicial approach in matters which are within the constraints of policy, for policy should be treated as a *fact* to be found and applied to the circumstances of the case.

My other point for the future is mundane. Parties in Court proceedings now use "skeleton arguments", a name for abbreviated arguments. It would make the task of Inspectors much easier in report writing if this is provided at Inquiries. Providing the Inspector with a skeleton of issues and submissions must be as useful at Inquiries as it is in Court.

This foreword is no place for dealing with the commendable achievements of the Inspectorate in reducing planning delays over the last decade; it is appropriate to mention that the new procedures dealt with by this book have made a contribution.

George Dobry

London, May 1990

NOTE

Where reference is made to the Town and Country Planning Acts 1990, the relevant section number of the 1971 Act is retained in square brackets for ease of use.

CONTENTS

APPENDICES' TABLE OF CONTENTS

Appendices A.2 to A.4, B.1 to B.8 and D.1 to D.3 are reproduced with the kind permission of Her Majesty's Stationary Office.

TABLE OF CASES

TABLE OF STATUTORY INSTRUMENTS

CHAPTER 1

INTRODUCTION

1.1. Scope of this book

This book is intended to provide a practice guide to the procedure and the method of presenting a case at the main types of planning inquiry. It is principally concerned with the stage which begins after a decision has been made to appeal to the Secretary of State or the matter has otherwise been taken out of the hands of the local planning authority. Accordingly, the earlier procedures before the local planning authority will only be dealt with so far as necessary to set the context. Similarly the general law of Town and Country Planning is not dealt with in this book and will have to be ascertained from other sources. The most comprehensive, up to date source is the *Encyclopedia of Planning Law and Practice*. A chapter has been included dealing with planning agreements which have become increasingly relevant in the context of planning appeals.

1.2. Recent changes in planning procedure

The most important change to take place recently has been the completely revised set of procedures for planning inquiries prescribed by the Town and Country Planning (Inquiries Procedure) Rules 1988.[1] The purpose of these changes is to provide for greater exchange of information between the parties about their cases before the inquiry takes place. A tight timetable for such exchange is laid down in the Rules which are fixed forward from the date of notification that an inquiry is to be held, *i.e.* the "relevant date", and not backward from the date of the inquiry.

1.3. Changes in practice

The Local Government (Access to Information) Act 1985 has provided those involved in the planning process with greater public access to local authority meetings, reports and documents. Further, in London boroughs and metropolitan districts a new system of development plans—unitary development plans—has been introduced. Unitary development plans will be the sole development plans for the areas to which they relate. Local planning authorities are also empowered to designate simplified planning zones, *i.e.*, areas in which development control does not apply as rigidly. Development control guidance for local planning authorities is contained in Government Circulars and more recently Planning Policy Guidance Notes. A Recent Consultation Paper entitled *Efficient Planning* sets out a number of proposals including charging fees for planning appeals. However, these proposals have not yet been implemented by legislation. The 1990 Consolidation Acts received the Royal Assent on May 24, 1990. Section numbers from the 1971 Act and other relevant Acts are retained in brackets for ease of reference.

---

[1] S.I. 1988 No. 944; see Appendix D.

1.4. Statutory sources and abbreviations

The following are the principal statutory sources for the law considered in this book and the abbreviations which will be used.

Acts of Parliament

Town and Country Planning Act 1971	1971 Act
Town and Country Planning (Amendment) Act 1972	1972 Act
Local Government Act 1972	Local Government Act 1972
Local Government, Planning and Land Act 1980	1980 Act
Local Government and Planning (Amendment) Act 1981	1981 Act
Housing and Planning Act 1986	1986 Act
Town and Country Planning Act 1990	1990 Act
Planning (Listed Buildings and Conservation Areas) Act 1990	1990 Listed Buildings Act
Planning (Hazardous Substances) Act 1990	1990 Hazardous Substances Act
Planning (Consequential Provisions) Act 1990	1990 Consequential Provisions Act

Statutory Instruments

Town and Country Planning (Tree Preservation Order) Regulations 1969 (S.I. 1969 No. 17, as amended by S.I.s 1975 No. 148, 1981 No. 14)	The Tree Preservation Order Regulations
Town and Country Planning General Regulations 1976 (S.I. 1976 No. 1419)	The General Regulations
Town and Country Planning (Fees for Applications and Deemed Applications) Regulations 1981 (S.I. 1981 No. 369, as amended by S.I.s 1982 No. 716, 1983 No. 1674, and S.I. 1989 No. 193)	The Fees Regulations
Town and Country Planning (Determination of Appeals by Appointed Persons) (Prescribed Classes) Regulations 1981 (S.I. 1981 No. 804, as amended by S.I. 1986 No. 623).	Determination Rules
Town and Country Planning (Enforcement Notices and Appeals) Regulations 1981 (S.I. 1981 No. 1742)	The Enforcement Notices Regulations
Town and Country Planning (Enforcement) (Inquiries Procedure) Rules 1981 (S.I. 1981 No. 1743)	The Enforcement Inquiries Procedure Rules
Planning (Listed Buildings and Conservation Areas) Regulations 1990 (S.I. 1990 No. 1519).	The Listed Building Regulations
Town and Country Planning (Use Classes) Order 1987 (S.I. 1987 No. 764)	The Use Classes Order

Town and Country Planning (Inquiries Procedure) Rules 1988 (S.I. 1988 No. 944)	The Secretary of State's Rules
Town and Country Planning (Determination by Inspectors) (Inquiries Procedure) Rules 1988 (S.I. 1988 No. 945)	The Inspector's Rules
Town and Country Planning General Development Order 1988 (S.I. 1988 No. 1813, as amended by S.I. 1989 No. 603 and S.I. 1989 No. 1590).	G.D.O.
Town and Country Planning (Control of Advertisements) Regulations 1989 (S.I. 1989 No. 670)	The Advertisement Regulations

References to "the Secretary of State" are to the Secretary of State for the Environment in respect of England and the Secretary of State for Wales in respect of Wales. References to "The Commission" are to the Historic Buildings and Monuments Commission for England.

Frequent reference will be made to Departmental guidance in the form of Circulars, Development Control Policy Notes, and Planning Policy Guidance Notes.

Where reference is made to the numbers of Departmental Circulars, for reasons of space only the Department of the Environment numbering for England is given, although comparable Circulars have been issued in the case of Wales by the Welsh Office since the transfer of functions to the Secretary of State for Wales on April 1, 1965.

It should be noted that such Circulars, although of considerable practical utility, have no statutory force and are not binding on inspectors or on the Secretary of State. The Secretary of State is in law entitled to change his policy without informing anyone,[2] but he must give adequate reasons for departing from policy.[3]

In view of the importance of Departmental guidance in relation to procedure and practices, we have included extensive reference to Circulars and Guidance Notes, as well as to relevant statutory instruments. It must, however, be borne in mind that these are subject to frequent change. The *Encyclopedia of Planning Law and Practice* provides the best up-to-date source.

---

[2] See *Lavender (H) & Son* v. *Minister of Housing and Local Government* [1970] 1 W.L.R. 1231; but see *Bromley L.B.C.* v. *Secretary of State for the Environment and Cope* [1990] J.P.L. 53.

[3] See *Save Britain's Heritage* v. *Secretary of State for the Environment, The Times,* April 4, 1990.

CHAPTER 2

PLANNING APPEALS

A. INTRODUCTORY

2.1. Appeal under section 79 and section 77 "call-in"

Section 79 of the 1990 Act [36/71] provides for appeals to the Secretary of State against a refusal, or grant subject to conditions, of planning permission whereby the applicant is aggrieved. The machinery of section 79 is made applicable to appeals against a refusal by the local planning authority of, or the imposition of conditions on, (a) any consent, agreement or approval required by a planning condition (for example, "reserved matters" under an outline permission), or (b) any approval required under a development order.[1] It also applies to appeals in default of a decision by the local planning authority.[2] The Secretary of State also has power to direct that an application is referred to him instead of being dealt with by the planning authority (s.77 [35/71]). Although not strictly on "appeal" (it is normally referred to as a "call-in"), the same procedures generally apply.

2.2. No appeal against grant of permission

The Planning Acts provide no statutory remedy for those aggrieved by the grant of permission (for example, neighbours, local amenity groups etc.). Indeed the statutory rights of such third parties, even to notification of applications and appeals, are very limited.[3] In practice most authorities make administrative arrangements for informing individuals or groups likely to have a special interest in planning proposals, and give them an opportunity to make representations before a decision is made. In the case of particularly controversial proposals of more than local significance, local groups (perhaps with the assistance of a local M.P.) may be instrumental in having the application "called-in" by the Secretary of State. It is also worth bearing in mind that the authority's decision is not binding until a notice of permission is actually issued. A sustained campaign may help to achieve a change of view, particularly when standing orders require a decision to go through more than one stage (for example, council ratification of a committee decision). Once a permission is issued the only courses of action open to aggrieved third parties are:

(1) *Judicial review* If there has been some procedural defect or other legal error, the potential grounds are in effect the same as those for challenging a decision of the Secretary of State (see paragraph 2.52) but examples of successful challenge to local authority permission are very rare.[4] If judicial review is

---

[1] See the 1990 Act, s.78 [36(1)/71].

[2] *Ibid.* ss.78, 79.

[3] See *R. v. Secretary of State for the Environment, ex p. Kent*, [1990] J.P.L. 53.

[4] See, *e.g. R. v. Great Yarmouth Borough Council, ex p. Botton Brothers Arcades* [1988] J.P.L. 18, where a permission was quashed because of a failure to consult local interest groups on a major change of policy approach.

contemplated, it is essential that it is commenced promptly since an application may be struck out for unjustified delay even within the normal three month period under the rules.[5] The making of the application will not prevent the implementation of the permission, unless a stay is specifically applied for (under Order 53, rule 3(10) of the Rules of the Supreme Court) and a stay will not normally be granted except on an undertaking to pay any damages resulting if the application is unsuccessful.

(2) *Revocation Order* In exceptional circumstances the Secretary of State or even the authority (for example, after a change of political control) might be persuaded to make an order under section 97 [45/71] revoking or modifying a permission (see Chapter 3, *post*). This is very rare in view of the compensation involved.

(3) *Local Ombudsman* If there has been a procedural failure or maladministration of some kind in the process leading to the issue of the permission, a complaint may be made to the Commissioner for Local Administration (see Chapter 7, *post*). This will not result in revocation of the permission, but may in special cases lead to a recommendation for monetary compensation.

B. PRELIMINARY CONSIDERATIONS

2.3. Refusals and deemed refusals

By far the largest category of appeals with which this book is concerned comprises appeals against a refusal or "deemed refusal" of planning permission by a local planning authority. The G.D.O. requires the authority to give notice of their decision within eight weeks of the receipt of a valid and complete application (article 23); and, if their decision is unfavourable, to state such reasons (article 25). The notice must also give details of any direction or adverse view given by a Government department, or any direction by the local highway authority or the county planning authority. The notice will explain the applicant's right of appeal. This time limit may be extended by agreement in writing. Section 79 of the 1990 Act [36/71] provides the procedure for appeal to the Secretary of State against a refusal of planning permission while section 78 [37/71] enables an applicant to take advantage of the same procedure where the authority have failed to give notice of their decision within the eight week period or such extended period as may have been agreed. This is usually referred to as an appeal against a "deemed refusal." An application for planning permission is treated as "received" when the authority has received a complete application together with any certificate and any fee

---

[5] See R.S.C., Ord. 53, r. 4(1): *R.* v. *Stratford-on-Avon District Council, ex p. Jackson* [1985] 1 W.L.R. 1319, C.A.

required.[6] The authority are required to send a form of acknowledgment of the application stating the date on which it was received (*ibid.*). The time for appeal can normally be taken as running from that date.

2.4. Grounds of refusal

The reasons given by the authority for refusing the application or, as the case may be, for imposing conditions, are the starting point for considering whether to appeal. They should indicate whether there is some objection in principle to the development or whether it is based purely on technical considerations (for example, access or drainage). In the latter case it is possible that the objection may be overcome by further consultations, whereas in the former it is likely that an appeal will present the only chance of a satisfactory resolution. If the refusal is based on some adopted policy, the opportunity should be taken of checking the status of the policy document (for example, is it statutory or non-statutory?) and ascertaining its precise effect (see below). For example, there may be stated exceptions to the policy, of which advantage can be taken. In the case of a deemed refusal, of course no such formal guidance as to the attitude of the planning authority will be available. However, it should be possible to obtain from the planning department some informal indication as to the main points of concern. Advantage should be taken of the Local Government (Access to Information) Act 1985 to obtain copies of relevant officers' reports and committee minutes.

2.5. The development plan

Section 70 of the 1990 Act [29(1)/71], which is applied to appeal decisions by section 79 [36(5)/71], requires the Secretary of State or as the case may be the inspector, when deciding an appeal, to "have regard to the provisions of the development plan, so far as material to the application, and to any other material considerations. . . . "

An important first step, therefore, when considering an appeal, is to find the development plan and discover whether it contains anything of relevance to the particular appeal. This is not always as easy as might be thought. Statutory development plans may take a number of different forms and may vary considerably in their degree of utility or contemporary relevance.

The present system of development plans derives from changes made by the 1968 Act and now embodied in Part II of the 1990 Act. A valuable guide to the workings of the system will be found in Circular 22/84.[7] Broadly, the scheme is that the statutory development plan for each area should consist of a "structure plan" setting out the general

---

[6] G.D.O., art. 10(2).

[7] *Memorandum on Structure and Local Plans: The Town and Country Planning Act 1971: Part II (as amended by the Town and Country Planning (Amendment) Act 1972, The Local Government Act 1972, and the Local Government, Planning and Land Act 1980)* and see PPG 15, *Regional Planning Guidance, Structure Plans and the Content of Development Plans.*

policy framework, together with a number of "local plans" dealing in more detail with a particular locality or subject-matter. The structure plan will normally be prepared by the county planning authority and is subject to approval by the Secretary of State following an "examination in public" (E.I.P.). In principle it should be kept up to date by a regular process of monitoring and review. Local plans will be prepared by county or district planning authorities to provide policies for particular districts ("district plans") or designate areas for comprehensive development ("action area plans"). Local plans will not normally be considered by the Secretary of State, but will be approved by the local planning authority following an inquiry before an inspector appointed by the Secretary of State.

Unless and until there is both a structure plan and a local plan formally approved for a particular area, the "old-style" development plan will remain in force and will continue to be part of the statutory development plan. However, its relevance to any current planning issue is likely to be small. In practice more importance is likely to be attached to the structure and local plans even before they have been formally adopted. The significance of such plans in the context of planning appeals will increase the further they have proceeded on the path towards formal adoption. This is explained in an important passage in the Memorandum which is often cited at inquiries and deserves quotation in full:

> "The absence of a local plan or relevant proposals in a local plan, or the fact that a local plan is in the offing or that there are proposals for alteration or repeal or replacement of a structure plan or a local plan, is not, in itself, a reason for refusing planning permission. A structure plan, a local plan and proposals for the alteration, repeal or replacement of such plans may be taken into account as a material consideration for development control purposes while going through the statutory procedures leading to approval or adoption. The weight to be accorded to such a plan or to such proposals will increase as successive stages are reached in the statutory procedures. The relevant stages for this purpose are all the subject of publicity or advertisement by the local planning authority under the 1971 Act or the Regulations. These stages are:
> (a) the matters publicised as proposed to be included in the plan . . .
> (b) the plan or proposals for alteration as submitted or placed on deposit . . .
> (c) the plan or proposals for alteration as proposed to be modified following an examination in public or local inquiry (if held) . . .
> (d) the plan or proposals for alteration as proposed to be adopted in the case of a local plan."[8]

PPG 12, *Local Plans* emphasises the additional weight to be given to up to date plans:

---

[8] Circ. 22/84, para. 1.12.

"8. In determining planning appeals the Secretaries of State, like the local planning authority, are required by the Act to have regard to the provisions of the development plan, and to any other material considerations. An up to date local plan which is consistent with national and regional policies and with the relevant provisions of the structure plan will therefore carry considerable weight. Where there is such a plan, together with properly substantiated reasons for the local authority's decision, the Secretaries of State and their Inspectors will be guided by it in dealing with planning appeals, particularly where the proposal in question raises purely local considerations."[9]

Conversely, the importance of even an approved plan will diminish as time elapses and circumstances change:

"14. Many development plans were approved several years ago, often several years after they had been prepared, and were based on even earlier information. The policies which they contain, and the assumptions on which they were based, may therefore be out of date and not well related to today's conditions. They cannot be adapted rapidly to changing conditions, and they cannot be expected to anticipate every need or opportunity for economic development that may arise. They should not be regarded as overriding other material considerations, especially where the plan does not deal adequately with new types of development or is no longer relevant to today's needs and conditions—particularly the need to encourage employment and to provide the right conditions for economic growth. However, there is a reciprocal point: where the plan is up to date and relevant to the particular proposal, it follows that the plan should normally be given considerable weight in the decision and strong contrary planning grounds will have to be demonstrated to justify a proposal which conflicts with it."[10]

The Local Government Act 1985 abolished the Greater London Council and Metropolitan County Councils. The Act provides for the replacement in their areas of the existing structure and local development plans by "unitary development plans." So far the Act has been brought into force in the West Midlands, Merseyside, Tyne and Wear, West Yorkshire, Greater London and Dudley.[11]

The only way to find out the up to date position in any area is to consult the planning department of the local authority in question.

---

[9] PPG 1, para. 14.

[10] PPG 1, para. 14.

[11] Unitary Development Plans (West Midlands) (Appointed Day) Order 1988 (S.I. 1988 No. 140); Unitary Development Plans (Merseyside) (Appointed Day) Order 1988 (S.I. 1988 No. 1179); Unitary Development Plans (Tyne and Wear) (Appointed Day) Order 1989 (S.I. 1989 No. 637); Unitary Development Plans (West Yorkshire) (Appointed Day) Order 1989 (S.I. 1989 No. 1065); Unitary Development Plans (Greater London and Dudley) (Appointed Day) Order 1989 (S.I. 1989 No. 1089).

Where there is any doubt about the status of a particular plan it is advisable to check the relevant minutes of the planning committee. It may be important, for example, to discover whether a draft plan has actually been adopted as an interim policy for development control purposes pending formal approval, or whether it has merely been approved for consultation. In the latter case its relevance in deciding any planning application will be limited.

The Government has published a White Paper on the *Future of Development Plans*. The document sets out proposals for a new system including wider coverage of regional guidance and streamlining of procedures for preparing and adopting development plans. The new system will require legislation but PPG 15 advises upon work which can be undertaken to implement changes proposed in the White Paper without the need for legislation.

2.6. Non-statutory policies and statements

It is not uncommon for authorities to adopt non–statutory policies to guide development. Such policies are of doubtful status in law[12] and are likely to be given little weight on appeal. As stated in the Memorandum:

> "1.13. Any plan containing proposals for the development and other use of land which is not included in the development plan scheme as a local plan, or as proposals for the alteration of a local plan, and which has not been subject to any of the stages in the statutory procedures identified above as giving weight to plan proposals can have little weight for development control purposes. It cannot be treated as an emerging local plan. Where there is a need to devote resources to the preparation of proposals for the use of land, these should be settled in the statutory plan."[13]

More weight is likely to be given to non-statutory statements where they relate to detailed matters, such as design standards, which are not normally suitable for inclusion in a plan:

> "1.14. There is, however, a continuing role for planning guidance which supplements the policies and proposals contained in structure and local plans. This may include, for example, practice notes for development control requirements, development briefs and detailed or sketch layouts for such developments as housing or open space. These documents should be published separately from the policies and proposals of the statutory development plan for the area and kept publicly available. They should be consistent with the structure plan and any local plan for the area.

---

[12] See *Great Portland Estates* v. *Westminster City Council* [1985] A.C. 661; [1985] J.P.L. 108, where a local plan policy providing for supplementary informal guidance as to acceptable forms of office development was held unlawful.

[13] Circ. 22/84, para. 1.13.

1.15. Supplementary planning guidance may be taken into account by the Secretary of State as a material consideration in matters which come to him for decision. The weight to be accorded to it will increase when it has been prepared in consultation with the public and has been made the subject of a council resolution. Where, however, unresolved planning issues are identified the local planning authority should reconsider the need for a local plan or proposals to alter a local plan. . . . The statutory process secures the rights of individuals and bodies to be involved in plan preparation; provides for the resolution of any controversy and for the co-ordination of the views of the planning authorities, statutory undertakers and Government departments; and secures general conformity with the structure plan."[14]

2.7. Circulars and policy notes

Of equal importance to the statutory development plan system in the determination of appeals, is the large body of Policy Notes, circulars and most recently Planning Policy Guidance Notes issued by the Department of the Environment. These have no formal statutory status, and in theory neither local authorities nor inspectors are bound by them. However, in practice they form the major source of guidance for inspectors on departmental practice and policy and since the inspector is acting in the name of the Secretary of State, any relevant circular or Planning Policy Guidance Note will be taken into account by him. Indeed a failure to do so may be a ground for quashing his decision[15]; and a failure by the authority to follow the advice in a relevant circular may be a ground for awarding costs against it (see paragraph 2.49 below). It is essential, therefore, for anyone involved in a planning appeal to have knowledge of relevant circulars and Planning Policy Guidance Notes. Draft circulars are usually issued for consultation in advance of formal adoption, but they have no status and inspectors will generally refuse to allow a draft circular to be cited. Circulars and Planning Policy Guidance Notes may relate to matters of general policy, to specific categories of development, or to matters of procedure and practice. Some of the more important—in the context of planning appeals—are listed in Appendix A.

2.8. The presumption in favour of development

From the point of view of general policy, the most important current advice is contained in PPG1, *General Policy and Principles*. This explains the general presumption in favour of development in words which are quoted regularly at inquiries:

"The planning system fails in its function whenever it prevents, inhibits or delays development which can reasonably be permit-

---

[14] Circ. 22/84, paras. 1.14, 1.15.
[15] See *Pye (J.A.) (Oxford) Estates* v. *West Oxfordshire District Council and the Secretary of State for the Environment* [1982] J.P.L. 577.

ted. There is always a presumption in favour of allowing applications for development, having regard to all material considerations, unless that development would cause demonstrable harm to interests of acknowledged importance. Except in the case of inappropriate development in the Green Belt the developer is not required to prove the case for the development he proposes to carry out; if the planning authority consider it necessary to refuse permission, the onus is on them to demonstrate clearly why the development cannot be permitted."[16]

Although the presumption has in effect acquired the status of law,[17] it is not always so clear what it means in practice. It is sometimes used to justify the proposition that even an approved policy is not by itself sufficient to justify refusal. Some of the Circulars appear to support this view, for example:

". . . planning applications for industry, as for all types of proposed development, should always be considered on their merits having regard to the development plan and other material considerations. In the modern economy, it is not always possible to anticipate in the development plan all the needs and opportunities which may arise. Thus where a developer applies for permission for a development which is contrary to the policies and proposals of an approved development plan this does not, in itself, justify a refusal of permission (although there will be a general presumption against inappropriate development where losses of countryside, Green Belt and agricultural land are at issue). While the decision will obviously be more difficult than in cases which conform to development plan policies, the onus nevertheless remains with the planning authority to examine the issues raised by each specific application and where necessary to demonstrate that a particular proposal is unacceptable on specific planning grounds . . . "[18]

". . . A refusal of planning permission which is based solely on development plan provisions may in some circumstances be regarded as unreasonable, for example where it is clear that no proper consideration has been given to the merits of the application before the planning authority, or the development plan was clearly out of date and changed circumstances or other material considerations were not taken into account."[19]

Such a proposition, however, is too wide and the words of the Circular are rarely applied literally so as to require authorities to provide

---

[16] PPG 1, para. 15.
[17] See *Thornville Properties* v. *Secretary of State for the Environment and Stafford Borough Council* [1981] J.P.L. 116.
[18] Circ. 16/84, *Industrial Development*, para. 9.
[19] Circ. 2/87, *Awards of Costs Incurred in Planning and Compulsory Purchase Order Proceedings*, para. 8.

independent justification for a policy refusal. An approved up to date policy restricting development is likely to be regarded by inspectors as an "interest of acknowledged importance" sufficient in itself to justify refusal. Indeed, it would nullify the purpose of the development plan system if the approved policies were open for review on every section 79 [36/71] appeal.

The presumption in favour of development is therefore important, but should not be overstated. The appellant must overcome any serious objections—aesthetic, technical and of policy; but, if he can do so, he does not have to establish *need*. He is entitled to a permission whether or not he can make out a positive case in favour. Furthermore, it may not be enough for the authority to rely on a literalistic application of the words of a policy if the latter's objectives would not be harmed.

2.9. Conflicts between plans and policies

Conflicts between national and local policies should be minimised by the procedure, on the one hand for approval of structure plans by the Secretary of State, and on the other for certification (by county planning authorities) of local plans as in "general conformity with the structure plan." Not infrequently, however, one will find conflicting policies or criteria in different documents or similar policies expressed in more or less restrictive terms. There is no clear guidance as to how these conflicts are likely to be resolved. The Act itself contains rules for reconciling conflicts between statutory plans: the effect of these is summarised as follows:

> "Within the provisions in the development plan, if there is a conflict:
> (a) a structure plan prevails over the old development plan (except in certain cases of compensation for compulsory purchase);
> (b) a local plan prevails over the old development plan . . .
> (c) a local plan prevails over the structure plan;
> (d) the more recently adopted or approved local plan prevails over another local plan."[20]

Any conflict between the written statement of a plan and the diagram or proposal map is resolved in favour of the written statement.[21]

This offers a reliable general guide. However, the apparent preference given to the most recent local plan can be misleading. Since no plan is legally binding as such, it is always open to an inspector to prefer the guidance in the structure plan, which will have the approval of the Secretary of State. Furthermore, the local planning authority is itself under a continuing duty in its development control functions (notwithstanding anything in its local plan) "to seek the achievement of the general objectives of the structure plan for the time being in force for their area."[22]

---

[20] Circ. 22/84, para. 1.8.

[21] *Ibid*. paras. 2.13, 3.30.

[22] 1990 Act, Sched. 1, para. 7 [Local Government, Planning and Land Act 1980, s.86(3)].

There is no guidance as to the reconciliation of conflicts between development plan policies and the guidance in Planning Policy Guidance Notes and Circulars. In theory, the development plan—as a statutory document—should have preference. In practice, that approach is not followed and much will depend on the nature of the advice and the chronology. In most cases a restrictive provision in a local plan is unlikely to be given much weight in the face of a later circular counselling a more liberal approach. On the other hand, if such a restrictive local policy could be shown to be based on special local factors justifying an exception to the national approach, it may well override the Circular.[23]

One of the hazards of the modern planning appeal is the proliferation of policy "guidance" from different sources and in different terms. Much of the art of the planning advocate lies in distilling from these sources a single coherent and defensible policy framework within which a decision favourable to his client can be made.

2.10. Decision whether to appeal

The decision whether to appeal, and as to the timing of an appeal, involves difficult questions of judgement. It is natural for an applicant, who feels frustrated by the apparent intransigence of the local planning committee, to assume that the justice of his cause will automatically shine through before a higher tribunal. However, it is worth bearing the following points in mind:

(1) On questions of judgement, inspectors are as prone to individual opinions as other people. Whilst it may be possible to ascertain the climate of opinion in a local planning committee, for example by talking to members or officers, the identity of the inspector will not be known until shortly before the appeal and even then there is no opportunity for "testing the ground" (other than by the generally fruitless exercise of examining previous decisions in which the inspector has been involved).

(2) When the application is before the local planning authority, there is generally an opportunity to discuss points of detail with the officers and to make suitable amendments to the plans before they go to committee. There is no equivalent opportunity to discuss matters on an informal basis with the inspector before the hearing, and the opportunity to make detailed amendments at that stage is limited.

(3) It must be remembered that the inspector or the Secretary of State is entitled to look at the matter afresh and is not bound by concessions which may have been offered by the local planning authority. For example, the authority may have refused a particular application but indicated that a compromise proposal would be favourably considered. If an appeal is pursued, there is always a risk that the inspector (or the Secretary of State) will not only dismiss the appeal, but also make it clear that even the compromise is objectionable.

---

[23] *Camden London Borough Council* v. *Secretary of State for the Environment* [1989] P.L.R. 79; but see *Charnwood Borough Council* v. *Secretary of State for the Environment* [1990] E.G.C.S. 26.

(4) On an appeal, particularly if there is a public inquiry, there is generally a greater opportunity for public involvement. This introduces a further element of unpredictability into the procedure, since, while the authority and the appellant are required to make their case known in advance of the inquiry, there is normally no such constraint on members of the public.

2.11. Timing of appeal

Although the authority are required to issue their decision within eight weeks, this is not a mandatory requirement. It carries no penalties for non-compliance and a decision issued outside this time limit is not void. In practice many applications are not decided within the statutory time limit. Because of the delay associated with an appeal, a judgement has to be made whether to allow the authority further time, or whether to take the matter out of their hands by appealing against a deemed refusal. If the indications from the local officers are generally favourable and the delay is caused by the need to sort out points of detail, it is obviously sensible to allow further time to resolve such matters. However, it is easy for time to be wasted by allowing negotiations to drag on when it is clear that there is a major point of difference which is only capable of being resolved on appeal.

This dilemma can often be avoided altogether by submitting to the local planning authority a second application in identical form—either at the same time as the first or at the time of lodging an appeal against a deemed refusal. This should enable consultations and negotiations to proceed at the local level without undue delay in the appeal process. However, it needs to be borne in mind that under the new procedures (see below) the appellant will need to be ready for preparation of evidence soon after submission of the appeal. If the negotiations are successful, a permission can be issued immediately on the second application and the appeal can be withdrawn. This practice is recognised in the Fees Regulations, which allow a second duplicate application to be lodged within 28 days of the first for one quarter of the normal fee, and, following an appeal against a deemed refusal, allow a second application of the same character to be made within 12 months without charge.[24] The applicant would be well advised to maintain his appeal until he has an actual permission in his hands. Negotiations with officers do not bind the authority which is free to change its mind at any time until a notice of decision is issued.

Where a decision has been given by the local planning authority the G.D.O. requires that the appeal should be lodged within six months. Although this period was intended to allow time for negotiations it may be wiser, in cases where an inquiry is likely to be involved, to lodge the appeal as quickly as possible in order to avoid delay with inquiry dates, but only if the appellant is ready to proceed with preparation of the evidence for the appeal. The time between lodging the appeal and the inquiry can be used for any negotiations, and the

---

[24] Circ. 5/89, *Town and Country Planning (Fees for Applications and Deemed Applications) Regulations 1989*, para. 21.

impending hearing will help to put pressure on all concerned. Where the appeal is to be by written representations, it is usually sensible to pursue any negotiations before appealing, since once the appeal is lodged the Department is reluctant to allow unnecessary delay in moving to a decision.

The Secretary of State has power to extend the time limit for the appeal beyond the six months, but he is normally unwilling to do so. However, it is always possible to submit a new application to the local planning authority and if necessary, to appeal against a deemed refusal of that application at the end of the eight week period.

2.12. Appeals against conditions

Section 79 [36/71] enables an applicant to appeal not only against an outright refusal of permission but also against the grant of permission subject to conditions. In deciding whether to appeal, similar considerations apply to those considered above. However three matters deserve particular mention in this context:

(1) *Circular 1/85.*[25] A comprehensive statement of the Secretary of State's policy as to the imposition of conditions, including model conditions, is to be found in this Circular. It should enable a judgement to be made as to the likelihood of a successful appeal against a particular condition. Where a condition is designed to secure some planning benefit for the authority, it should be tested against the principles laid down in Circular 22/83[26] (see Appendix A).

(2) *High Court action.* Where it is thought that the condition is not merely objectionable as a matter of policy, but is invalid in law, it may be possible to make an application to the High Court for a declaration to that effect by judicial review. In some circumstances this may be a quicker and simpler remedy and may be particularly appropriate where it is important to obtain an early decision on a matter of legal principle.[27] However, it must be borne in mind that the result may well be that the whole permission is nullified, unless the invalid condition can be "severed." The test of severability is somewhat imprecise, but generally the invalidity of a condition is likely to be held to invalidate the whole permission, unless it can clearly be said that the authority would have reached the same decision without the condition.[28]

(3) *Re-opening the merits.* It is essential to bear in mind that, on an appeal against a condition, the Secretary of State is entitled to investigate the merits of the decision as a whole. He may, for example, impose more onerous conditions or even refuse permission altogether.[29] It is often a better and less risky course to submit a fresh

---

[25] *The Use of Conditions in Planning Permissions.*
[26] *Planning Gain. Obligations and Benefits which Extend Beyond the Development for which Planning Permission has been sought.*
[27] See, *e.g.* R. v. *Hillingdon London Borough Council, ex p. Royco Homes* [1974] 1 Q.B. 720.
[28] See *Kent County Council* v. *Kingsway Investments (Kent)* [1971] A.C. 72.
[29] See, *e.g.,* [1974] J.P.L. 739; [1975] J.P.L. 556.

application to the authority for a permission free from the objectionable condition (under section 73 of the 1990 Act [31A/71]. This will give an opportunity not only for the specific objections to the condition to be stated more fully to the authority with a view to changing their mind, but also, if the decision is unfavourable, to appeal against it without putting in jeopardy the first permission.

Whatever its outcome, the mere fact that the applicant has made the second application and appeal does not prevent him subsequently implementing and relying on the first permission.[30]

2.13. No appeal against section 106 agreements

Local planning authorities sometimes seek to supplement the control of development available under planning conditions, by inviting applicants to enter section 106 agreements [52/71] incorporating the same or additional restrictions. Such invitations should be treated with caution. Departmental policy discourages the use of section 106 agreements in cases where a condition can be used:

> "It may be possible to solve a problem posed by a development proposal equally well by imposing a condition on the planning permission or by concluding an agreement under section 52 of the Act or under other powers. The Secretaries of State consider that in such cases the local planning authority should impose a condition rather than seek to deal with the matter by the making of an agreement, since the imposition of restrictions by means of an agreement deprives the developer of the opportunity of seeking to have the restrictions varied or removed by an application on appeal under Part III of the Act if they subsequently become inappropriate or too onerous."[31]

The lack of any right of appeal against restrictions in an agreement can turn out to be a serious impediment to the free use or disposal of the land. Other than by consent such restrictions can only be lifted by the Lands Tribunal (under section 84 of the Law of Property Act 1925) but the grounds on which the Tribunal has jurisdiction to do so are very limited and it will not necessarily regard itself as bound to follow a favourable planning appeal decision. If an agreement is to be entered into, it is advisable to incorporate a specific provision allowing for reasonable variation (for example, to take account of a subsequent planning appeal decision) with provision for arbitration. A Consultation Paper on *Planning Agreements* was published in July 1989 and proposes that unilateral undertakings be given as an alternative to section 106 agreements. The advantage of this procedure is that it would enable a developer to give an undertaking, which would be enforceable by the local authority, but it would not be necessary for the local planning authority to agree the terms. The subject of planning agreements is dealt with further in Chapter 8.

---

[30] See Circ. 19/86, *Housing and Planning Act 1986: Planning Provisions*, para. 13.
[31] Circ. 1/85, Annex, para. 10.

2.14. Appeals against refusal of approval of "reserved matters"

The section 79 [36/71] appeal procedure (including the deemed refusal procedure under section 79 [37/71]) is available where an approval required by a condition is refused or granted by the local planning authority subject to conditions. The most familiar example of this is the approval of "reserved matters"[32] under the conditions of an "outline permission" also available in any case where any condition on a permission requires subsequent approval or agreement of any matter.[33]

It should be noted that the term "outline planning permission" is defined in article 1(2) of the G.D.O.; see also section 92 of the 1990 Act [42(1)/71], which provides that a permission for a building granted subject to a condition requires subsequent approval for any "reserved matter." Reserved matters are matters of siting, design, external appearance, means of access, or landscaping of which details were not given in the original application (*ibid.*). It follows, on the one hand, that a permission for a building is still technically "outline" so long as there remains only one of the listed matters (for example, landscaping) to be settled, but not if some other matter (for example, drainage) remains to be approved; and, on the other, that a permission for something other than a building (for example, a mineral operation) is not strictly an "outline permission" even though the conditions leave a number of detailed matters to be settled. These points of terminology sometimes cause confusion; their practical significance is reduced since the amendment (in 1980) of section 79 [36/71] to cover appeals against all forms of approval or consent required by condition. They may, however, have relevance to the question of time limits (see below) and they also are relevant to the question of fees.[34]

The issues arising on a reserved matter appeal will be much narrower, since the principle of development is already established, and a refusal or the imposition of conditions can only be justified by considerations relevant to the particular matters reserved for approval.[35] The application for approval cannot be used as an opportunity to re-open the merits of the permission itself.

In deciding whether to appeal the following points should be borne in mind:

(1) *Policy guidance.* In so far as the decision is based on matters of design or aesthetics, guidance in assessing the prospects of an appeal will be found in PPG1,[36] paragraphs 27 to 29 (see Appendix A).

(2) *Time limits.* Every outline planning permission (see above) is subject to a time limit for the submission of details of reserved

---

[32] "Reserved matters" are defined by G.D.O., art. 1(2).
[33] See, *e.g., Roberts* v. *Vale Royal District Council and the Secretary of State for the Environment* (1977) 39 P. & C.R. 514; [1977] J.P.L. 369.
[34] Circ. 5/89, para. 40.
[35] *Hamilton* v. *West Sussex County Council* [1958] 2 Q.B. 286.
[36] *General Policy and Principles.*

matters. Unless otherwise specified this will be three years from the date of the outline permission.[37] In the case of other approvals required by condition there is no time limit for submission unless one is specifically expressed in the permission. However, if the condition requires approval before commencement of works, details will have to be submitted in time to allow approval before the expiry of the time limit for the commencement of the development. Once the time limit for submission of details has expired, no further details can be submitted.[38] On the other hand, there is no limit to the number of different sets of details that can be submitted before the time limit expires. If an appeal is contemplated, therefore, it is important to ensure (a) that details of all reserved matters are submitted with in the time limit, and (b) that consideration is given to the possibility of submitting within the time limit alternative plans which are likely to be acceptable to the authority, as a precaution in case the appeal fails. Otherwise the permission as a whole may lapse and it may become necessary to make a complete fresh application for planning permission.

(3) *Judicial Review.* If the grounds of the refusal or the conditions indicate clearly that the authority has gone outside the scope of the reserved matters or otherwise erred in law, an alternative remedy would be to apply to the High Court for judicial review to quash the decision. The streamlining of High Court procedures makes this a much more attractive remedy than formerly. However, the High Court cannot itself grant permission,[39] and there is no guarantee that the authority, on reconsideration, may not find a legally valid basis of refusal. A written representation appeal will usually be as quick and more effective.

2.15. Form of notice of appeal

In respect of the categories of appeal dealt with in this chapter it is required that the notice of appeal shall be given on a form obtained from the Secretary of State.[40]

The form is obtained by writing to the Secretary of State for the Environment, Tollgate House, Houlton Street, Bristol BS2 9DJ or (in Wales) to the Secretary of State for Wales, Welsh Office, Summit House, Windsor Place, Cardiff CF1 3BX. A useful booklet, *Planning Appeals—A Guide to Procedure*, will be supplied with the forms. Where the appeal relates to a refusal, deemed refusal or conditional grant of planning permission (as opposed to an approval of reserved

---

[37] 1990 Act, s.92 [42(1)/71].

[38] See 1990 Act; s.93 [43(7)(b)/71]; see also *Heron Corporation* v. *Manchester City Council* [1978] 1 W.L.R. 937.

[39] See *Shemara* v. *Luton Corporation* (1967) 18 P. & C.R. 520.

[40] G.D.O., art. 26(1).

matters or other details) it is necessary for the appeal to be accompanied by a certificate under section 66 [27/71] relating to notification of owners and other interests.[41] The form of certificate is prescribed by the G.D.O. and is included in the standard appeal form.

2.16. Who decides the appeal?

Appeals under sections 78 and 79 [36, 37/71] are made nominally to the Secretary of State. However, the vast majority are now transferred for decision to "a person appointed by the Secretary of State" (by virtue of Schedule 6 to the 1990 Act [Sched. 9/71] and Regulations made under it). Apart from certain appeals by statutory undertakers, the only appeals which will come to the Department itself for decision are those where the Secretary of State has specifically recovered jurisdiction (Schedule 6, paragraph 3). In such cases he is required to give his reasons (paragraph 3(2)). In 1986[42] the following criteria were generally regarded as justifying recovery of jurisdiction:

(a) residential development of 150 or more houses;

(b) proposals for development of major importance having more than local significance;

(c) proposals giving rise to significant public controversy;

(d) proposals which raise important or novel issues of development control;

(e) retail development over 100,000 sq. ft.;

(f) proposals for significant development in the Green Belt;

(g) major proposals for the winning and working of minerals;

(h) proposals which raise significant legal difficulties;

(i) proposals against which another government department has raised major objections;

(j) cases which can only be decided in conjunction with a case over which inspectors have no jurisdiction.

As can be seen these are not precise categories, and it is always open to an appellant or the authority to ask for a particular appeal to be recovered if it is thought to involve important points of principle. Even where jurisdiction is recovered by the Secretary of State, the appeal will normally be decided without reference to the Secretary of State or any Minister in person. Only the following categories, it seems,[43] are as a matter of practice referred to Ministers:

(a) where the decision branch propose to go against the inspector's recommendation on the planning merits;

---

[41] See 1990 Act, s.79 [36(5)/71]; the requirements are applicable to appeals.

[42] *Planning: Appeals, Call-in and Major Public Inquiries* (1986) Cmnd. 43, p. 10.

[43] See *Planning: Appeals, Call-in and Major Public Inquiries*, Cmnd. 43, p. 10.

(b) significant development in the Green Belt;

(c) where the proposed decision is to refuse permission for a development involving more than 150 dwellings, or covering more than six hectares;

(d) where it appears that there is considerable political interest because of representations received from a Member of Parliament;

(e) sensitive or major appeals.

2.17. Inquiry or written representations

The appeal form requires the appellant to indicate whether he would be willing to have his appeal dealt with by written representations rather than by a hearing or local inquiry. The written representations procedure is non–statutory and can only be adopted with the consent of both the appellant and the local planning authority since either has the right to require a hearing.[44] The practice is explained in Circular 18/86[45] (see paragraph 2.21 *infra*). Even if the parties agree on written representations, the Secretary of State may still decide that an inquiry should be held.

Before deciding to accept that an appeal should be dealt with by way of written representations rather than public inquiry, the advantages and disadvantages should be weighed up.

From the point of view of speed and expense, written representations are to be preferred. In 1988/9 the average time from notice of appeal to decision in transferred cases was 23 weeks for written representation appeals as compared to 37 weeks for inquiry appeals; and the Department are hoping to reduce the time for written representation appeals still further. From the appellant's point of view the written representations procedure may also have the advantage of reducing the scope for intervention by third parties—which can be a highly unpredictable element in a public inquiry. Although an opportunity is given for third party representations such an invitation is likely to attract less public attention than a full inquiry.

In many cases the factual and policy issues are clear-cut and the decision will depend principally on the inspector's impression of the site. In such cases there is generally little advantage in seeking an inquiry. There are two main disadvantages of the written representation procedure. First, the parties lose the practical and psychological effects of a presentation in person. In more complex or unusual cases it is important not only to be able to ensure that the case has been fully absorbed and understood by the inspector, but also to be able to bring the project and its participants to life by an oral presentation. Second, the inquiry offers the opportunity to deal with the grounds of refusal and give notice of the challenge and test the opposing case by cross-examination. This is a factor the importance of which is often over-

---

[44] 1990 Act, s.79 [36(4)/71].
[45] *Planning Appeals Decided by Written Representations.*

estimated (see paragraph 2.48 below) but is again more significant in complex or unusual cases where cross-examination can be a useful means of refining and clarifying the issues.

Overall the great majority of appellants opt for written representations (85 per cent of appeals were decided in this way in 1988/9) and the Department strongly encourages this procedure (see Circular 18/86). From a statistical point of view, the success rate for written representation appeals is slightly lower than inquiries but this may reflect the fact that in marginal cases appellants are more willing to risk the lower costs of a written representation appeal.

2.18. Drafting the grounds of appeal

The Department's form provides limited space for the grounds of appeal. Where an inquiry is proposed, the grounds of appeal can be given in outline, but they should deal with the grounds of refusal and give notice of the main lines of argument and evidence that will be advanced at the inquiry. Where the appeal is against a deemed refusal, "non-determination by the authority" is a sufficient ground of appeal in itself.

Where the appeal is to be by written representation the grounds of appeal will normally form the appellant's principal statement of case; and, if so, a much fuller submission is appropriate.

2.19. Service of documents

The notice of appeal served by the Secretary of State must be accompanied by the following documents[46]:

(a) the application made to the local planning authority which has occasioned the appeal;

(b) all plans, drawings and documents sent to the authority in connection with the application;

(c) all correspondence with the authority relating to the application;

(d) any notice provided to the authority in accordance with section 65 of the Act [26/71];

(e) any certificate provided to the authority in accordance with sections 65 or 66 of the Act [26, 27/71];

(f) any other plans or drawings relating to the application which were not sent to the authority;

(g) the notice of the decision or determination, if any;

(h) if the appeal relates to an application for approval of certain matters in accordance with a condition on a planning permission, the application for that permission, the plans submitted with that application and the planning permission granted.

---

[46] G.D.O., art. 26(3).

At the same time the applicant must send to the local planning authority copies of the notice of appeal and copies of any documents sent to the Secretary of State under paragraph (f) (*i.e.*, plans or drawings not previously supplied to the authority).[47]

Before sending the documents, care should be taken to ensure that they are complete, legible and up to date and that the plans sent are the appropriate revisions.[48]

It is strongly advisable for a detailed list of the documents supplied to the Secretary of State (include dates of letters, number of plans etc.) to be prepared and for copies of the list to be included with the notice sent to the Secretary of State and the authority. This should ensure that everyone at least starts with the same basic documents.

2.20. Procedural pitfalls

Once a decision has been made in principle to appeal, it is important to check that the application is procedurally in order. The following points sometimes give rise to problems:

(1) *The identity of the appellant.* Section 79 [36/71] does not enable an appeal to be made by anyone other than the original applicant. Accordingly where, for example, a prospective purchaser of land wishes to proceed with an appeal on an application made by the owner, he cannot do so in his own name but must obtain the consent of the owner to lend his name to the appeal.

(2) *The applicant must be "aggrieved" by the decision.* The right of appeal is only given to the applicant if he is "aggrieved" by the decision.[49] This is a technical expression whose meaning has been subject to much debate, but broadly requires that he should have some real and not merely theoretical interest in the decision.[50] A prospective purchaser would qualify, but not a complete stranger to the land. This point may cause difficulties if the original application was made by an owner who has since disposed of any interest in the land. If there is provision for the price to be readjusted in the event of permission being granted, he is clearly "aggrieved" by the refusal and can lend his name to the appeal. Otherwise it may be necessary for the new owner to make a new application in his own name and appeal against a refusal or deemed refusal of that application.

(3) *Scope of the application.* A basic point, but one often overlooked, is to ensure that the application does in fact correspond to the development which the prospective appellant wishes to carry out. In the course of consultations with the

---

[47] G.D.O., art. 26(3).
[48] See para. 2.20(3) below.
[49] 1990 Act, s.79 [36/71].
[50] See *Bizony* v. *Secretary of State for the Environment* [1976] J.P.L. 306.

authority ideas may have changed and amendments may have been made and new plans submitted. A refusal may be issued by the authority, or an appeal lodged against a deemed refusal, without anyone taking the trouble to ascertain precisely what development is covered by the application or which plans are included in it. This can cause difficulties on appeal because powers of amendment at this stage are limited. As far as possible these points should be settled at the outset, if necessary by agreement with the authority. Particular points are:

    (a) whether the application is for full or outline permission— and in the latter case, which matters are to be treated as "reserved". Note that where, on a detailed application for permission, the grounds of refusal raise points of both principle and detail, it is often sensible to agree on appeal to treat it as pure "outline" with all detailed plans being treated as "illustrative" only. This will enable the inquiry to concentrate on the points of principle, leaving the details for subsequent consideration;

    (b) the precise description of the proposed development;

    (c) which of the submitted plans or other documents are to be treated as part of the application and which are to be treated as purely illustrative;

    (d) whether the proposed arrangements for access, drainage, etc., are accurately described.

(4) *Technical matters.* In some cases the Secretary of State accepts the appellant's case on the main issues of principle but is forced to dismiss the appeal because there are outstanding technical difficulties (for example, of access, drainage, etc.) which cannot be dealt with by a condition on a planning permission. Although such a decision is usually expressed to be made "without prejudice" to the submission of a new application to the local planning authority when the problems are resolved, time is wasted and there is always the risk that policies may change in the meantime. The basic rule is that a planning condition can relate only to land which is either included in the application site or within the "control" of the applicant.[51] Thus if, for example, land outside the application site is required to provide sightlines for an access to the development, the applicant must ensure that he has secured "control" of that land. The term "control" is not defined, but normally the applicant should ensure that he has the legal means to secure performance of the condition at least by the time of the inquiry.[52] Where "control" in this sense has not

---

[51] 1990 Act, s.72 [30/71]; Circ. 1/85, para. 32.

[52] See *Wimpey (George) & Co.* v. *New Forest District Council* [1979] J.P.L. 314; *Atkinson* v. *Secretary of State for the Environment and Leeds City Council* [1983] J.P.L. 599.

been obtained, but there is a reasonable prospect of obtaining it, it may be possible to overcome the problem by use of a so-called *"Grampian"* condition.[53] Similarly, suitable drainage arrangements may require off-site works to lay sewers or clear drainage channels. This matter is often covered by an agreement with the water authority. However, the water authority cannot be compelled to enter an agreement. If a binding agreement with the water authority cannot be achieved, the applicant must either obtain binding agreements with the landowners involved or make alternative arrangements which he can achieve on land within his control, assisted if necessary by the statutory rights conferred on owners of land in relation to drainage.[54]

(5) *Revised applications.* In some cases it will become apparent, after submitting the appeal, that the case at the inquiry will be improved if a revised application is submitted (for example, to show revised details where design is an important factor, or to include additional land needed to accommodate an agreed solution for access). With the co-operation of the local planning authority and the Department it is usually possible to arrange for such a revised application to be processed so that it can be dealt with at the same inquiry (whether or not the first application is withdrawn). However, it is important that as much notice as possible should be given. It is usually desirable to allow about five months between submission of the application and the inquiry (that is, two months for consideration by the authority, nine weeks from the notice of the inquiry plus a margin of flexibility). This time can be shortened if the Department agrees to call in the application, or if the authority consent to abridge notice of the inquiry. It must be remembered that the Department's current practice is not to call in the application if it is of only local importance. Consequently, it will not be easy to persuade the Department to call in an application for administrative convenience so that it can be conjoined to an existing appeal.

(6) *Certificates under the 1971 Act, sections 65 and 66 [26, 27/71].* Section 65 requires applications for certain classes of "unneighbourly" development to be accompanied by a certificate as to completion of certain prescribed publicity requirements.[55] The G.D.O. specifies the following classes:

(a) the construction of buildings for use as public conveniences;

---

[53] See Circ. 1/85, para. 34. See also *Grampian Regional Council* v. *City of Aberdeen* (1984) 47 P. & C.R. 633 and *Jones* v. *Secretary of State for Wales, The Times*, June 13, 1990.

[54] For example, Public Health Act 1936, s.34 (right to connect to public sewers); Water Act 1989, s.71 (right to requisition sewer).

[55] G.D.O., art. 11.

(b) the construction of buildings or other operations or the use of land for the disposal of waste materials or the use of land as a scrap yard;

(c) the winning or working of minerals or the use of land for mineral working deposits;

(d) the construction of buildings or other operations or the use of land for retaining, treating or disposing of sewage, trade waste or sludge (other than the laying of sewers, the construction of pumphouses in a line of sewers or the construction of septic tanks and cesspools serving single dwellinghouses, single buildings or single caravans in which not more than 10 people will normally reside, work or congregate, and works ancillary thereto);

(e) the construction of buildings to a height exceeding 20 metres;

(f) the construction of buildings or the use of land for the purposes of a slaughterhouse or knacker's yard or for killing or plucking poultry;

(g) the construction of buildings or the use of land for the purposes of a casino, a funfair or a bingo hall, a theatre, a cinema, a music hall, a dance hall, a skating rink, a sports-hall, a swimming bath or gymnasium (not forming part of a school, college or university), or a Turkish or other vapour or foam bath;

(h) the construction of buildings or the use of land as a zoo or for the business of boarding or breeding cats or dogs;

(i) the construction of buildings or the use of land for motor car or motorcycle racing, including trials of speed;

(j) the construction of a stadium;

(k) the use of land as a cemetery or crematorium.

This requirement is sometimes overlooked by both applicant and authority (for example, where a sewage plant forms an incidental part of a larger development). However, since it is a matter affecting jurisdiction, the Secretary of State will not entertain an appeal if this requirement has not been fulfilled at the application stage, and it cannot be corrected except by making a new application. Section 66, which requires a similar certificate relating to notices to owners, is less likely to be overlooked in practice since it applies to all applications.

(7) *Environmental Impact Assessment.* The Town and Country Planning (Assessment of Environmental Effects) Regulations 1988,[56] which implement the requirements of the European Community Directive 85/337, require an assessment of certain projects on the environment to be submitted with the application.

---

[56] S.I. 1988 No. 1199. Circ. 15/88 is a comprehensive explanation of the procedures and criteria, see also DOE, *Environmental Assessment—A Guide to the Proceedings*, HMSO, 1989.

C. Written Representations

2.21. Regulations

Procedure in written representation cases is now subject to strict timetables imposed by the Written Representations Procedure Regulations 1987.[57] Advice on practice is given there and in Circular 18/86[58]: Circular 11/87 also contains a diagram illustrating sequence and timescale for steps to be taken by the appellant, the Department, the local planning authority, and third parties respectively (see Appendix B). The following paragraphs consider the action required by each party.

2.22. The appellant

The first task is for the appellant to submit the notice of appeal and accompanying documents to the Secretary of State and the local planning authority.[59] The intention is that the grounds of appeal should represent the appellant's case and it is desirable that it should do so since attempts to adduce new material at a later stage will be resisted and will certainly cause delay. Accordingly, the preparation of the case should be given as much care as would be given to preparing for an inquiry (including, where appropriate, the involvement of specialist solicitors and counsel). If necessary submission of the appeal should be delayed until all the required material is available. The form of the case will normally be a written submission with supporting appendices and illustrative material. Before drafting the statement it is advisable to obtain copies of any relevant report to the local authority committee which dealt with the application. Such a report will often contain a full statement of the main facts and policies relevant to the appeal. If so the report can be appended to the notice of appeal with an indication of any points of difference. This will enable the statement of case to be limited to the points in issue. Where technical issues are involved on which experts have advised, copies of these reports can be appended to the case with statements of their qualifications and experience. However, such material should be limited as far as possible to evidence relevant to the points actually in dispute. The bulk of material should be kept to a minimum (bearing in mind that the authority is likely to want to reply in kind). Where supporting reports or other documents are referred to, they should be fully paginated and the relevant parts should be clearly referenced in the text of the case.

Once he has submitted his notice of appeal with supporting documents, the appellant should receive in turn, (i) a notification from the Department of the "starting date" (that is, the date of receipt of the papers by the Department); (ii) 14 days from the starting date, a questionnaire and supporting documents from the authority (see below); and (iii) 28 days from the starting date, the local authority's

---

[57] S.I. 1987 No. 701. Circ. 11/87, *Town and Country Planning (Appeals) (Written Representations Procedure) Regulations 1987.*
[58] *Planning Appeals Decided by Written Representations.*
[59] See para. 2.15 above.

statement of case (if any): the questionnaire will indicate whether a further statement is intended. The appellant then has 17 days from the receipt of the questionnaire or statement (if any) to submit any response which should be copied to the Department and the authority. The following advice is given in Circular 11/87:

"11. Where the LPA[60] indicates on the questionnaire that it intends to make a further statement, the appellant should wait for that statement before responding. However, the details included in the questionnaire, and the documents accompanying it, should give the appellant sufficient information to enable him to begin to prepare any response he may feel is required in advance of receiving the authority's further statement of case.

12. Unless the appeal is against non-determination, the LPA should have set out the reasons for refusal fully and clearly in its notice of decision. . . .

Equally the appellant should have set out his grounds for appeal in the original appeal form and any attachments. Failure to complete the form may render the appeal invalid. There should be no new points in the LPA's statement, but the 17 day period following that statement is intended to allow the appellant to comment on anything new that does appear. There is no obligation on the appellant to comment; indeed, the sooner he notifies the Department if he has no comments the sooner the ultimate decision is likely to be given."

2.23. The local planning authority

Circular 11/87 sets out clearly the responsibilities of the local planning authority ("LPA") on receipt of the notice of appeal[61]:

"(i) Within five working days of receipt of the appeal form to notify those who are required to be consulted on the application under an Act or Order and those who made representations that an appeal has been made. The notification must give the appeal reference, a description of the application, the name of the appellant, the address of the appeal site and the starting date. The notification should state that earlier representations will be forwarded to the Department and that any modification, elaboration or withdrawal of those representations should be sent direct to the appropriate room at the Bristol or Cardiff Office within 28 days of the starting date. At Annex B is a model letter[62] providing the information required by the Regulations.

(ii) Within 14 days of the starting date to complete and send to the Department and at the same time to the appellant a questionnaire enclosing copies of any papers required by the questionnaire. These will be copies of correspondence or directions from

---

[60] Local Planning Authority.
[61] Circ. 11/87, para. 3.
[62] See Appendix B.2.

statutory consultees about the application, copies of relevant representations from other interested persons, the planning officer's report to committee (if any), any relevant committee minute and extracts from the relevant plans or policies on which the decision relied. Copies of all this material should be sent to the appellant. LPAs should also indicate whether they intend to prepare any further statement to explain the reasons for their decision.

(iii) Within 28 days of the starting date, to send to the Department any further specially prepared statement of case and at the same time send a copy to the appellant. . . ."

"8. LPAs must themselves judge what sort of submission they wish to put forward in the time-scale laid down by the Regulations. In many cases, Planning Inspectors are capable of appraising the LPA's case from the questionnaire and other key documents; they do not need a full and free-standing statement of case. The relevant background documents to the planning committee's decision and the planning officer's report to the committee, where available, may often be sufficient to present the authority's case. Where the authority chooses not to submit a full statement, the questionnaire must state that fact clearly to enable the appellant (if he so chooses) to reply to the questionnaire without awaiting a further statement."[63]

After receipt of the appellant's response (see above) the authority has seven days to submit comments on any new material that has emerged.

2.24. Other parties

The authority will give notice of the appeal to parties who made representations on the application and to other parties who are required to be consulted on the application. Other parties or groups will not necessarily be made aware of the appeal unless they have made prior arrangements with the authority. Circular 18/86 comments:

"21. There should generally be no need for LPAs to consult anyone at the appeal stage who has not already been consulted at the application stage. The responses to the earlier consultation ought to give the views of the statutory and other consultees. At the appeal stage the LPA need only notify those who responded to consultation at the application stage; and send copies of the relevant previous correspondence to the Department and to the appellant. The onus would then be on those parties who wish to make additional comments to send these direct to the Department. Whenever an inspector finds there is insufficient information on which to take a decision, it is always possible for him to ask for more. The change in procedure will mean that LPAs no longer need to hold up the notification of interested parties until their statements are available for public inspection, nor interested

---

[63] Circ. 11/87, para. 8.

parties hold up their comments until they have seen the LPA's statement. If adequate reasons for refusal have been given by the LPA, there should be nothing more of substance for the interested parties to see."

Because of the tight time limits involved in the procedure, any local groups or interests who wish to submit new material on the appeal will need to be prepared to move very quickly.

2.25. Site view

A site visit will normally be arranged within a target period of two weeks from the close of the period for representations. The actual date will be arranged two weeks in advance.

The purpose of the site view is simply to ensure that the inspector is made aware of the characteristics and relevant features of the site and its surroundings. No discussion of the merits of the appeal is allowed, and it is in fact unnecessary for the inspector to be accompanied by either party unless access to private land is required or if these are features of the site which need to be pointed out.[64] However, it is advisable for the parties to be represented to ensure that relevant viewpoints are properly identified.

2.26. Extension of time period

Circular 11/87 indicates the limited circumstances in which extensions of time will be allowed:

"14. The time limits will be extended only in exceptional circumstances. Such circumstances might include:
(i) the failure of another party to abide by a time limit at an earlier stage of the process;
(ii) the appellant's need for extra time to respond to the authority's statement in an appeal following the failure of an LPA to determine the application (where the appellant has been unable to obtain an earlier indication of the nature of the authority's case); or
(iii) the linking of the appeal to another type of appeal process where different time limits apply.

The Department will notify principal parties of such extensions."

2.27. Decision or report

The intention is that within two weeks of the site view the inspector's decision (in transferred cases) will be issued or a report (in recovered cases) submitted to the Department.[65] No time limit is given for the issue of the Secretary of State's decision. The 1990 Act provides for a legal challenge to the decision. At present costs are only awarded in the case of appeals dealt with by public inquiry, but the

---

[64] Circ. 18/86, para. 25.
[65] Circ. 11/87, para. 15.

1986 Act allows for extending costs awards to cases dealt with by written representation although this provision has not yet been brought into operation.

D. LOCAL INQUIRIES—PRE-INQUIRY PROCEDURE

2.28. Different types of hearing

Section 79 [36/71] merely specifies that the appellant and the local planning authority are entitled to be "heard": it does not specify the procedure. The procedures have been developed through practice and are only partially covered by statutory provisions. The following categories of hearing can be identified:

(1) *Planning Inquiry Commission* A special form of hearing before a panel (appointed under the 1990 Act, section 101 and Schedule 8 [47, 48/71]) to inquire into appeals involving items of special importance or technical novelty.

The procedure is never used in practice and need not be considered further.

(2) *Standard Local Inquiry* A local inquiry held under the Inquiries Procedure Rules. This is the normal procedure used for sections 78 and 79 appeals [36, 37/71], and is described fully in the following sections of this book.

(3) *Major Planning Inquiries* This is a term used to describe those inquiries which the Department has decided are suitable for the application of the special procedures outlined in the Code of Practice for Major Planning Inquiries.[66] The Code is "intended for application in cases of major public interest because of its national or regional implications, or the extent or complexity of the environmental, safety, technical or scientific issues involved, and where for these reasons there are a number of third parties involved as well as the applicant and the local planning authority.[67] The statutory framework, including the statutory rules, is the same as for standard inquiries, although some rules (for example, as to pre-inquiry meetings) are of particular relevance to major inquiries. The Department will inform the parties at an early stage if the Code is to be applied. The Code itself is set out in full in Appendix B.6 and accordingly is not dealt with separately in this chapter.

(4) *Informal Hearings* In simpler cases, where either of the main parties has requested a hearing or inquiry under section 79,

---

[66] Circ. 10/88, *Town and Country Planning (Inquiries Procedure) Rules 1988, Town and Country Planning Appeals (Determination by Inspectors) (Inquiries Procedure) Rules 1988*, Annex 1, Appendix B.6.

[67] Circ. 10/88, Annex 1, para. 3.

the Department may invite them to agree to the use of the "informal hearing" procedure. A Code of Practice[68] for such informal hearing has been issued by the Department and is reproduced at Appendix B.7. The statutory rules do not apply to such hearings.

As indicated above, the Inquiries Procedure Rules apply to inquiries held in all appeals being considered in this chapter (other than informal hearings). The Secretary of State's Rules apply where the decision is to be taken by the Secretary of State. The Inspector's Rules apply where it is to be taken by an inspector.[69]

2.29. Section 71(2) parties

Although the principal parties at the inquiry will be the appellant and the local planning authority, the Rules also give a special status to "section 71(2) parties," [29(3)/71] *i.e.*, those with an interest in the land who have made representations within the 21 day period.

2.30. 1988 Procedure Rules

The Secretary of State's Rules apply to local inquiries held into, (i) planning appeals arising out of a refusal, conditional grant of planning permission or non-determination of the application which are decided by the Secretary of State rather than an inspector; (ii) planning applications which are called in by the Secretary of State; and (iii) applications decided by the Secretary of State in relation to listed building consent, conservation area consent and tree preservation orders. The Inspector's Rules apply to local inquiries held into planning appeals arising out of a refusal or conditional grant of planning permission into non-determination appeals, and into appeals in relation to listed building consent and conservation area consent which are decided by inspectors. The new Rules replace the "1974 Rules."[70] The purpose of these changes is set out in the accompanying Circular.[71]

> "6. Many of the changes to the Rules respond to the growing concern about the time taken to decide planning cases which go to local inquiry, particularly those about major development proposals. They also take account of changes since 1974 in inquiry practice and in the relevant law. The main objective of the new Rules is to make the inquiry process at all stages as efficient and effective as possible, whilst impairing neither the fairness and impartiality of the proceedings, nor the ability of participants to make representations which are relevant to the decision.
> 7. In particular, effective use of the period before the inquiry opens can make a crucial contribution to the speed and efficiency

---

[68] Circ. 10/88, Annex 2, Appendix B.7.
[69] The Rules are reproduced in full in Appendix D.
[70] Circ. 10/88, paras. 2–5.
[71] Circ. 10/88.

of the inquiry proceedings themselves. Early exchanges of information before the inquiry can help the inspector and the parties to identify the principal issues on which the inquiry should concentrate, thus avoiding needless discussion of matters which are not relevant or can be resolved in advance. At a local inquiry there should be no place for surprise tactics.

8. The pre-inquiry procedures have therefore been substantially revised with a view to securing early and full exchanges of information between the principal parties and reducing the time taken between submission of the appeal (or referral of the application) and the opening of the inquiry. There are specified periods within which statements have to be exchanged, which are fixed forward from the date of notification that an inquiry is to be held (the "relevant date") and not backward from the date of the inquiry as in the 1974 Rules. The Rules also specify the period within which the inquiry is to open. The effect of these timetabling arrangements, which are explained in more detail later in this Circular and which are illustrated on the flow charts at Annexes 3 and 4, is to provide from the beginning predetermined dates by which action has to be taken. Under the 1974 Rules there was no clear timetable until the inquiry date had been fixed, often some time after the application or appeal had been received."

2.31. Appeals determined by the Secretary of State
The various procedural steps before an inquiry are as follows:

(1) *Acceptance of appeal by the Secretary of State.* The Secretary of State will notify the parties that he intends to proceed with the consideration of the appeal. If the Secretary of State refuses to accept the appeal for some reason, his decision may be open to challenge by judicial review.

(2) *"Relevant notice" and "relevant date".* A key element in the new Rules is the definition of the "relevant date" which is the starting-point of time limits for the various procedural steps. The "relevant date" is the date of issue of the "relevant notice" by the Secretary of State, that is, the notice informing the parties of his intention to hold an inquiry.[72] The Secretary of State is under no specific time limit for the service of this notice, but it is important that the parties are ready to proceed with preparation of their statement of case as soon as it is received.

(3) *List of "section 71(2) parties" who have made representations.* On receipt of the relevant notice, the local planning authority must forthwith inform the Secretary of State and the appellant in writing of the names and addresses of all section 71(2) [29(3)/71] parties (see above). The Secretary of State shall as

---

[72] Secretary of State's Rules, r. 4.

soon as practicable thereafter inform the applicant and the local planning authority in writing of any section 71(2) party who has made representations to him. This rule applies where:

(a) the Secretary of State or any local authority has given to the local planning authority a direction restricting the grant of planning permission;

(b) in a listed building consent case, the Commission has given a direction to the local planning authority as to how the application is to be determined;

(c) the Secretary of State or any other Minister of the Crown or any government department or local authority has expressed in writing to the local planning authority the view that the application should not be granted either wholly or in part, or should be granted only subject to conditions, or, in the case of an application for consent under a tree preservation order, should be granted together with a direction requiring replanting; or

(d) any authority or person consulted in pursuance of a development order has made representations to the local planning authority about the application.[73]

The appellant should in any event request the authority to supply copies of the officers' report in the application and of all representations received. When necessary the Local Government (Access to Information) Act 1985 can be relied on.

(4) *Direction restricting the grant of permission.* Where (3)(a) to (d) above apply, the local planning authority must inform the person or body of the inquiry and, unless they have already done so, that person or body shall then provide the local planning authority with a statement of the reasons for making the direction.

(5) *Pre-inquiry meetings.* The Secretary of State may cause one or a number of pre-inquiry meetings to be held if it appears to him desirable. If he does so the following procedure applies[74]:

(a) The Secretary of State shall serve with the relevant notice notification of his intention to call a pre-inquiry meeting and a statement of the matters which appear to him likely to be relevant to his consideration. Any view expressed by another Minister or government department expressed in writing shall be set out by the Secretary of State in his statement, a copy of which shall be supplied to the Minister or government department.

(b) The local planning authority shall place a notice in a local newspaper of the pre-inquiry meeting and the Secretary of State's statement. The Secretary of State may specify the form of the notice.

---

[73] Secretary of State's Rules, r. 4(2).
[74] *Ibid.* r. 5.

(c) The local planning authority and the applicant shall not later than eight weeks after the relevant date each serve an outline statement on the other and on the Secretary of State.

(d) Where 3(a) to (d) above apply the local planning authority shall:

(A) include in their outline statement the terms of
  (i) any direction given together with a statement of reasons therefor; and
  (ii) any view expressed or representation made on which they intend to rely at the inquiry

(B) supply a copy of the statement within eight weeks of the relevant date to the person or body concerned.

(e) Other persons who have notified the Secretary of State of their wish to appear at the inquiry may be required by him to serve, within four weeks of being so required, an outline statement on him, the applicant and the local planning authority.

(f) The pre-inquiry meeting (or, where there is more than one, the first meeting) shall be held not later than 16 weeks after the relevant date.

(g) The Secretary of State shall give not less than 21 days written notice of the meeting to those entitled to appear at the inquiry and any other persons whose presence at the meeting seems to him to be desirable; and may require the local planning authority to make arrangements to publicise the meeting.

(h) The inspector shall preside over the meeting and has powers to control procedure and conduct.

(i) Provision is made for further pre-inquiry meetings if they appear necessary to the inspector.

If the Secretary of State does not hold a pre-inquiry meeting under rule 5 an inspector has a further power to hold such a meeting. Then, 14 days written notice must be given and the same procedure is followed.[75]

(6) *Service of statement of case.*[76]

(a) The local planning authority shall not later than
  (i) six weeks after the relevant date, or
  (ii) where a pre-inquiry meeting is held, four weeks after the conclusion of that meeting,
  serve a statement of case on the Secretary of State, the applicant and any section 71(2) party.

(b) Where 3(a) to (d) above apply, the local planning authority shall include in their statement of case such matters and supply a copy to those bodies within the same time period.

---

[75] Secretary of State's Rules, r. 7.
[76] *Ibid.* r. 6.

The purpose of the service of statements of case and guidance as to contents is in Circular 10/88:

> "28. The statement of case should contain the full particulars of the case which a party proposes to put forward at the inquiry, together with a list of relevant documents. If the parties know as much as possible about each other's case at an early stage, this will ensure that, where there is scope for negotiation, it takes place well before the inquiry is due to commence, thereby avoiding late cancellations or requests for postponement of inquiries. It will also help the parties to concentrate on the matters which are really in dispute and help the inquiry to run efficiently: this can help to avoid unnecessary adjournments, which can lead to awards of costs. It will often be helpful if parties can provide with their statements the data, methodology and assumptions used to support their submissions. This is particularly important for major inquiries. If extensive tables, graphs, diagrams, maps etc. are not produced until after the inquiry has opened, the other parties might well need time, by means of an adjournment, to study these. To assist in ensuring that adequate information is supplied in advance of the inquiry, there is now a power in rule 6(6) enabling the Secretary of State or the inspector to require the provision of such further information as may be specified."

(c) The applicant shall not later than:

    (i) in the case of a referred application where no pre-inquiry meeting is held, six weeks after the relevant date; or

    (ii) in the case of an appeal where no such meeting is held, nine weeks after the relevant date; or

    (iii) where a pre-inquiry meeting is held, four weeks after the conclusion of that meeting,

serve a statement of case on the Secretary of State, local planning authority and any section 71(2) party.

(d) Any other person who notify him of an intention or wish to appear at any inquiry may be required by the Secretary of State to serve a statement of case within four weeks of being so required. Copies of any relevant documents referred to must be served.

(e) In the case of a "called-in" application (see paragraph 2.1 above) the Secretary of State must serve a statement not later than 12 weeks after the relevant date.

(f) A reasonable opportunity for inspection of documents must be provided.[77]

(7) *Statements of Relevant Matters.* Unless he has already done so, the Secretary of State in the case of a referral application and

---

[77] Secretary of State's Rules.

in the case of an appeal, may, not later than 12 weeks after the relevant date, provide the parties with a written statement of the matters which appear to him to be relevant to the appeal.[78]

(8) *Inquiry Timetable.* Where a pre-inquiry meeting is held an inspector shall and in other cases may arrange a timetable of the procedures.[79]

(9) *Notification of Appointment of Assessor.* Where the Secretary of State appoints an Assessor he shall notify any person entitled to appear of the Assessor's name and the matters on which he is to advise the inspector.[80]

(10) *Date and notification of inquiry.* The date fixed by the Secretary of State unless he considers it impracticable for holding the inquiry must be (a) not later than 22 weeks after the relevant date (currently in some areas dates are being offered much later than this target); or (b) where a pre–inquiry meeting is held under rule 5, eight weeks after the conclusion of the meeting. In either case where those provisions cannot be met the Rules require that the date otherwise be fixed at the earliest practicable date. Not less than 28 days written notice of the date, time and place must be given to every person entitled to appear. The time and place for the holding of the inquiry may be varied by the Secretary of State if this is necessary or advisable, but reasonable notice of the variation must be given.[81]

In practice, normally the Department seek to offer a date and obtain agreement to it first to the local planning authority and then to the appellant. Repeated rejections will lead to a date being imposed on the parties.

(11) *Public notice of inquiry.* The Secretary of State may require the local planning authority to take any of the following steps:
   (a) to publish not later than 14 days before the date fixed for the inquiry in one or more newspapers circulating in the locality in which the land is situated such notice of the inquiry as he may direct;
   (b) to serve such notice of the inquiry as the Secretary of State may specify on whomsoever the Secretary of State may specify;
   (c) to post such notices of the inquiry as he may direct in a conspicuous place near to the land. There is no penalty prescribed for non-compliance with this requirement, but it may result in the need for adjournments.

In addition the Secretary of State may require the applicant to affix a notice of the inquiry on the land.[82]

---

[78] Secretary of State's Rules, r. 6(8).
[79] *Ibid.* r. 8.
[80] *Ibid.* r. 9.
[81] Secretary of State's Rules, r. 10(1)–(5), and see *Lambeth London Borough Council* v. *Secretary of State for the Environment* [1990] J.P.L. 196.
[82] *Ibid.* r. 10(6)–(7).

(12) *Statements of evidence.* Proofs of evidence must be sent to the inspector and the other parties not later than three weeks before the date on which the person is due to give evidence, or the date fixed for the inquiry. The inspector can direct a written summary to be prepared although this is unusual in practice.

2.32. Appeals determined by an Inspector

The various procedural steps before an inquiry described in paragraph 2.31 *supra* are similar to those which apply to appeals determined by an inspector. Such appeals are governed by the Inspector's Rules and the procedure is set out below.

(1) The Secretary of State must notify the name of the inspector to all parties. If the Secretary of State appoints a different inspector it is sufficient for him to announce his name and appointment at the beginning of the inquiry.[83]

(2) Statements of case must be served by the local planning authority not later than six weeks after the relevant date, and by the appellant not later than nine weeks thereafter.[84] Copies of documents must be served with the statement of case.

(3) A statement of relevant matters may be served by the inspector not later than 12 weeks after the relevant date.[85]

(4) An inspector has power to hold a pre-inquiry meeting giving not less than 14 days notice.[86]

(5) An inspector may arrange a timetable for proceedings.[87]

(6) If an Assessor is appointed the parties must be notified.[88]

(7) The date fixed by the Secretary of State, unless he considers it impracticable, for holding the inquiry must be:

(a) not later than 20 weeks after the relevant date (currently in some areas dates are being offered much later than this target); and

(b) 28 days written notice of the date, time and place having been given.

The Secretary of State may vary the date, time and place for holding an inquiry but must give 28 days written notice of so doing. He may also require the local planning authority to publicise the inquiry (see paragraph 2.31 *supra*).[89]

---

[83] Inspector's Rules, r. 5.
[84] *Ibid.* r. 6.
[85] *Ibid.* r. 7.
[86] *Ibid.* r. 7.
[87] *Ibid.* r. 8.
[88] *Ibid.* r. 9.
[89] *Ibid.* r. 10.

(8) Statements of evidence and, if so required, summaries of evidence must be supplied not later than three weeks before evidence is given in accordance with the timetable or if there is no such timetable three weeks before the date fixed for the inquiry.[90]

E. LOCAL INQUIRIES—PREPARATION OF CASE

2.33. The authority's case—general comments

Reference has been made in paragraph 2.29 to the written statement of case which the local planning authority must serve before the inquiry. The statement of case should contain the full particulars of the case which the local planning authority intends to put forward and any omission of a major issue which the local planning authority intend to put forward at the inquiry can result in an application for an adjournment and a consequent award of costs.[91] Much time can be saved at an inquiry if the statement is carefully thought out and the real issues between the parties clarified and narrowed down.

The local planning authority's statement must be accompanied by a list of documents which it is proposed to put in evidence. "Documents" in this context is not confined to maps and plans but cover all forms of documentary material, including letters, minutes, appeal decisions etc. In preparing the authority's case it is important to bear in mind the cardinal principle that planning permission should always be granted "unless there are sound and clear-cut reasons for refusal" and that the onus lies on the authority to support those reasons. It is no use putting forward technical objections, unless the authority will have available qualified technical evidence to support them. If the support of another authority is going to be required to justify an objection (for example, the water authority or the Ministry of Agriculture), it is essential to check that they are willing to provide a suitable witness. These matters should be checked well before the statement is prepared. If it becomes clear that the authority will not be able to support any of the grounds of refusal, the appellant should be informed as soon as possible. Otherwise the authority may risk an award of costs.

2.34. The appellant's case—general comments

The authority's statement of case and the documents referred to in it should be investigated by the appellant as soon as possible. The appellant must serve his statement of case three weeks after the local planning authority and it must include full particulars of the case and a copy of any document referred to in it. It is important, therefore, for the appellant to familiarise himself at an early stage with the policy documents on which the authority are relying and to establish their

---

[90] Inspector's Rules, r. 14.
[91] Circ. 2/87, *Awards of Costs Incurred in Planning and Compulsory Purchase Order Proceedings*: see Appendix A.3.

status. For example, if there is a recently approved development plan for the area, the appellant should, if possible, prepare his case so as to bring himself within those policies. If he cannot, he will need to find some policy help from another source (for example, a Circular) or some other special reason to justify a departure. If the authority are seeking to rely on an informal policy statement or a plan which has not yet been fully tested by public consultation, it may be easier to justify a departure from it. Copies of any relevant officer's report and of all representations received by the authority should be requested. Since the Local Government (Access to Information) Act 1985, there is no justification for authorities declining to make copies available. It may also be useful to obtain copies of the relevant minutes by which the particular policy was adopted. Both appellants and local planning authorities must provide statements of evidence and a written summary of the evidence three weeks before giving evidence if a timetable for evidence has been fixed, but otherwise three weeks before the start of the inquiry. For this reason it is imperative that preparation of evidence and accumulation of documents begins at an early stage. However, it should be noted that an inspector has no effective power to enforce these time-limits apart from his general power to award costs in cases in which one of the parties has behaved unreasonably.

2.35. Defining the issues

Unlike the practice in ordinary litigation in the courts, there are no strict pleadings in a planning appeal although as outlined above the new Rules now require pre-inquiry statements with full particulars to be produced by both sides. In addition, the Rules make provision for a pre-inquiry meeting to be held in appropriate cases and for proofs of evidence to be exchanged. However, informality of the appeal proceedings may well make inevitable some uncertainty as to the precise issues particularly where there is significant public involvement. In any event, before evidence for an appeal can be prepared, the appellant must decide whether he has sufficient information as to the grounds of refusal and facts relied upon by the planning authority in support. Similarly, the local planning authority may consider that the grounds of appeal are not sufficiently explicit. In such event either party should ask the other for further information. Indeed, in this respect greater freedom is allowable than in the courts; and an inquiry can properly be made in appropriate cases, even before the formal statement as to:

   (i) any planning decisions of the authority or that the Secretary of State relied upon;

  (ii) which, if any, Department Circulars and selected planning appeal decisions will be relied on;

 (iii) whether any governmental publications are germane to the issues;

 (iv) whether any departmental witnesses will be called by the local planning authority;

  (v) what documents, if any, other than those in the appellant's possession, will be produced.

It is particularly important that an attempt be made to agree technical and statistical material well in advance of the inquiry. In housing appeals, when need is likely to be an issue, the Department generally invites the parties to agree basic data, but this should be the norm in any case where such matters are in issue.

Where there is likely to be significant involvement on the part of other interests (for example, parish councils, amenity groups), it is often useful to write to them in advance of the inquiry and ask for clarification of their position. The new Procedure Rules enable the Secretary of State to require any other person who wishes to appear at the inquiry to produce a statement of case within four weeks of such a request. If it is known that a third party is likely to play a major role, the appellant should request the Secretary of State to request such a statement.

2.36. Pre-inquiry meetings

Sometimes, the inspector will hold a pre-inquiry meeting (see paragraph 2.31) at which an attempt may be made to define issues and work out a reasonable programme.

This is a standard practice at "major inquiries." Such meetings are valuable in principle, but they can easily be a pure waste of time unless their purpose is adequately thought out in advance by the inspector and the parties. It is generally essential that an agenda should have been circulated before the meeting, and that the main parties should have been asked to provide information as to the nature and likely length of their cases and also to give notice of any procedural points which they wish to raise at the meeting. Only in this way will the inspector be at all adequately equipped to conduct the meeting. The meeting should result in precise guidelines and time limits for the exchange of documents and material production of proofs. General exhortations to co-operation are unlikely to achieve anything. Parties should be given specific responsibilities for carrying out specific steps within a particular timetable. It may be necessary for the authority to take a lead in this respect, and also to ensure that after the meeting a record of the matters decided is circulated.

2.37. Choice of representative

A local authority may appear at the inquiry by their clerk or any other officer appointed for the purpose, or by counsel or a solicitor. Other parties (including the appellant) may appear at the inquiry by counsel or a solicitor or any other person.[92] Normally the decision will depend on the complexity and importance of the case. In simple cases the appellant should not be afraid of appearing for himself; and in general inspectors will do their best to help with procedural difficulties. In choosing a professional representative care should be taken to select someone, (a) who is familiar with the law and practice of planning inquiries; and (b) who is at the right level (in terms of experience and

---

[92] Inspector's Rules, r. 11(3).

cost) for the case. On the former point, it must be remembered that planning can be a technical subject; and, whilst an inspector will expect to assist an appellant in person, he will assume that a professional representative knows his job. On the latter point, it is a waste of time and money to choose a well-known name if the appellant cannot afford to pay for sufficient of his time to enable him to prepare the case properly, or if the case does not raise problems requiring his particular expertise. Sometimes the function of advocate and expert witness can be combined. In smaller cases this may help to save expense. However, it is not advisable in larger cases. The advocate has a specialised function involving skills of presentation, tactics and cross-examination. He is the spokesman of the appellant, and his role is quite distinct from that of the expert witness who is, or should be, giving his own professional opinions on the particular aspect of the case with which he is called on to deal. It is now possible for certain "approved professionals" in addition to solicitors to instruct counsel.[93]

2.38. Choice of witnesses

Except where the project is of a relatively standard character, it will usually be necessary to call a representative of the appellant to explain the nature of the proposed development and the need for it. Apart from this, in most planning appeals the principal issues will be generally ones of expert opinion: for example, the planning merits of a proposal, the acceptability of its design, its drainage requirements, the adequacy of its access. In all but the simplest cases it will be necessary for each side to call suitably qualified expert witnesses to deal with these matters. As much care is necessary in selecting such witnesses as in selecting the advocate. It is normal to have one main planning witness (who may be a qualified planner or surveyor) whose evidence will cover the issues generally, and he will be supplemented by other technical witnesses as necessary. Where more than one expert is involved, it is often helpful to choose witnesses who have some experience of working together. It will usually be apparent from the grounds of refusal which issues need to be covered by expert evidence, but attention should also be given to points which have been raised by third parties in letters of objection.

Where experts are to be instructed, they should be brought into the case as early as possible, and certainly as soon as a decision to appeal is made. Not only will this give them time to assemble adequate material (for example, traffic figures at different times of the year) but it will also enable any recommendations they make to be incorporated in the plans which eventually come before the inquiry and give time for any necessary amendments to the application.

2.39. Preparation of proofs

It is customary at planning inquiries for proofs of expert witnesses to be put in and read, except where the inspector has ordered written

---

[93] Members of a number of bodies including the Royal Institute of Chartered Surveyors and the Royal Town Planning Institute may now instruct barristers directly.

summaries to be produced. In practice if there are members of the public present who have not had an opportunity to read the proof it may often have to be read in full. Proofs should be kept as short as possible and repetition avoided. For example, there is no need to describe the site at length, if it is adequately described in the statement of case. Reading time can often be saved by putting uncontentious material in appendices. Particular attention should be given to headings, paragraph numbering and general clarity of presentation. Statistics should be avoided unless they clearly prove something material to the case.

2.40. Preparation of plans and documents

The local authority should set out in its statement of case what plans will be produced at the inquiry and should have them available for inspection and copying. Too often they are not available with the result that two sets of plans and documents are produced. This tends to make the paperwork of the proceedings unnecessarily cumbersome and confusing. The plan or plans submitted with the application are often sufficient for the conduct of the inquiry, and some, if not most, of the plans submitted are non-controversial: in many cases such additional plans as are produced by the authority would in fact suffice and it may be possible to agree them, if they are available in time. What is essential is that well before the inquiry all concerned (witnesses and advocates) have available one or more clear plans which show the site and the area and identify relevant features, policy areas, roads, etc. Generally documents should be simply and attractively presented and kept to a minimum: do not submit a complete study where an extract will suffice; do not prepare elaborate photographic presentations which cannot readily be folded up and fitted into the inspector's brief case; and do not produce documents in heavy expensive binders which will only add to the weight of the inspector's luggage. Where it is necessary to produce correspondence, a bundle should be agreed if possible and page numbered (make sure that all copies are legible and have the same page numbers). As far as possible all documents should be produced in a common A4 format, and plans should be capable of being readily folded to the same format (see Appendix B.9).

2.41. Numbers of copies

Where proofs and other documents are produced, sufficient copies should be available for the appellant's own team, for the inspector and for the local authority's advocate and witnesses. This means a minimum of five copies—one for the inspector, one each for the witness and his advocate, and two for the opposing party. It is always desirable for some spare copies to be available for members of the public and the Press and in ordinary cases it would be sensible to prepare at least five such copies. There can be no absolute guide and the decision as to numbers is a matter of common sense. In a case which may generate substantial public interest, good relations will be assisted if there are plenty of copies to distribute. However, the Rules provide for copies of proofs of evidence to be sent before the inquiry to any other party who has given notice of his intention to appear.[94] Expense on copying of photographs and other illustrative matter can be cut down by restricting separate copies to the inspector and main parties and preparing one set for general display in the inquiry hall.

2.42. Preparation of case—other parties

Any person who has served a statement of case is entitled to appear at the inquiry and other third parties may appear at the inspector's discretion. The Secretary of State may require a party who has notified him of a wish to appear at an inquiry to serve a statement of case within four weeks of being so required and to supply a proof of evidence and, if required by the inspector, a written summary of the evidence not later than three weeks before giving evidence.[95] Copies of statements of case and proofs must be served on the appellant and local planning authority. Other parties who have notified the inspector that they wish to appear must be served with the appellant's and the local planning authority's statements of case and proofs of evidence.

Third parties should make use of their rights of access to documents of the local authority registers and other documents available under the Local Government (Access to Information) Act 1985,[96] as well as their right under the Inspector's Rules to request and take copies of documents referred to in the authority's statement of case. Where third parties are supporting the authority's case, it is sensible to concentrate on those matters of which local groups are likely to have special knowledge (views of importance, local road hazards, etc.)

There is no provision for financial assistance to third parties in planning cases. Where funds are available, it may be possible to instruct specialist advocates and expert witnesses. However, this may be wasted expenditure if it will merely duplicate the case being put by the planning authority. It is in any event no substitute for effective presentation of the individual points of view and strength of feeling of those directly affected.

Representatives of parish councils, amenity groups or other bodies should ensure that they have been properly authorised to express the views of their organisation. It is desirable to have available an appropriate minute of a recent meeting.

2.43. Representatives of government departments and other authorities at inquiry

Where either:

(a) the Secretary of State, any local authority or the Commission has given a direction restricting the grant of planning permission in a listed building consent case, the commission has given a direction as to how the application is to be determined; or

(b) the Secretary of State or any Minister of the Crown or government department or local authority has expressed in

---

[94] Inspector's Rules, r. 14.
[95] Inspector's Rules, r. 14.
[96] See Chap. 1.

writing to the local planning authority the view that the application should not be granted, either wholly or in part, or should be granted only subject to conditions,

the appellant may, not later than 14 days before the date of the inquiry, apply in writing to the Secretary of State for a representative of his Department or other government department concerned to be made available to the inquiry.[97] The Secretary of State forwards the application and a representative of the Department in question will then attend the inquiry.[98] There is no longer a requirement in the Rules that such a representative be called as a witness by the local planning authority to state the reasons for the direction or view expressed although it remains open to the local planning authority to call such a representative in appropriate circumstances. He will give evidence and be subject to cross-examination to the same extent as other witnesses, but questions which in the opinion of the inspector are directed to the merits of Government policy will be disallowed.[99]

2.44. Witnesses representing the Ministry of Agriculture

Arrangements for involvement of the Ministry of Agriculture ("MAFF") in appeals are explained in Circular 16/87[1]:

"Appeals
9. It will be open to the Secretary of State, or, in cases decided by inspectors, the inspector to ask MAFF to provide a technical appraisal, if he considers this necessary to ensure that agricultural issues are fully covered in the course of an appeal. Such a technical appraisal would be made available to the parties on the same basis as if it had been requested by the local planning authority at application stage.
Pre-inquiry Statements and Representations at Inquiries
10. Where an application is called in for the Secretary of State's determination or goes to appeal, any views which MAFF may have expressed to the effect that permission should not be granted, either wholly or in part, or should only be granted subject to conditions, will be treated as an expression of view within the meaning of rule 8(1) of the Inquiries Procedure Rules. Where any such views expressed by MAFF have had a material bearing on the authority's decision, and the applicant subsequently appeals, those MAFF views should be included in the authority's rule 6(2) statement. The appellant will be able to require MAFF to provide a representative to appear at the inquiry. These arrangements apply whether or not the consultation with MAFF has been carried out under statutory arrangements. The local planning authority may also wish to ask MAFF to be represented at an inquiry."

---

[97] Inspector's Rules, r. 12(1).
[98] Inspector's Rules, r. 12(2).
[99] *Ibid.* r. 12(3), (4).
[1] *Development Involving Agricultural Land.*

2.45. Information as to progress of appeal

Appellants in the past often felt frustrated by the lack of apparent progress in the processing of their appeal. The 1988 Rules should help by providing for early fixing of an inquiry date and fixed dates for exchange of pre-inquiry statements in order to speed up the inquiry process and statements of evidence. However, if the appellant is concerned about any delay or there are special reasons for requiring an early hearing, he or his advisers should contact the "case officer" dealing with his case at the Department. The name of the case officer should have been notified to the appellant but otherwise he can be identified by an enquiry to the Department under the appropriate appeal reference number. Some local planning authorities have a back-log of planning appeals and have considerable difficulty in fixing an early inquiry date. Circular 10/88 makes it clear that authorities should take urgent steps to remedy the position:

> "38. In such cases, the determination of the appellant's case is delayed, and—where the appeal is successful—the economic benefits of development are delayed. It is clearly undesirable that despite the best efforts of the Department, there should be wide variations around the country in the time taken for planning appeals to be heard. It is therefore important that those local authorities who are at present providing insufficient capacity to keep pace with the number of local inquiries which need to be programmed in their areas should take urgent steps to remedy the position. Planning authorities may wish to consider whether the position could be eased by making more use of consultants to prepare and present the authority's case at public inquiries."

F. THE INQUIRY

Generally, the inquiry follows the same procedure whether or not the matter is to be determined by an inspector or the Secretary of State. The procedural steps are set out below and references generally give the relevant rule number in both the Secretary of State's and the Inspector's Rules.

2.46. Persons entitled to appear

The applicant and the local planning authority which refused permission are the principal persons entitled to appear. In addition, the council of the county or the council of the district in which the land is situated, or the national park committee where the land is in a national park, a joint planning board or any urban development corporation also have the right to be represented if they are not the local planning authority.

Section 71(2) parties,[2] any person who has served a statement of case, the council of the parish or community in which the land is

---

[2] See para. 2.29 above.

situated (if that council has made representations to the local planning authority in respect of the application), and, where the land is in an area designated as the site of a new town, the development corporation of the new town, and the New Towns Commission if required to be notified, complete the list of persons and authorities entitled to appear.[3]

2.47. Other appearances

Any other person may appear at an inquiry at the discretion of the inspector.[4] The established practice is that all persons with a genuine interest in the application (for example, neighbours who fear that their property may be affected and persons or representatives or bodies of persons concerned to preserve the amenities of the district) are allowed to appear and take part in the inquiry. But this is by administrative concession. Third parties, even when allowed to appear at an inquiry, may not be allowed to take as full a part in it as they might wish. For instance, they may be denied rights to cross-examine the witnesses.[5]

2.48. Procedure at the inquiry

(A) *Outline of the procedure*. Except as otherwise provided in the 1988 Rules, the procedure at the inquiry is in the inspector's discretion.[6] He opens the inquiry by stating his name, qualifications and terms of appointment, and by describing the applications before the inquiry. He then takes appearances, and the advocates or representatives of the appellant and of the local planning authority should give their names and those of their witnesses; the names of local objectors are then recorded. The inspector also inquires whether representatives of the press are present and whether they wish to obtain a copy of the report. Except that the appellant has the right to begin and the right of final reply, the order of appearance is at the discretion of the inspector.[7] The normal sequence is, (1) the appellant; (2) the local planning authority; (3) section 71(2) parties [29(3)/71] and any public bodies; (4) other interested parties; (5) appellant's reply. In cases where there are many parties involved, the inspector may begin by inviting the representatives of each to make a short (10 minute) summary of his case. At larger inquiries more elaborate arrangements will have to be made for programming, after including the appointment of a programme officer. Although the initiative will usually be taken by the inspectorate, it is open to the main parties to suggest suitable arrangements where they anticipate problems.

In the standard inquiry, the normal procedure is as follows. The appellant opens his case and calls evidence in support. The examina-

---

[3] Secretary of State's Rules, r. 11; Inspector's Rules, r. 11.
[4] *Ibid*. r. 11(2).
[5] See para. 2.48 below.
[6] Secretary of State's Rules, r. 14; Inspector's Rules, r. 15.
[7] Secretary of State's Rules, r. 14(2); Inspector's Rules, r. 15(2).

tion-in-chief of witnesses may be conducted by question and answer in the same way as in court, or more usually they will read proofs or summaries of proofs. The appellant's witnesses are then cross-examined. The local planning authority then open their case, call their evidence in the same way, and make their closing statement. Other parties follow in the above sequence. The local planning authority are normally required to close their case before other parties are heard. This is not a hard and fast rule and, in appropriate cases, closing speeches of the main parties may be reserved until all evidence has been given. In any event the inspector will normally allow individual parties to be fitted into the programme at times convenient to them. The advocate for the appellant makes the final closing speech.[8]

(B) *Times of sittings.* Inquiries usually sit from 10 a.m. to about 5 p.m. each day, with a break for lunch of about one hour, usually from 1 p.m. to 2 p.m. These times can be varied by the inspector. The lunch-break is a valuable time for reviewing the case, planning additional evidence and preparing submissions. This is assisted if arrangements are made beforehand for a simple meal to be available somewhere locally, with room to write and spread papers. Smoking is not allowed during inquiries. Inspectors sometimes allow a short break in the middle of the morning and afternoon sittings, particularly if the authority can make arrangements for tea or coffee to be available. These breaks can be useful occasions for informal exchanges of views and information. Inspectors are sometimes asked to sit late to complete an inquiry. In spite of the convenience, the practice is generally undesirable, since the inspector's ability to absorb information and take adequate notes will inevitably be reduced.

(C) *Inspectors' practice advice.* Guidelines for parties at inquiries have been given by the Chief Inspector. They are reproduced at Appendix B.8. Particularly noteworthy is the relative importance given to opening and closing statements. The appellant's opening statement is a useful opportunity to set the scene, and catch the attention of the press and public (if any). However, in most planning cases its value from the inspector's point of view is limited if, as is usually the case, the issues are fully covered in the written evidence which the inspector will have had the opportunity of reading beforehand. A short statement (not more than 30 minutes) is usually sufficient, summarising the issues and evidence, and drawing attention to any procedural points or unusual features. At long inquiries or inquiries where complex issues of law or policy interpretations arise, a fuller opening presentation may be appropriate.

Closing statements can be of much more importance since, by reviewing all the evidence both written and oral, they provide a real opportunity to influence the form of the inspector's decision or report. This is particularly important where reliance is to be placed on admissions made in cross-examination or as the result of prolonged debates on technical or statistical issues. Inspectors frequently ask to

[8] Secretary of State's Rules, r. 14(2); Inspector's Rules, r. 15(2).

be given written notes of the final submissions; and it is good practice in any event to offer some form of written summary even if it is in manuscript. Exclusive reliance on the inspector's note-taking capacity at the end of the inquiry may lead to omissions or misunderstandings. It is always worth producing written summaries of any statistical material (insofar as it qualifies or differs from material in the written proofs) and of any other matters of which a precise record is important (for example, legal submissions). There is often a temptation to rush the final submissions in order to complete an inquiry at the end of a long day: such practice should be resisted.

(D) *Rules of evidence.* The Rules[9] provide that evidence is admitted at the discretion of the inspector, who can direct that documents tendered in evidence may be inspected by any person entitled or permitted to appear at the inquiry and that facilities be afforded to him to take or obtain copies thereof. When new documents are produced, the other parties must be given adequate time to consider them, although often a slightly prolonged lunch adjournment will be enough.[10] The rules of evidence which are applied in courts of law do not apply at planning inquiries, where any evidence may be admitted which is probative of some fact in issue before the inquiry.[11] It is unusual, therefore for any material to be excluded altogether although the inspector can be addressed as to the limited weight which should be given to evidence not subject to cross-examination.

(E) *Amendment of statement of case and consequential adjournment of inquiry.* The inspector may allow the local planning authority or the applicant or both of them to alter or add to the statement of case or to the list of documents which accompanied the statement.[12] Such leave should only be given "so far as may be necessary for considering any of the matters under inquiry."[13] The inspector must give every person entitled to appear an adequate opportunity of considering any fresh matter or document and if necessary must adjourn the inquiry.

In practice it is unusual for such adjournments to be requested, in view of the practical inconvenience it causes. If an adjournment does become necessary the inspector may make in his report a recommendation as to payment of any additional costs occasioned by the adjournment.

(F) *Adjournment of inquiry for other reasons.* The inspector has also a general power to adjourn the inquiry. If the time, date and place are announced before the adjournment, no further notice is required.[14] If a new notice is necessary, a reasonable time should be given, although there is no specific requirement in the Rules.

---

[9] Secretary of State's Rules, r. 13; Inspector's Rules, r. 14.

[10] See *Performance Cars* v. *Secretary of State for the Environment* (1977) 34 P. & C.R. 92; [1977] J.P.L. 585.

[11] *Miller (T.A.)* v. *Minister of Housing and Local Government* [1968] 1 W.L.R. 992.

[12] Secretary of State's Rules, r. 14(8); Inspector's Rules, r. 15(8).

[13] Inspector's Rules, r. 15(8).

[14] Secretary of State's Rules, r. 14(11); Inspector's Rules, r. 15(11).

(G) *Absence of persons entitled to appear*. The inspector can adjourn the inquiry if any person entitled to appear is not present; alternatively he may proceed with the inquiry at his discretion.[15] In practice, if one of the main parties fails to appear without prior warning or explanation, and attempts to trace him are unsuccessful, the inspector is likely to proceed with the appeal on the material before him, rather than adjourn.

(H) *Acceptance of written representations and statements*. The inspector is entitled to take into account any written representations or statement received by him before or during the inquiry from any person.[16] In practice all such representations are taken into account. The documents in question must be disclosed at the inquiry. The usual practice is that the documents are not read aloud but are passed among the interested parties who may comment on them, if they wish, at an appropriate time in the presentation of their case. The Rules imply that documents received after the inquiry should not normally be taken into account, but sometimes it will be essential to do so when, for example, some new point of importance has arisen.[17] The inspector may refuse to permit the giving or production of evidence, cross-examination or the presentation of any other matter which he considers irrelevant or repetitious. But where he refuses to allow oral evidence to be given, any person may submit the evidence or other matter in writing before the close of the inquiry.[18]

The inspector may require a person who is behaving in a disruptive manner to leave, may refuse to permit his return or may permit it subject to conditions: such a person has a right to submit evidence or any other matter in writing before the close of the inquiry.[19]

(I) *Evidence on oath*. The inspector may take evidence on oath and for that purpose administer oaths or may, instead of administering an oath, require the person examined to make and subscribe a declaration of the truth of the matter respecting which he is examined (Local Government Act 1972, section 250). This power is not generally used other than in connection with appeals against enforcement notices under sections 174 and 175 or determination under section 64 of the 1990 Act [88, 53/71], where evidence on the facts relative to the past user of the premises is crucial. This will also apply to established use certificate appeals.

(J) *Witness summonses and production of documents*. If a local inquiry is ordered, advantage may be taken of the provisions of section

---

[15] Secretary of State's Rules, r. 14(9); Inspector's Rules, r. 15(9).

[16] Secretary of State's Rules, r. 14(10); Inspector's Rules, r. 15(10).

[17] See *Whitecroft* v. *Bolton Metropolitan Borough Council* [1984] J.P.L. 875; *Reading Borough Council* v. *Secretary of State for the Environment and Commercial Union Properties (Investments)* [1986] J.P.L. 115; and *Prest* v. *Secretary of State for Wales* [1983] J.P.L. 112, where a compulsory purchase decision was quashed for failure to take account of a point raised in post-inquiry correspondence.

[18] *Ibid*. r. 14(4); r. 15(4).

[19] *Ibid*. r. 14(7); r. 15(7).

250 of the Local Government Act 1972 (applied by the 1990 Act, section 320 [282(2)/71]). The person appointed to hold the inquiry may issue a summons to any person, subject to payment of expenses, to attend at a time and place specified in the summons to give evidence or to produce any documents in his custody or under his control which relate to any matter in question at the inquiry (1972 Act, section 250(2)). The power is rarely exercised and it is likely to be more relevant in enforcement appeals where disputed facts are in issue (see Chapter 5, *post*). Its exercise is within the sole discretion of the "appointed person", *i.e.* the inspector, who holds the inquiry; and therefore becomes exercisable as soon as the inspector is appointed. The inspector has no power to require the production of documents of title to any land which is not the property of the local authority.[20]

(K) *Amendment of application for permission.* The power of the Secretary of State to reverse or vary any part of the decision of the local planning authority and to deal with the application as if it had been made to him in the first instance[21] in theory gives him wide powers to consider amendments on appeal. In practice the power is restrictively exercised.[22] Amendments will not be accepted if they extend the scope of the development specified in the application or if they "materially change the character of the development" as originally applied for. Furthermore, inspectors are often unwilling to accept amendments at inquiries except with the consent of the local planning authority, even though this is not strictly necessary.[23] Ample notice should therefore be given of any proposed amendments, and copies sent to the Department well in advance.[24] As far as possible the amendments should be discussed and agreed with the authority before the inquiry.

(L) *Cross-examination.* The appellant, the local planning authority and section 71(2) parties have the right to cross-examine witnesses. In practice a party is restricted to questioning witnesses opposing his case. However, evidence produced by supporting parties may be questioned to clarify particular points or where the evidence is hostile on a particular issue. Cross-examination by other parties is at the discretion of the inspector. The inspector may refuse to permit cross-examination when he considers it to be irrelevant or repetitious (see Appendix B.8). The practice varies considerably. Where a main group of objectors is represented by a professional advocate, it would be unusual not to allow him a full opportunity for cross-examination.

---

[20] 1972 Act, s.250(2), proviso (b).

[21] 1990 Act, s.79 [36/71].

[22] For the principles see *Kent County Council* v. *Secretary of State for the Environment and Burmah-Total Refineries Trust* (1976) 33 P. & C.R. 70; [1976] J.P.L. 755; *Wheatcroft (Bernard)* v. *Secretary of State for the Environment* [1982] J.P.L. 37, C.A.

[23] *Kent County Council* v. *Secretary of State for the Environment and Burmah-Total Refineries Trust* [1976] J.P.L. 755.

[24] In practice, at least a week has to be allowed simply to ensure that the matter reaches the inspector.

Conversely, where there are a number of individual objectors, the inspector is much more likely to seek to restrict questioning. The inspector will usually indicate at the outset of the inquiry what the practice is going to be, and, if not, he can be asked to do so.

The value of cross-examination at local inquiries can be over-estimated. At its best it can be a useful method of clarifying the issues, narrowing the differences and exposing weaknesses in the opposing case. At its worst it can be time-wasting and counter-productive. The following points should be borne in mind:

> (i) Aggressive cross-examination techniques tend to be unpopular with inspectors, who are often unimpressed by apparently damaging answers forced from the witness in this way. Perhaps because many of them will have been at the receiving end of cross-examination in their former professional lives, their sympathies are likely to be with the witness.
> (ii) Differences in interpretation of development plans or other documents are rarely a useful subject for cross-examination. The arguments can be fully explained in submission.
> (iii) Much of the evidence of inquiries is in the nature of opinion evidence by professional witnesses. If it is based on faulty data or mistaken premises, it may be possible to undermine it. However, an expression of view on a purely subjective matter (for example, aesthetics) is unlikely to be altered by cross-examination and, even if it is, the inspector is likely to form his own view in any event.
> (iv) Extensive cross-examination of non-professional local witnesses is usually a profitless exercise and may be dangerous. Lay witnesses who are not particularly good at spontaneous self-expression often respond better to the stimulus of cross-examination, and they may bring out points of local knowledge previously overlooked. Usually it is better to leave any new points of substance to be covered in submission or, if necessary, to ask the inspector for leave to recall an appropriate witness to deal with them.
> (v) Since there is usually no transcript, note-taking is a problem. A careful watch should be kept on the inspector's pen. If he has stopped writing, it usually means one is wasting one's time. If he is writing vigorously, it may mean that he is interested—or that he is trying to keep awake. Since inspectors will usually use the written proof as the basis for drafting their reports or decision letters it helps if cross-examination follows generally the sequence of the proof and is directed to particular paragraphs in it, and if the advocate gives a specific indication when he thinks he has received an answer of particular significance. In any event, he should ensure that someone on his side takes a full note so that relevant answers can be referred to in closing submissions.

(M) *Re-examination.* Following cross-examination, the advocate who called the witness is given the opportunity to re-examine him. The purpose of this is to give him an opportunity to clarify or qualify (but not contradict) answers given in cross-examination. "Leading" questions (*i.e.*, questions which suggest the appropriate answer) are not permitted. For this reason, re-examination can be an unpredictable exercise, particularly as the witness will have become mentally adjusted to protecting himself against a hostile examination and may not readily adjust to the more friendly approach of his own advocate. Re-examination, therefore, is usually best kept to a minimum.

(N) *Inspector's questions*. After the completion of cross-examination and re-examination the inspector will usually ask his own questions. The purpose of this is to complete his record of the basic information required for his decision or report, rather than to suggest conclusions on the main issues. However, it can sometimes be a useful pointer to aspects which need to be covered fully. If the inspector's questions raise new matters, an opportunity will usually be given to the main parties to ask any further questions arising out of them.

(O) *Third party involvement*. As stated above, third parties (including individual objectors and groups) are usually heard after the other parties but before the appellant's final submissions. This can be a considerable advantage, in that it gives them a full opportunity to analyse and exploit the weaknesses in the other cases. However, other arrangements may be made to suit the convenience of the parties, for example, at longer inquiries or where there is more than usual public interest, an evening session may sometimes be arranged. This is usually only done where it is specifically requested. Inquiry practice has not yet evolved a very satisfactory format for such meetings, and the initiative tends to be left to those requesting the meeting to ensure that it is effective. Accordingly, any local representative who makes such a request should be sure that the meeting will be well attended and that people come prepared to make short statements (preferably with copies of written notes for the inspector and the main parties). A badly attended meeting will be counter-productive in that it will create an unfavourable impression of the degree of real public concern. It is also important that people are given some prior information about the project and the inquiry so far. People who come to such a meeting expecting to be given a presentation of the main cases will usually be disappointed. If they make representations on a mistaken basis of fact, they will be open to attack.

(P) *Fairness*. Quite apart from the Rules, there is a general requirement that the inquiry should not only be fair, but be seen to be fair.[25] The former requires the inspector to ensure that all parties are given a reasonable opportunity to present their case and to challenge and respond to points made in opposition. The latter requires the inspector not to give even the appearance of undue favour or hostility to either party. An inspector's decision was quashed where the chairman of the local planning committee, who was thought to have been instrumental in the authority's refusal of permission, was seen in conversation with the inspector after the end of the inquiry.[26] Another

---

[25] See *Bushell* v. *Secretary of State for the Environment* [1981] A.C. 75; [1980] J.P.L. 458.
[26] *Simmons* v. *Secretary of State for the Environment* [1985] J.P.L. 253.

was quashed when the inspector gave the impression of extreme hostility and unwillingness to listen to the appellant's case at the inquiry.[27] Even though there had been no injustice, a compulsory purchase order was quashed as a result of a conversation held by the inspector in the absence of the applicants.[28]

(Q) *Conditions*. Inspectors will normally ask the parties to seek to agree a list of conditions to be imposed if the appeal is successful. Normally the authority will produce a draft list and ask the appellant for comments: this should preferably be done before the inquiry. Authorities have a tendency to produce over-elaborate lists of conditions which do not conform to the strict standards set by Circular 1/85 (see Appendix A, *post*) and can lead to excessive control of detailed implementations. Such lists should, therefore, be examined carefully and judged against the advice of the Circular.

(R) *Site inspections*. The Rules make provision for inspection of "the land."[29] The inspector may make an unaccompanied inspection before or during the inquiry without giving notice of his intention to the persons entitled to appear. He may also inspect after the close of the inquiry, and he must do so if either the appellant or the local planning authority so request before or during the inquiry. In all cases where he intends to make an inspection after the inquiry he must announce at the inquiry the date and time.[30] The appellant, the local planning authority and the section 71(2) parties [29(3)/71] are entitled to accompany the inspector on any inspection after the close of the inquiry but he need not defer his inspection if any person entitled to accompany him is not present at the time appointed. In practice, whether or not requested, a formal site inspection accompanied by the parties is almost always held, usually immediately after the end of the inquiry. Normally attendance will be by one representative (usually the main witness) on behalf of each of the main parties, but the inspector will generally offer third parties the opportunity to attend if they wish. "The land" is defined in rule 2 as "the land, tree or building to which an inquiry relates." There is, therefore, no express duty to inspect other land or premises mentioned at the inquiry either as alternative sites for the proposed development or as likely to be affected by it; but in practice the inspector will normally visit any relevant viewpoint or site within the locality if he is requested to do so. Discussion of the issues is not permitted during the site inspection.

2.49. Procedure after the inquiry—Secretary of State's decisions

(A) *Inspector's report*. After the close of the inquiry, the inspector makes a written report to the Secretary of State including his findings

---

[27] *Halifax Building Society* v. *Secretary of State for the Environment* [1983] J.P.L. 816.
[28] *British Muslims Association* v. *Secretary of State for the Environment* (1987) 55 P. & C.R. 204.
[29] Secretary of State's Rules, r. 15; Inspector's Rules, r. 16.
[30] *Ibid.* r. 15(3); r. 16(3).

of fact and his recommendations or his reason for not making any recommendations.[31] These reports follow a standard form. They begin with a description of the site and surroundings. Then follows a summary of the cases presented respectively by the appellant, the local planning authority and any other parties. The report ends with the inspector's conclusions and his recommendations. A list of the parties, their representatives and witnesses, and of the documents submitted in evidence, is appended to the report. Where an Assessor has been appointed he may make a report to the inspector. The inspector will append it to his own report where he will set out how far he agrees or disagrees (giving reasons) with the Assessor's report.[32]

(B) *Procedure where the Secretary of State disagrees with the inspector: re-opening of inquiry.* The Secretary of State is not bound by the views expressed by his inspector. As a matter of law, the Secretary of State must form his own independent view giving such weight as thinks proper to the findings and recommendations of the inspector.[33] However, in certain circumstances, the Inquiries Procedure Rules require him to notify the parties if he proposes to disagree with the inspector's recommendation. Rule 16(4) stipulates that where the Secretary of State:

(a) differs from the inspector on any matter of fact[34]; or

(b) after the close of the inquiry takes into consideration any new evidence (including expert opinion on a matter of fact) or any new matter of fact (not being of government policy),

and is for that reason disposed to disagree with a recommendation made by the inspector, he must not come to a decision which is at variance with any such recommendations without first notifying the appellant, the local planning authority, and any section 71(2) party who appeared at the inquiry, of his disagreement and the reasons for it and giving them an opportunity of making written representations within 21 days or of asking for the inquiry to be re-opened. If any party does so ask, the Secretary of State must re-open it.[35]

Even where the Rules do not in terms demand it, fairness may require that the parties be given a chance to comment on such matters and ventilate them at an inquiry.[36]

(C) *General power to re-open inquiry.* In addition to the cases where he may be required to re-open the inquiry (paragraph (B), *supra*), the

---

[31] Secretary of State's Rules, r. 16(1).

[32] *Ibid.* r. 16(2), (3).

[33] See *Continental Sprays* v. *Minister of Housing and Local Government* (1968) 19 P. & C.R. 774. *R.* v. *Secretary of State for the Environment, The Times* July 14, 1989.

[34] As to what is a "matter of fact," see *Pyrford Properties* v. *Secretary of State for the Environment* [1977] J.P.L. 724. It does not depend on the particular heading under which the item comes in the inspector's report: *Luke (Lord) of Pavenham* v. *Minister of Housing & Local Government* [1968] 1 Q.B. 172.

[35] Secretary of State's Rules, r. 16(5).

[36] See *Fairmount Investments* v. *Secretary of State* [1976] 1 W.L.R. 1255.

Secretary of State has a general power to cause the inquiry to be re-opened in any case where he thinks fit.[37] Where an inquiry is re-opened the provisions as to the notice to be given to various persons and the mode of giving notice apply (paragraphs 2.30–2.32 *ante*).

(D) *Notification of decision with reasons*. Rule 17 requires the Secretary of State to notify his decision and his reasons for it in writing to all persons entitled to appear at the inquiry who did appear. The statutory duty to give reasons is of particular importance when considering the possibility of challenging the Secretary of State's decision in the High Court (see below). The reasons must be clear and adequate and deal with the substantial issue in the case.[38]

Where any person entitled to be notified of the Secretary of State's decision has not received a copy of the inspector's report and makes a written application to the Secretary of State within four weeks from that date of the decision, the Secretary of State must supply him with a copy. "Report" includes any Assessor's report but not any other documents so appended; and any person who has received a copy of the report may apply to the Secretary of State for an opportunity of inspecting such documents and the Secretary of State must give him the opportunity.

(E) *Costs*. In the case of a local inquiry (but not a hearing) the Secretary of State may make orders as to the costs of the parties (Local Government Act 1972, section 250(5)). Costs will not normally be awarded except where one party has acted "unreasonably." The principles upon which awards are made are set out in Circular 2/87 (see Appendix A, *post*). The application for costs should be made to the inspector immediately before the close of the inquiry.[39] He will give the other party an opportunity to respond, and will report the submissions and his recommendation to the Secretary of State. Late applications for costs will not be entertained unless there was a good reason for not applying earlier.[40] An award is intended to cover "the cost necessarily and reasonably incurred in relation to the proceedings."[41] In the case of disagreement as to amount, it will be determined by a Taxing Master. In some cases (for example, where the authority failed to present evidence on a particular issue) a partial award may be made.

In addition to ordering one party to pay the costs of another, the Secretary of State may recover his administrative expenses of the inquiry at a standard daily amount.[42]

---

[37] Secretary of State's Rules, r. 16(5).

[38] See *Givaudan* v. *Minister of Housing and Local Government* [1967] 1 W.L.R. 250; *French Kier Developments* v. *Secretary of State for the Environment* [1977] 1 All E.R. 296, and *Save Britain's Heritage* v. *Secretary of State for the Environment, The Times*, April 4, 1990.

[39] Advocates must put aside any superstitions they may have about applying for costs before they know the result of the appeal.

[40] Circ. 2/87, para. 27, and see Appendix A.3.

[41] *Ibid*. para. 28.

[42] Housing and Planning Act 1986, s.42; Fees for Inquiries (Standard Daily Amount) Regulations 1988 (S.I. 1988 No. 1788).

2.50. Procedure after the inquiry—Inspectors' decisions

(A) *New evidence etc.* In cases decided by inspectors similar rules apply in relation to the notification of the parties and the re-opening of the inquiry where the inspector "proposes to take into consideration any new evidence (including expert opinon on a matter of fact) or any new matter of fact (not being a matter of government policy) which was not raised at the inquiry and which he considers to be material to his decision."[43] There is a similar general power to re-open the inquiry, with equivalent provision for notice.[44]

(B) *Decision.* There is no report to the Secretary of State, but the inspector is under a duty to notify the parties of his decision with adequate reasons.[45] The decision-letter will usually incorporate a short summary of the cases of the parties, but will not contain a detailed report of the proceedings. Similar provision is made for inspection of documents.[46]

(C) *Advance notice of decision.* In cases to be decided by the inspector, he may, at the end of the inquiry, indicate that he is prepared to give the parties advance notice of his decision. This is a non-statutory procedure and can only be adopted with the consent of the parties. Where it is adopted, the inspector will, immediately following his site view, send to the parties a notice stating whether he proposes to allow or dismiss the appeal; and, if the former, whether he proposes to allow it subject to conditions. His formal decision-letter with the details of any conditions and his reasons will follow in due course in the normal way (usually about three to four weeks later). It should be noted that the decision is that contained in the formal decision-letter, and technically there is no permission until that is received.

(D) *Costs.* Similar principles apply to the award of costs, save that the award will normally be made by the inspector himself rather than the Secretary of State.

G. Applications To The High Court

2.51. High Court remedies under the 1990 Act

The Act of 1990 in Part XII contains provisions which entitle the decision of the Secretary of State on section 79 appeals [36/71] to be challenged in the High Court. For these purposes, an inspector's decision is treated as though it were a decision of the Secretary of State.[47] The challenge to a section 79 appeal decision is by way of an application to quash the decision.[48]

---

[43] Inspector's Rules, r. 17.
[44] *Ibid.* r. 17(3).
[45] *Ibid.* r. 18(1).
[46] *Ibid.* r. 18(2).
[47] 1990 Act, Sched. 6, para. 2 [Sched. 9, para. 2(3)/71].
[48] *Ibid.* s.288 [245/71].

2.52. Grounds

The application may be on one or both of two grounds: first, that the Secretary of State's decision was not within the powers of the Act; second, that any of the "relevant requirements"[49] in relation to the decision have not been complied with. In practice, the two grounds are not clearly distinguished, and the same complaint may fall under both heads. They are generally interpreted as similar to the grounds on which decisions may be challenged by judicial review. The best summary of the circumstances in which the court will quash a decision under this procedure is as follows (the principles apply equally to inspectors' decisions):[50]

"(1) The Secretary of State must not act perversely. That is, if the court considers that no reasonable person in the position of the Secretary of State, properly directing himself on the relevant material, could have reached the conclusion which he did reach, the decision may be overturned. See, for example, *Ashbridge Investments* v. *Minister of Housing and Local Government* [1965] 1 W.L.R. 1320, *per* Lord Denning M.R. at 1326F and Harman L.J. at 1328H. This is really no more than another example of the principle enshrined in a sentence from the judgment of Lord Greene M.R. in *Associated Provincial Picture Houses* v. *Wednesbury Corporation* [1948] 1 K.B. 223 at 230: "It is true to say that, if a decision on a competent matter is so unreasonable that no reasonable authority could ever have come to it, then the courts can interfere."

(2) In reaching his conclusion the Secretary of State must not take into account irrelevant material or fail to take into account that which is relevant: see, for example, the *Ashbridge Investments* case *per* Lord Denning M.R., *loc. cit.*

(3) The Secretary of State must abide by the statutory procedures, in particular by the Town and Country Planning (Inquiries Procedure) Rules 1974 [now the 1988 Rules]. These rules require him to give reasons for his decision after a planning inquiry (rule 13) and those reasons must be proper and adequate reasons which are clear and intelligible, and deal with the substantial points which have been raised: *Re Poyser and Mills Arbitration* [1964] 2 Q.B. 467.

(4) The Secretary of State in exercising his powers, which include reaching a decision such as that in this case, must not depart from the principles of natural justice: *per* Lord Russell of Killowen in *Fairmount Investments* v. *Secretary of State for the Environment* [1976] 1 W.L.R. 1255 at 1263D.

(5) If the Secretary of State differs from his inspector on a finding of fact or takes into account any new evidence or issue of fact

---

[49] *I.e.*, any requirements of the 1990 Act or of the Tribunals and Inquiries Act 1971 or of any Order, Regulations or Rules made under either Act.

[50] *Per* Forbes J. in *Seddon Properties* v. *Secretary of State* [1978] J.P.L. 835.

not canvassed at the inquiry he must, if this involves disagreeing with the inspector's recommendations notify the parties and give them at least an opportunity of making further representations: rule 12 of the Inquiries Procedure Rules.

There are other peripheral principles. If he differs from the inspector on an inference of fact he must have sufficient material to enable him to do so: *per* Lord Denning M.R. in *Coleen Properties* v. *Minister of Housing and Local Government* [1971] 1 All E.R. 1049 at 1053C. Otherwise the courts can interfere in accordance with the first principle stated above. If it is a matter of planning policy he is free to disagree with the inspector's conclusions or recommendations without bringing into operation rule 12: *Luke (Lord) of Pavenham* v. *Minister of Housing and Local Government* [1968] 1 Q.B. 172; but, of course, he must make clear what the policy is and its relevance to the issues raised at the inquiry in accordance with the third principle above. If there has been conflicting evidence at the inquiry it seems to me that he may, if he wishes, prefer one piece of evidence to another, though the material must be there to enable him to do so, he must give reasons for doing so, and if he is disagreeing with a finding of fact by the inspector he must apply the procedure of rule 12. Since the courts will interfere only if he acts beyond his powers (which is the foundation of all the above principles) it is clear that his powers include the determination of the weight to be given to any particular contention; he is entitled to attach what weight he pleases to the various arguments and contentions of the parties; the courts will not entertain a submission that he gave undue weight to one argument or failed to give any weight at all to another. Again in doing so he must, at any rate if substantial issues are involved, give clear reasons for his decision.

In considering whether or not the Secretary of State has acted contrary to any of these principles the materials upon which the court may come to a conclusion are, in general, the inspector's report and the letter of the Secretary of State setting out his decision. In approaching this task it is no part of the court's duty to subject that decision letter to the kind of scrutiny appropriate to the determination of the meaning of a contract or a statute. Because the letter is addressed to parties who are well aware of all the issues involved and of the arguments deployed at the inquiry it is not necessary to rehearse every argument relating to each matter in every paragraph.''

2.53. Procedure

The detailed procedure for making an application is covered by Order 94 of the Rules of the Supreme Court. The application must be made by originating motion to a single Judge of the Queen's Bench Division. (An illustrative form of notice of motion is given in Appendix C.) This must be filed in the High Court and served on the other parties within the six week period. This time limit cannot be extended.[51] The Rules require service on the Secretary of State and the authority directly concerned.[52] If the application is made by the authority or some other party, the appellant in the appeal should also be served. Evidence is by affidavit, which should be filed and served within 14 days of the notice of motion,[53] but this time limit can be extended by consent or leave of the court. Any affidavit in opposition should be filed within 21 days thereafter.[54] A copy of any affidavit filed and of the exhibits must be left with the court for use of the judge.[55]

In practice evidence is usually limited to a short affidavit (sworn by the solicitor handling the case, or some other person with knowledge of the case) which will exhibit the decision and report (if any), and such of the documents including a plan as are necessary to understand the grounds. Reference to documents or other matters not before the inspector is not normally permitted. Where, however, some aspect of the proceedings before him is not fully reported in the decision letter or report, additional evidence may exceptionally be given.[56]

2.54. Application must be by a "person aggrieved"

As with an appeal to the Secretary of State (see paragraph 2.20, *ante*), it is essential that the applicant to the High Court should have a sufficiently direct interest in the matter. It used to be considered that a legal interest was necessary, so that, for example, an application could not be made by a neighbouring landowner.[57] This rigid view is, however, unlikely to be followed today.[58] In any event, it has been held that anyone who is permitted to appear at the inquiry (for example, a representative of a local residents' group) has a sufficient legal interest in the decision to enable him to make an application to the High Court.[59] An authority directly concerned may make an application to the High Court under section 288(2) of the 1990 Act [245(2)/71] in the same way as may a person aggrieved.

2.55. Powers of the High Court

Where an application is made to the High Court to quash the decision of the Secretary of State the court has power to make an interim order suspending the operation of the decision pending the final determination of the proceedings.[60] This power is rarely invoked

---

[51] R. v. *Secretary of State for the Environment, ex p. Ostler* [1977] Q.B. 122. R. v. *Secretary of State for the Environment, ex p. Kent, The Times*, May 14, 1989.

[52] R.S.C., Ord. 94, r. 2(2)(*d*).

[53] *Ibid.* Ord. 94, r. 3.

[54] *Ibid.* r. 3(3).

[55] *Ibid.* r. 3(4). See Appendix C, *post*, for illustrative drafts.

[56] See *East Hampshire District Council* v. *Secretary of State for the Environment and Josephi (C.H.)* [1979] J.P.L. 533; affirming [1978] J.P.L. 182.

[57] *Buxton* v. *Minister of Housing and Local Government* [1961] 1 Q.B. 278.

[58] See *Att-Gen. (Gambia)* v. *N'Jie* [1961] A.C. 617.

[59] *Turner* v. *Secretary of State for the Environment* (1973) 28 P. & C.R. 123. See also *Bizony* v. *Secretary of State for the Environment* [1976] J.P.L. 306, (1976) 239 E.G. 281; and *Hollis* v. *Secretary of State for the Environment* [1983] J.P.L. 164.

[60] 1990 Act, s.288(5)(*a*) [245(4)(*a*)/71].

and generally only relevant where a permission has been granted and the authority or any other interested person is seeking to challenge its validity and wishes to prevent its being implemented in the meantime. An undertaking in damages is likely to be required (conditional upon the developer actually deferring implementation following the suspension). If the court is satisfied that the decision was not within the powers of the Act or that the applicant's interests have been substantially prejudiced by failure to comply with the "relevant requirements" it may quash the decision.[61] The requirement for "substantial prejudice" is satisfied if there is a significant chance that the decision would have been more favourable to the applicant if made on the correct basis,[62] although a non-stringent test may be applied where the local authority is the applicant.[63] The decision must be quashed as a whole, it cannot be quashed in part.[64]

The exercise of the court's power is in any event discretionary. However, where the statutory requirements for quashing the decision are satisfied the court will not refuse an order except in general circumstances.[65]

2.56. Appearance and costs

Where the application is made by the original appellant, the decision will normally be defended by the Treasury Solicitor for the Secretary of State. If so, the planning authority will not normally be represented; and, if it is, is unlikely to be awarded costs even if successful. Where the authority is the applicant, the original appellant is justified in appearing even if the Secretary of State is represented, and since they have separate interests two sets of costs will usually be awarded.

2.57. Procedure following quashing of decision

Where a decision of the Secretary of State or an inspector is quashed, he must send to persons entitled to appear at the inquiry and who appeared at it a written statement of matters upon which further representations are invited for his further consideration. An opportunity is provided for those persons to make such representations in writing or of asking such for the re-opening of the inquiry within 21 days and he may as he thinks fit cause the inquiry to be re-opened (whether by the same or a different inspector).[66]

---

[61] 1990 Act, s.288(5)(b) [245(4)(b)/71].

[62] See *Hibernian Property Co.* v. *Secretary of State for the Environment* (1973) 27 P. & C.R. 197; *Performance Cars* v. *Secretary of State for the Environment* (1977) 34 P. & C.R. 92.

[63] See, *e.g., Greenwich London Borough* v. *Secretary of State for the Environment and Spar Environments* [1981] J.P.L. 809; but compare *Preston Borough Council* v. *Secretary of State for the Environment and E.L.S. Wholesale (Wolverhampton)* [1978] J.P.L. 548.

[64] *Hartnell* v. *Minister of Housing & Local Government* [1963] 1 W.L.R. 1141, 1154.

[65] See *Kent County Council* v. *Secretary of State for the Environment and Burmah-Total Refineries Trust* (1976) 33 P. & C.R. 70.

[66] Secretary of State's Rules, r. 18; Inspector's Rules, r. 19.

2.58. Judicial review

Review by the High Court under section 288 [245/71] excludes any rights to impugn the Secretary of State's action or decision by *certiorari* or declaration.[67] However, the right to apply for mandamus to compel the Secretary of State to carry out his duties is not excluded.

Mandamus can be directed against Ministers of the Crown to hear and entertain appeals and applications in respect of which they have, expressly or by implication, refused jurisdiction.[68] The statutory procedure applies only to a final decision on the appeal. Thus, a refusal of an adjournment may be challenged by judicial review.[69] It seems also that a refusal to entertain the appeal altogether is a matter for judicial review rather than the statutory procedure.[70]

In any other case where the statutory procedure does not apply there is no reason why judicial review should not be available.[71]

2.59. Practical considerations

It must always be borne in mind that, even where a decision of the Secretary of State or the inspector is successfully challenged, it merely results in the matter being remitted to him for redetermination. Normally the interested parties are given an opportunity to make further representations, or sometimes to have the inquiry re-opened, although this is not usually necessary. Before incurring the expense of the application to the High Court, careful thought should be given to the question whether the decision is likely to be any different even when the error of law or procedure is corrected. It may well be open to the Secretary of State or inspector to reach the same conclusion on the planning merits. It should also be remembered that new facts or policies can always be taken into account up to the date of the new decision.[72] The application may prove fruitless if new policies have been adopted which would rule out the development when reconsidered.

---

[67] 1990 Act, s.284 [242/71].

[68] *R. v. Minister of Health, ex p. Rush* [1922] 2 K.B. 28.

[69] *Co-operative Retail Services v. Secretary of State for the Environment and City of Wakefield Metropolitan District Council and William Morrison Supermarkets* [1980] 1 W.L.R. 271; [1980] J.P.L. 111.

[70] *Co-operative Retail Services v. Secretary of State for the Environment*, doubting *Chalgray v. Secretary of State for the Environment* (1976) 33 P. & C.R. 10.

[71] See, *e.g.*, *R. v. Secretary of State for the Environment, ex p. Reinisch* (1971) 22 P. & C.R. 1022 (decision on costs).

[72] See *Price Bros. (Rode Heath) v. Secretary of State for the Environment* (1979) 38 P. & C.R. 579; [1979] J.P.L. 387.

CHAPTER 3

OTHER OBJECTIONS AND APPEALS

A. OBJECTIONS TO REVOCATION AND MODIFICATION ORDERS

3.1. Power of planning authority to revoke or modify permissions

A local planning authority may by order revoke or modify a planning permission granted on an application made under Part III of the Act. When making a revocation or modification order the authority must have regard to the development plan and any other material considerations.[1] The order may revoke or modify the permission wholly or to such extent as appears expedient, but an order may only be made under this section before the permitted building or other operations have been completed or the permitted change of use has taken place and such order cannot affect so much of the permitted operations as have previously been carried out.[2] If it is desired to terminate a use already commenced or to alter or remove operations which are already carried out, the appropriate machinery is the making of a discontinuance order under sections 102 and 103 of the 1990 Act [51/71]. A revocation order or modification order requires the confirmation of the Secretary of State unless it takes effect as an unopposed order under section 99 of the 1990 Act [46/71]. Interests affected by the order have the right to object and to require to be heard by a person appointed for the purpose.[3] If the order is confirmed there is a right to compensation.[4]

3.2. Procedure for making of the order

There are no procedural steps which the local planning authority need take before the making of the order, and an owner of land has no right under the 1990 Act to a notice that it is intended to make the order and no opportunity of making representations to the local planning authority. Subject to section 99 of the 1990 Act [46/71] (see preceding paragraph) an order, once made, must be submitted to the Secretary of State for confirmation.[5] There is no time limit within which such submissions must be made; but, on submission, notice must be served by the local planning authority both on the owner and the occupiers of the land affected and on any other person who (in the opinion of the local planning authority) will be affected by the order.[6]

The notice served on an affected person must be in writing, and must specify the period (not less than 28 days) within which the person

---

[1] 1990 Act, s.97 [45(1)/71].
[2] *Ibid.* s.97(3) [45(4)/71].
[3] *Ibid.* s.98 [45(3)/71].
[4] *Ibid.* s.107 [164/71].
[5] *Ibid.* s.98 [45(2)/71].
[6] *Ibid.* s.98 [45(3)/71].

affected may require the Secretary of State to hold a hearing by a person appointed for the purpose, before confirming the order.[7]

3.3. Objections—preliminary considerations

An owner faced with the revocation or modification order should consider carefully before deciding to object. A serious drawback of the procedure is that there is no provision for suspending the permission while the order is being considered and, as a corollary, there is no right to compensation for delay or other losses suffered during that period. Thus, a developer faced with such an order, when he is on the point of implementing the permission, has little choice but to proceed with the development even though the statutory procedure is being gone through and, if the order is confirmed, to claim compensation for the abortive expenditure.[8] This is clearly an unsatisfactory position and there may be cases where, to avoid such delay and uncertainty, he would be better advised to accept the order and take his compensation immediately.

The Department offers no specific guidance on the criteria used in considering confirmation of such orders. Generally, it seems that the Secretary of State will give weight to the earlier decision to grant permission, and will not confirm the order unless that decision can be shown to have been a serious error or there has been some fundamental change in policies or circumstances. He will also give weight to the disruption which would be caused to those who have acted in reliance on the permission. It is not clear to what extent the Secretary of State regards the level of compensation and the consequent burden on ratepayers as relevant factors in the balance. However, it may have an effect on potential supporters of the order. A prospective objector would be well advised, therefore, at an early stage to obtain expert advice on the amount of compensation likely to be involved, both to assist him in his decision whether to object and also for possible use at the inquiry.

3.4. Form of objection and preparation of case

There is no prescribed form for an objection. A letter setting out shortly the main grounds of objection will suffice. The Inquiries Procedure Rules do not apply to inquiries held into objections into revocation or modification orders. However, in accordance with the ordinary practice the authority should provide a statement of its case, together with an indication of the documents on which it will rely. The preparation of the objector's case will follow the same lines as the preparation of the case for a planning appeal.

3.5. The inquiry

Although there are no inquiry procedure rules, the ordinary rules of natural justice impose similar requirements and in practice the pro-

---

[7] 1990 Act, s.98 [45(3)/71].

[8] Compare *K. & B. Metals* v. *Birmingham City Council* (1976) 33 P. & C.R. 135.

cedure follows that of a planning appeal. However, the order is reversed. Since the authority is promoting the order, it will normally have the right to begin. The statutory objectors will be heard next, and then any other members of the public who support or oppose the scheme. Where the order has been made by the authority largely in response to an initiative by a local group, the inspector can be asked to hear their case before that of the objectors, so that the objectors know the full case they have to meet. However, this is at the discretion of the inspector.

3.6. Procedure after inquiry

The inspector's report and the Secretary of State's decision in practice follow the same lines as on a planning appeal. By virtue of section 12 of the Tribunals and Inquiries Act 1971, the Secretary of State is under a duty to give reasons only if requested to do so. However, in practice he invariably gives his reasons automatically as on a planning appeal. Where a local inquiry is held, the Secretary of State has the same powers to award costs as on a planning appeal (see paragraph 2.49, *ante*). However, in this case a successful objector will normally be awarded costs, whether or not the authority have acted unreasonably.[9]

3.7. Orders made by Secretary of State

By sections 100 and 104 of the 1990 Act [276(2)/71] the Secretary of State is empowered to make such an order himself in default of action by the local planning authority. In this case the order is first made in draft and there is then an opportunity for objections before the Secretary of State decides whether or not formally to make the order. The procedure for such objections is essentially the same as in the case of an order made by the local planning authority. However, it is not unusual for the Secretary of State, before beginning the statutory procedure, to hold an "exploratory inquiry" by virtue of his general powers to hold inquiries under section 320 of the 1990 Act [282/71]. There is no standard procedure for such inquiries. From a potential objector's point of view it must be emphasised that the holding of such a preliminary inquiry does not detract from this right to object formally to the draft order if and when it is published.

3.8. Registration of Revocation Order as a local land charge

By the Local Land Charges Rules 1977,[10] an entry must be made in Part III of the Register of Local Land Charges, containing particulars of the order, a sufficient description identifying the land affected, notice of the place where the order may be inspected and the date of the registration of the charge. The entry should be made when the order takes effect, *i.e.* when it is confirmed by the Secretary of State (see paragraph 3.1, *ante*).

---

[9] Circ. 2/87.
[10] S.I. 1977 No. 985.

3.9. Application to the High Court

After the confirmation of the Revocation Order by the Secretary of State it may be challenged by an application to the High Court under section 288 of the 1990 Act [245/71] on the ground that the order is not within the powers of the Act, or that any of the relevant requirements in relation to the order have not been complied with (see also paragraph 2.51 *et seq.*, *ante*).

B. OBJECTIONS TO DISCONTINUANCE ORDERS

3.10. Order to discontinue an existing use or remove buildings

Once a development has been carried out lawfully,, whether by the carrying out of operations or by a change of use, the planning permission can no longer be revoked, but a local planning authority has the power to make a discontinuance order, which must be confirmed by the Secretary of State. Additionally, a discontinuance order can apply to development which, although it was commenced without planning permission, has acquired immunity from enforcement action through passage of time.

A discontinuance order can be made if it appears to a local planning authority that it is expedient in the interests of the proper planning of their area (including the interests of amenity), regard being had to the development plan and to any other material considerations.[11] Affected interests have a right to compensation.[12]

3.11. Scope of order

A discontinuance order may require that any use of land should be discontinued or it may impose conditions on the continuance of the use. Alternatively, the order may require steps to be taken for the alteration or removal of any buildings or works.

3.12. Procedure

The local planning authority has no actual duty to consult with the owner prior to the making of a discontinuance order or to give him any advance notice that it is considering the making of an order. Once the order is made by the local planning authority, it must be submitted to the Secretary of State for confirmation and a notice must be served on the owner and occupier of the affected land and on any other person who in the opinion of the local planning authority will be affected by the order.

3.13. Objection

Any person on whom the notice is so served may require an opportunity to appear before and be heard by a person appointed by the Secretary of State for that purpose. The notice must specify a

---

[11] 1990 Act, s.102(1) [51(1)/71]. Anologous procedures are available under Sched. 9, paras. 3 to 6 [51A, 51B/71] to require the cessation or suspension of mineral workings.
[12] *Ibid.* s.115 [170/71].

period not less than 28 days from the service of a notice within which the request for a hearing must be made.[13] No form of notice requiring a hearing has been laid down or prescribed, and an ordinary letter would suffice. It is preferable—though not, it would seem, necessary—to state in the letter the grounds on which the order would be opposed, and it seems that there is no good reason why the general practice applicable to appeals to the Secretary of State should not be followed. The Secretary of State may order a local inquiry under section 320 of the 1990 Act [282/71]. The Inquiries Procedure Rules do not apply to inquiries or hearings concerned with the confirmation of discontinuance orders. The basis of procedure and the considerations applicable to making an objection and preparing the case follow those for revocation or modification orders.

3.14. Confirmation of order by the Secretary of State

The order may be confirmed by the Secretary of State with or without such modifications as he considers expedient, or he may refuse to confirm it. When confirmed, a copy must be served by the authority on the owner and occupier of the land to which it relates.[14] The order must be registered in the Register of Local Land Charges.

3.15. Planning permission granted by Discontinuance Order for different development

The local planning authority when making a discontinuance order may, without any application made in that behalf, grant permission for any development of land to which the order relates, either unconditionally or subject to conditions specified in the order. This can have the effect of reducing the compensation payable as a result of the making of the order.

The Secretary of State has power to include in the confirmed order any grant of permission for the development of the land which might have been included in the order submitted to him. Further, he may modify the planning permission granted by the local planning authority.[15] In either event a permission for retention of unauthorised development commenced before the date of submission of the order to the Secretary of State may also be granted.[16] Where the effect of a discontinuance order is that persons will be displaced from residential accommodation and there is no suitable alternative accommodation the local planning authority must see that such accommodation is provided in advance of the displacement.[17]

3.16. Enforcement of a Discontinuance Order—criminal liability

Any person who uses the land for any purpose which is required to be discontinued by the order or in contravention of the conditions

---

[13] 1990 Act, s.103(3) to (6) [51(6)/71].

[14] *Ibid.* s.103(7) [51(7)/71].

[15] *Ibid.* s.103(2) [51(5)/71].

[16] *Ibid.* s.102(4), (5) [51(3)/71].

[17] *Ibid.* s.102(6) [51(8)/71].

imposed by it, or causes or permits the land to be so used, is guilty of an offence and is liable on summary conviction to a fine not exceeding £2,000 or on conviction on indictment to a fine. If the use is continued after conviction a further offence is committed; it is punishable with a fine on summary conviction of £50 for every day on which the use is continued or on conviction on indictment to a fine.[18]

3.17. Removal of buildings by local planning authority
Further, if an order to alter or remove any buildings under section 51 has not been complied with, the local planning authority may enter on the land and carry out the works and thereafter sell materials removed in executing the works, subject to accounting for the periods of sale.[19]

3.18. Application to the High Court
Any person aggrieved by a discontinuance order who desires to question its validity on the ground that the order is not within the powers of the 1990 Act, or that any relevant requirements have not been complied with in relation to the order, may within six weeks from the date on which the order was confirmed make an application to the High Court under section 288 [245/71] (see paragraph 2.51 *et seq.*, *ante*).

C. TREE PRESERVATION ORDERS

3.19. Power to make Tree Preservation Orders
If it is expedient in the interests of amenity a local planning authority may make a tree preservation order in respect of trees, groups of trees or woodlands.[20] The order may make provisions for prohibiting the cutting down, topping, lopping, uprooting, wilful damage or wilful destruction of trees except with the consent of the local planning authority, and for securing the replanting of a woodland area which is felled pursuant to a permission granted by or under the order.[21] The order may also prohibit the causing or permitting of such cutting down.[22] The order must be in the form (or substantially in the form) set out in the Schedule to the Tree Preservation Order Regulations 1969.[23] This form adapts the usual planning application procedure for applications for cutting down trees and makes provisions as to compensation in respect of damage or expenditure caused or incurred in consequence of the refusal of any consent required under the order, or of the grant of consent subject to conditions. The order must include a map defining the position of the trees.

---

[18] 1990 Act, s.189 [108/71].
[19] *Ibid.* s.189(2) [108(2)/71].
[20] *Ibid.* s.198(1) to (3) [60(1)/71].
[21] S.I. 1969 No. 17, as amended by S.I. 1975 No. 148 and S.I. 1988 No. 963.
[22] *R.* v. *Bournemouth Justices, ex p. Bournemouth Corporation* (1970) 21 P. & C.R. 163.
[23] Town and Country Planning (Tree Preservation Order) Regulations 1969. (S.I. 1969 No. 17), as amended by Town and Country Planning (Tree Preservation Order) (Amendment) Regulations 1988 (S.I. 1988 No. 963)

3.20. Practice

The practice as to the making and confirmation of tree preservation orders and as to applications under them is fully explained in Circular 36/78. The following criteria are suggested by the Department for authorities when considering whether to make such an order:

"Authorities have a duty to make such orders, where appropriate, when granting planning permission. . . . More generally, orders should be used to protect selected trees and woodlands if their removal would have a significant impact on the environment and its enjoyment by the public. The Secretaries of State consider that authorities ought to be able to show that a reasonable degree of public benefit would accrue before orders are made or confirmed. The trees—or at least part of the them—should therefore normally be visible from a public place (such as a road or footpath), although, exceptionally, the inclusion of other trees may be justified. The benefit may be present or future (for example, when proposed development has taken place). Trees may be worthy of preservation for their intrinsic beauty or for their contribution to the landscape; or because they serve to screen an eyesore or future development; the value of trees may be enhanced by their scarcity; and the value of a group of trees or woodland may be collective only. Other factors (such as importance as a wildlife habitat) may be taken into account which alone would not be sufficient to warrant an order. Although the loss of trees would need to be significant, the risk of felling need not be imminent before an order is made and trees may be regarded as at risk generally from development pressures; changes in property ownership and intentions to fell trees are not often known in advance and the preservation of selected trees by precautionary orders may therefore be considered to be expedient. In some cases an order may not be expedient; for example, there is little risk to trees owned by or managed under agreement with the National Trust. An order may not be appropriate where owners are known to manage their estates acceptably with proper regard for amenity where such management is expected to continue . . ."[24]

3.21. Confirmation procedure

Generally, by section 199 of the 1990 Act [60(4)/71], a tree preservation order does not take effect until confirmed by the local planning authority. However, by virtue of section 201 of the 1990 Act [61/71], the local planning authority can include in the order a direction that the order shall apply immediately. The order does then take effect provisionally and it remains in effect for a maximum of six months. If within that six months the authority confirms the order or decides not to confirm it the provisional order then either takes effect as a

---

[24] Circ. 36/78, *Trees and Forestry*, para. 40.

confirmed order or, as the case may be, lapses.[25] The purpose, of course, is that people can be prevented from felling valuable trees in the period while confirmation is awaited. If the six months elapses without a decision the provisional order lapses.

As stated above the order must be substantially in the form in the Schedule to the Tree Preservation Order Regulations (as amended) and must define the trees by a map.[26] The local planning authority must place the order and map on deposit for inspection and a copy must be sent to the Conservator of Forests and the District Valuer.[27] A copy of the order and the map must be served on the owners and occupiers of the land affected by the order and on any person entitled to fell any of the trees affected or to work by surface working any minerals in the land affected by the order. There must also be served on the same persons a notice stating the grounds for making the order, the address at which and the hours during which the deposited order may be inspected, that objections and representations may be made to the local planning authority, and the effect of a direction under section 201 of the 1990 Act (see above) if there is one.[28] Objections or representations may be made to the local planning authority within 28 days from the service of the above notice. They must be in writing and must state their grounds and specify the particular trees, groups of trees or woodlands in respect of which they are made.[29]

Before deciding whether to confirm an order the local planning authority must take the objections and representations into account.[30] The authority is not bound to hold an inquiry into objections or give objectors any formal hearing. The Regulations contemplate that an inquiry may be held, since it is provided that, if an inquiry is held, the local planning authority must consider the report of the inquiry.[31] If they did hold an inquiry or a hearing the Inquiries Procedure Rules would not apply, and the procedure would be entirely within their discretion.

3.22. Notification of decision

The local planning authority must inform the owners and occupiers of the land to which the order relates, the Conservator of Forests, the District Valuer and any other person served with a notice under regulation 5 of their decision. If the order is confirmed in a modified form the same persons must be served with a copy of the order and map as confirmed.[32]

3.23. Consents under Tree Preservation Orders

The prescribed form of tree preservation order (Schedule to the Tree Preservation Order Regulations (as amended)) provides that an

---

[25] 1990 Act, s.201 [61(2)/71].
[26] Tree Preservation Order Regulations, reg. 4.
[27] *Ibid.* reg. 5(*a*).
[28] *Ibid.* reg. 5(*c*).
[29] *Ibid.* reg. 7.
[30] *Ibid.* reg. 8(2), as amended.
[31] *Ibid.*
[32] *Ibid.* reg. 9.

application may be made to the local planning authority for consent to cut down trees within the order. Certain parts of sections 75, 77 to 81, 97 and 99 of the 1990 Act [33, 35, 39, 45, 46/71] are with modifications applied to applications for consent. The general scheme is that such applications are treated as applications for planning permission. Thus, the Secretary of State may "call in" an application for his own decision. The applicant may appeal to the Secretary of State against a refusal or conditional grant of consent. Appeals are usually dealt with by written representations but either party may insist on a hearing by a person appointed by the Secretary of State and the advice given in Chapter 2 of this book will apply. The Inquiries Procedure Rules (dealt with under Chapter 2) apply to such hearings and inquiries. There may be an appeal in default of a decision, and the provisions of sections 97 and 99 of the 1990 Act as to revocation and modification of consent apply (see paragraph 3.1 *et seq., ante*).

When consent is refused or granted subject to conditions compensation may be claimed[33] unless the authority have certified that their decision is in the interests of good forestry or, except in the case of woodlands, that the trees have an outstanding or special amenity value.[34] There is the same right of appeal against such a certificate or against a refusal of consent.

3.24. Criteria for grant of consent

The principles upon which authorities should act in considering applications for consent are described in Circular 36/78.

> "58. The form of a tree preservation order which appears as a Schedule to the Regulations (S.I. 1969 No. 17) lays down the procedure for the granting of consent to cut down, uproot, top or lop a protected tree required under an order. An authority may grant consent unconditionally, or subject to conditions including a condition to replant. . . . It must be recognised that the mere preservation of existing trees would lead to their decay and ultimate loss. There are occasional examples where preservation far beyond maturity for timber purposes may be justified (for example, the old oak in a village green) but even in such cases the need for felling and replanting will arise sooner or later. Management is important in all woodlands—not only productive ones—and, unless there are nature conservation reasons for leaving a completely undisturbed unit, trees must be felled from time to time and replaced. A tree preservation order should be used to ensure that these operations take place in an orderly fashion so as to maintain the amenity of the woodland as far as possible. The principles of good forestry do not generally conflict with the long term aim of an order. Consideration of applications will often require a balance to be struck between amenity and other factors, such as potential or actual damage to buildings or

---

[33] 1990 Act, s.203 [174/71].
[34] *Ibid*. art. 5.

change of land use. Where proposals are not in conflict with the long term purpose of an order (such as suitable tree surgery or selective felling and replanting), the grant of consent should normally be straightforward: special considerations may justify the issue of a certificate under article 5(*b*) of the Order. In respect of woodlands, the Regulations require authorities to grant consent so far as accords with the principles of good forestry, except where, in their opinion, it is necessary to maintain the special character of an area in the interests of amenity; they may not otherwise impose replacement conditions on consents in respect of woodlands. . . ."

Evidence and submissions will need to be prepared with these considerations in mind.

3.25. Applications to the High Court
If any person is aggrieved by a tree preservation order and desires to question the validity of the order on the grounds that the order is not within the powers of the 1990 Act or that any of the relevant requirements have not been complied with in relation to that order, he may make an application to the High Court within six weeks from the date on which the order is confirmed (see paragraph 2.51 *et seq.*, *ante*). A decision by the Secretary of State on an application for consent under a Tree Preservation Order may be challenged in the same way.[35]

D. BUILDINGS OF SPECIAL ARCHITECTURAL OR HISTORIC INTEREST

3.26. Principles of control
"Listing" under sections 1 and 2 of the Planning (Listed Buildings and Conservation Areas) Act 1990 [54/71] is the basis of the control.[36] The foundation is section 7 of the Listed Buildings Act 1990 [55(1)/71] which provides that it is an offence to carry out without authority any works for the demolition of a listed building or for its alteration or extension in any manner which would affect its character as a building of special architectural or historic interest. For these purposes any object or structure fixed to a building or within its curtilage and forming part of the land since before July 1, 1948, is treated as part of the building.[37] The Secretary of State compiles the lists or approves, with or without modifications, such lists as are prepared by the Commission.

The works to a listed building are authorised where the local planning authority or the Secretary of State have granted listed building consent for the works.[38] In addition, where the proposed works include the demolition of the listed building there are provisions

---

[35] 1990 Act, s.284 [242/71]. Also see the Listed Buildings Act 1990, s.62.
[36] *Ibid.*
[37] Planning (Listed Buildings and Conservation Areas) Act 1990, s.1(5) [54(9)/71].
[38] *Ibid.* s.8 [55(2)/71].

for giving notice to the Commission and giving them reasonable access to the building for at least one month before the works are commenced.

There is an emergency procedure whereby the local planning authority can serve a building preservation notice. It applies where the building in question is not listed, and it can be used to prevent a person executing works to the building while the Secretary of State is considering whether to list the building. The building is deemed to be listed while the notice is in force. The notice can remain in force for a maximum of six months, but lapses earlier if the Secretary of State decides to list or to refuse to list the building. If the building is not listed the local planning authority will have to compensate anyone with an interest in the building for any loss he has suffered.[39]

There are two methods of enforcing the above provisions: one is by a prosecution for unauthorised works, while the other is by service of a listed building enforcement notice. Both can be operated simultaneously.

3.27. Objection to listing

There is no statutory provision for objection to listing as such.[40] Informal representations can be made to the Secretary of State and in an appropriate case these may result in a building being removed from the list, if for example it can be shown clearly that the building does not come within the normal criteria.[41] The only formal procedure for "de-listing" a building is to apply for listed building consent and, if necessary, appeal. Such an appeal can be based on the ground that the building should not have been listed in the first place.[42]

3.28. Certificate under section 18 [56A/71]

Where an unlisted building is already subject to planning permission for works involving demolition or other alterations, protection against listing can be obtained by acquiring from the Secretary of State a certificate under section 18 of the Planning (Listed Buildings and Conservation Areas) Act 1990 [56A/71].[43] Such a certificate provides immunity from listing for five years. The application can be made by anyone (for example, a prospective purchaser). Notice must be given to the local planning authority[44] but otherwise no special procedure or form of application is prescribed.

---

[39] See Planning (Listed Buildings and Conservation Areas) Act 1990, ss.3, 27 [58, 173/71].

[40] For a detailed explanation and criticism of listing procedure, see *Amalgamated Investment & Property Co. Limited* v. *Walker (John) & Sons* [1976] 3 All E.R. 509.

[41] See Circ. 8/87 *Historic Buildings and Conservation Areas—Policy and Procedures*, for the criteria generally applied in listing buildings, but note that these are revised from time to time.

[42] Planning (Listed Buildings and Conservation Areas) Act 1990, ss.20, 21, 22 [Sched. 11, para. 8(2)/71].

[43] S.56A of the 1971 Act was added by Local Government, Planning and Land Act 1980, Sched. 15.

[44] *Ibid.* s.18(3).

3.29. Application for listed building consent

The local planning authority have power on an application therefore to grant listed building consent unconditionally or subject to conditions.[45]

The rules which govern applications for such consent, its grant, and appeals against refusal are very similar to the rules governing planning permission. The rules are contained in Part I of Schedule 11 to the 1971 Act and in the Listed Building Regulations.[46] A condition may be imposed prohibiting demolition until a contract for the carrying out of redevelopment works for the site has been made and planning permission obtained for those works.[47]

3.30. "Call-in" and appeal

The Secretary of State may "call-in" an application for his own decision. He must hold a hearing or inquiry if the applicant or the local planning authority desire it.[48] The Inquiries Procedure Rules apply to such a hearing or inquiry.

An appeal may be made to the Secretary of State against the refusal or the grant subject to conditions of listed building consent. The same form is used as for planning appeals. The appeal must be made within six months of the decision or of the expiry of the period for the giving of a decision.[49] The Secretary of State can extend the time but will be reluctant to do so since six months should normally be an ample period. The following documents should accompany the appeal:

(i) the application made to the local planning authority;

(ii) relevant plans, drawings, particulars and documents submitted with the application, including a copy of the certificate given on the making of the application (under section 66 of the 1990 Act [27/71]);

(iii) the notice of the decision;

(iv) all other relevant correspondence with the local planning authority.[50]

It has already been mentioned that one ground of appeal may be that the building ought not to have been listed. Where there is a building preservation notice in effect another possible ground is that the building should not be listed.[51] It has also been mentioned that a

---

[45] Planning (Listed Buildings and Conservation Areas) Act 1990, s.17 [56(4), (5)/71].

[46] *Ibid.* s.17 [56(5)/71].

[47] Town and Country Planning (Listed Buildings and Conservation Areas) Regulations 1990 (S.I. 1990 No. 1519).

[48] Planning (Listed Buildings and Conservation Areas) Act 1990, s.12 [Sched. 11, para. 4/71].

[49] Listed Building Regulations, reg. 8(1).

[50] *Ibid.* reg. 8(2).

[51] Planning (Listed Buildings and Conservation Areas) Act 1990, ss.20, 21 [Sched. 11, para. 8(2)(*b*)/71].

building which was subject to a building preservation order is deemed to be listed.[52] The Secretary of State can give a direction that this deemed listing shall not apply, and it is a further possible ground of appeal that there should be such a direction.[53] Of course, these are exceptional grounds, and the usual basis of the appeal will be that in the circumstances consent should be granted or be granted free of conditions.

The Secretary of State must hold a hearing or inquiry if either party desires it.[54] Hearings and inquiries are governed by the Inquiries Procedure Rules 1988. The procedure on such inquiries is therefore identical to that followed in planning appeals (see Chapter 2, *ante*). There is also similar provision for challenging the Secretary of State's decision in the High Court.

3.31. Preparation of appeal

Essential guidance as to the Secretary of State's policy in dealing with applications for listed building consent will be found in Circular 8/87.

> "90. The following guidance on criteria may prove helpful to local authorities when considering applications for listed building consent to demolish or alter listed buildings:
>
> (a) the importance of the building, both intrinsically and rela- tively bearing in mind the number of other buildings of special architectural or historic interest in the neighbour- hood. In some cases a building may be important because there are only a few of its type in the neighbourhood or because it has a fine interior, while in other cases its importance may be enhanced because it forms part of a group or series. Attention should also be paid to the contri- bution to the local scene made by a building, particularly if it is in a conservation area; but the absence of such a contribu- tion is not a reason for demolition or alteration;
>
> (b) in assessing the importance of the building, attention should be paid to both its architectural merit and to its historical interest. This includes not only historical associations but also the way the design, plan, materials or location of the building illustrates the character of a past age; or the development of a particular skill, style or technology;
>
> (c) the condition of the building, the cost of repairing and maintaining it in relation to its importance, and whether it has already received or been promised grants from public funds. In estimating cost, however, due regard should be paid to the economic value of the building when repaired and to any saving through not having to provide alternative

---

[52] Planning (Listed Buildings and Conservation Areas) Act 1990, Sched. 1, paras. 1, 2(1), (2) and Sched. 4, para. 2 [54(10)/71].

[53] *Ibid.* ss.20, 21 [Sched. 11, para. 8(2)(*a*)/71].

[54] *Ibid.* s.22(2) [Sched. 11, para. 8(4)/71].

accommodation in a new building. Old buildings generally suffer from some defects but the effects of these can easily be exaggerated;

(d) the importance of any alternative use for the site and, in particular, whether the use of the site for some public purpose would make it possible to enhance the environment and especially other listed buildings in the area; or whether, in a rundown area, a limited redevelopment might bring new life and make the other listed buildings more economically viable.

91. Generally, it should be remembered that the number of buildings of special architectural and historic interest is limited. Accordingly, the presumption should be in favour of preservation except where a strong case can be made out for granting consent after application of the criteria mentioned. Preservation should not be thought of as a purely negative process or as an impediment to progress. The great majority of listed buildings are still capable of beneficial use and, with skilled and understanding treatment, new development can usually be made to blend happily with the old. The destruction of listed buildings is very seldom necessary for the sake of improvement; more often it is the result of neglect, or of failure to appreciate good architecture. Local authorities should be particularly vigilant. As owners of many listed buildings themselves, they should set an example to other owners."

The principal issues, therefore, will generally be the importance of the building on the one hand and, on the other, the likely alternative uses of the building and the cost of restoring it for such use. Expert evidence on these points will normally be essential (from, for example, architectural historians or surveyors with special experience of historic buildings). Generally there is a strong presumption against the grant of listed building consent and therefore, unless the appellant can establish either that the building should never have been listed in the first place or that it has no feasible alternative use, consent is likely to be refused. To establish the latter point the Secretary of State will normally require evidence that the freehold has been offered for sale on the open market.[55] The importance of an alternative use for the site may also be a material factor. The preparation and presentation of evidence will follow the same lines as for a planning appeal.

3.32. Development in conservation areas
Section 74 of the Planning (Listed Buildings and Conservation Areas) Act 1990 [277A/71] also applies the requirement for listed building consent (now called "conservation area consent") to proposals for the demolition of any buildings in a conservation area (other than the classes prescribed by Circular 8/87, paragraph 97). The

---

[55] Circ. 8/87, para. 89.

application and appeals procedure follows the procedure described above with some modifications. In particular it should be noted that the guiding consideration is not the character and importance of the building itself but its contribution to "the character or appearance of the conservation area in which it is situated." The quality of a proposed replacement building may be a very material factor (see generally Circular 8/87, paragraph 95 *et seq.*).[56]

In addition, local planning authorities must give special consideration to applications for developments in conservation areas and apply the positive test of whether a development will preserve or enhance the character or appearance of the conservation area.[57]

3.33. Revocation of listed building consent

A further occasion on which a hearing or inquiry may arise is when it is intended to revoke a listed building consent. The procedure is similar to that on the revocation of planning permission (see paragraph 3.1, *ante*). The local planning authority may make an order modifying or revoking consent. They then submit the order to the Secretary of State for confirmation.[58] Notice must be served on the owner and the occupier of the building affected and on any other person who in the opinion of the local planning authority will be affected by the order. If any such person requires it the Secretary of State must hold a hearing or inquiry before confirming the order. The Secretary of State may himself make an order or direct the local planning authority to submit an order to him for confirmation. In such cases there is the same opportunity to require a hearing or inquiry.[59] There is also a procedure whereby an order can take effect without the necessity of ministerial confirmation when the owner, the occupier and any other person affected have notified the local planning authority that they have no objection to the order.[60]

E. ADVERTISEMENT APPEALS

3.34. Control of advertisements

The control of advertisements is exercised by regulations made by the Secretary of State under sections 220 and 221 of the 1990 Act [63/71]: the Town and Country Planning (Control of Advertisements) Regulations 1989.[61] The law and practice are described in Circular 15/89.[62]

---

[56] *Save Britain's Heritage* v. *Secretary of State for the Environment, The Times*, April 4, 1990.

[57] Planning (Listed Buildings and Conservation Areas) Act 1990, ss.69, 70 [277/71] and *Steinberg and Sykes* v. *Secretary of State for the Environment and Camden London Borough Council* [1989] J.P.L. 258.

[58] Planning (Listed Buildings and Conservation Areas) Act 1990, ss.23, 24 [Sched. 11, para. 10/71].

[59] *Ibid.* s.26 [Sched. 11, para. 11/71].

[60] *Ibid.* s.25 [Sched. 11, para. 12/71].

[61] S.I. 1989 No. 670.

[62] Circ. 15/89, *Town and Country Planning (Control of Advertisements) Regulations 1989.*

Control extends generally to the display of advertisements on all sites (which include land and buildings) in England and Wales. There are certain exceptions such as, for example, advertisements on enclosed land not visible from outside and advertisements displayed on or in a vehicle.[63]

Subject to exemptions, some of which are mentioned above, an advertisement may not be displayed without either express or deemed consent. Express consent may be granted on an application to the local planning authority or to the Secretary of State.[64] Deemed consent is granted by the Regulations for various classes of advertisement,[65] including for example, advertisements on business premises, an advertisement on an hotel relating to its purpose, miscellaneous temporary advertisements, advertisements announcing local events, directional advertisements, advertisements for neighbourhood watch and similar schemes. All of these classes of deemed consent are subject to various conditions and limitations.[66]

Deemed permissions are generally open to the right of the local planning authority to serve a discontinuance notice which is subject to a right of appeal to the Secretary of State.[67]

The various steps of procedure for obtaining express consent are laid down in the Regulations.[68] The decision of the local planning authority must be in writing and if consent is refused or is conditional, reasons must be given. The decision must be given within eight weeks from the date of the receipt of the application, or within that time the applicant must be notified that the application has been called in by the Secretary of State under regulation 28. Every grant of express consent is limited to five years.[69] The system of advertisement control is complex and consequently the Department have published several useful booklets which contain a summary of controls.

3.35. Criteria

Advertisements are subject to planning control only in the interests of "amenity" and public safety.[70] It follows that the content or subject of an advertisement cannot be controlled under the Regulations and express consent cannot be refused because the local planning authority consider the advertisement "to be unnecessary or offensive to public morals." (Circular 15/89, paragraph 3).

3.36. Areas of special control

Rural areas and areas "which appear to require special protection on grounds of amenity" may be designated "areas of special control."

---

[63] Advertisement Regulations, reg. 3(2).

[64] *Ibid.* reg. 9(1).

[65] For a full description of the advertisements comprised within these classes, see reg. 6 and Part 1 of Sched. 3 to the Control of Advertisements Regulations 1989.

[66] Advertisement Regulations, reg. 6. Sched. 3.

[67] *Ibid.* reg. 16.

[68] *Ibid.* regs. 9–15.

[69] *Ibid.* reg. 13.

[70] 1990 Act, s.220(1) [63(1)/71] and Advertisement Regulations, reg. 4.

Such an area is defined by the local planning authority and approved by the Secretary of State.[71] The effect of designation is that the range of deemed consents is reduced;[72] that the power of the local planning authority to grant express consent is restricted;[73] and that existing advertisements which are no longer authorised must be removed.[74]

3.37. The right of appeal to the Secretary of State

There is a right of appeal to the Secretary of State if a local planning authority refuses express consent, imposes a condition or fails to give a decision within two months.[75]

3.38. Notice of appeal and supporting documents

The notice of appeal must be in writing and given within two months of the receipt of the notification of the decision of the local planning authority; the Secretary of State may extend the time. The following documents must be enclosed: (i) the application made to the local planning authority; (ii) all relevant plans and particulars submitted to them; (iii) the notice of decision, if any; (iv) all other relevant correspondence with the authority.[76] The new Procedure Rules require the local planning authority not later than six weeks from "the relevant date," *i.e.*, the date of notification that an inquiry is to be held, to serve a statement of case. The appellant must also serve such a statement nine weeks after the relevant date. The Rules also provide for other persons to be required by the Secretary of State to serve a statement of case.

3.39. The choice of appeal procedures

The available appeal procedures are:

(1) by written representations made by the appellant and the local planning authority, followed by an unaccompanied site inspection;

(2) by written representations made by the appellant and the local planning authority, followed by consideration of photographs of the appeal site, provided both parties agree to this procedure;

(3) by a "special procedure" for written representations and an unaccompanied site inspection. The "special procedure" has a tighter timetable of submission of documents and representations which should produce a quicker decision;

(4) by a hearing of the parties' oral representations, and an accompanied inspection of the appeal site, which is then

---

[71] Advertisement Regulations, reg. 18.

[72] *Ibid.* reg. 19(1).

[73] *Ibid.* reg. 19(2).

[74] *Ibid.* reg. 19(5).

[75] The provisions of ss.78 and 79 of the 1990 Act [36, 37/71] are modified for this purpose and are set out in Sched. 4 to the Advertisement Regulations.

[76] 1990 Act, s.79 [36(3)/71].

reported to the Secretary of State. Normally a hearing is held rather than a public inquiry. However, the majority of cases are dealt with by way of written representations. Guidance about appeal procedures is contained in Circular 15/89.

3.40. The Secretary of State's decision
The Secretary of State may allow or dismiss the appeal or reverse or vary any part of the decision of the local planning authority (whether or not the appeal relates to that part) or deal with the application as if it had been made to him in the first instance.[77]

3.41. Application to the High Court
The decision of the Secretary of State on appeal is final.[78] However, under section 288(1)(b) of the 1990 Act [245(1)(b)/71], a remedy in the High Court is available to any person aggrieved by the decision of the Secretary of State who desires to question its validity on the grounds that the decision is not within the powers of the 1990 Act or that any of the relevant requirements have not been complied with.

3.42. Revocation or modification of consent
Consent to the display of advertisements which involve building or similar operations may be revoked or modified at any time before those operations have been completed without affecting so much of those operations as have been carried out; where no such operations have been involved the revocation or modification may be at any time before either in any case which involves building operations before completion and in any other case the display has begun.[79] The procedure is similar to that for revocation of a planning permission (see paragraph 3.2., *ante*).

The local planning authority may make the modification or revocation order, but it does not take effect until it is confirmed by the Secretary of State, who may vary it as he considers expedient.[80] Notice in writing of the submission of the order to the Secretary of State must be served on (i) the person who had applied for the consent, (ii) the owner and occupier of the land, and (iii) any other person affected. If within such a period, not less than 28 days, as is specified in the notice the person on whom the notice is served requests a hearing, the Secretary of State must order a hearing before an inspector.

3.43. Powers of Secretary of State
The Secretary of State has power to serve a discontinuance notice, designate an area of special control or make a revocation order.[81] In such cases the Secretary of State may provide for a public inquiry to be held. The Secretary of State's decision is final and has the same effect

---

[77] 1990 Act, s.79 [36(3)/71].
[78] *Ibid.*
[79] Advertisement Regulations, reg. 16.
[80] *Ibid.* reg. 16(2).
[81] Advertisement Regulations, reg. 22.

as a decision of the local planning authority, subject always to an appeal to the High Court under section 288 of the 1990 Act [245/71], and see the Planning (Listed Buildings and Conservation Areas) Act 1990, section 63.

3.44. Directions to local planning authorities to supply information

The Secretary of State has a wide power to require local planning authorities "to furnish him with such information as he may require for the purpose of exercising any of his functions under the Regulations."[82] There is no reason why any applicant should not in a particular case request that the Secretary of State should issue such a direction.

3.45. Discontinuance Notice

A local planning authority has power to serve a discontinuance notice requiring the discontinuance of the display of an advertisement which is displayed with deemed consent.[83] An appeal lies to the Secretary of State and the notice is of no effect until the notice is finally determined or withdrawn.[84] An appeal to the Secretary of State against a discontinuance notice operates as a deemed application for planning permission. If the Secretary of State is satisfied that it is necessary to remedy a substantial injury to the amenity of the locality or a danger to members of the public he may serve a discontinuance notice.

A person who displays an advertisement in contravention of the Regulations is liable to a fine not exceeding £400 and in the case of a continuing offence, £40 for each day during which the offence continues after conviction.[85] A local planning authority has power to remove or obliterate placards and posters displayed in contravention of the Advertisement Regulations.[86] A person is deemed to display an advertisement if it is displayed on land of which he is the owner or occupier or if it gives publicity to his goods, trade, business or other concerns.[87] It is a defence to such a charge to prove that the advertisement was displayed without his knowledge or consent.[88]

F. APPEALS AGAINST NOTICES AS TO LAND ADVERSELY AFFECTING THE AMENITY OF THE NEIGHBOURHOOD

3.46. Amenity notices under section 215 of the 1990 Act

Local planning authorities have power to deal with land in bad condition by serving an abatement notice under section 215 of the 1990 Act.[89] These powers can be exercised in relation to land in the area of

---

[82] *Ibid.*

[83] Advertisement Regulations, reg. 8.

[84] *Ibid.* reg. 15.

[85] 1990 Act, s.224(3) [109(2)/71] and Advertisement Regulations, reg. 26.

[86] *Ibid.* s.225 [109A/71].

[87] *Ibid.* s.224 [109/71].

[88] *Ibid.* s.224(4) [109(3)/71].

[89] 1971 Act, s.65 was substituted by the Housing and Planning Act 1986.

the authority if it appears to the local planning authority that the amenity of any part of the area of that authority or of any adjoining area is adversely affected by the condition of that land.[90] The power is exercisable in respect of any land in the area of the authority; it does not normally extend to land within the curtilage of a building.

The consent of the Secretary of State to the service of an abatement notice is not required. The notice takes effect at the expiration of the period (not less than 28 days) specified therein, unless the person on whom the notice is served appeals to a magistrates' court.

3.47. Right of appeal to magistrates' court

A person on whom an abatement notice is served, or any other person who has an interest in the land to which the notice relates, may appeal. The right of appeal is governed by sections 217 and 218 of the 1990 Act [105, 106/71]. The appeal must be made within the time specified in the notice and the court has no power to extend it; it must be made to a magistrates' court for the area in which the land is situate.

The appeal is by way of complaint and an ordinary form should be used. An appeal lies on any of the following grounds:[91]

(a) that the condition of the land does not adversely affect the amenity of the area of the local planning authority or of any adjoining area; or

(b) that the condition of the land is attributable to and is such as results in the ordinary course of events from the carrying on of operations or a use of land which is not in contravention of Part III of the 1990 Act;

(c) that the land does not constitute a garden, vacant site or other open land; or

(d) that the requirements of the notice exceed what is necessary to prevent the condition of the land from adversely affecting amenity; or

(e) that the period specified in the notice for taking steps to comply with it is too short.

The operation of the notice is suspended until the final determination or withdrawal of the appeal.[92] On an appeal the court may correct any informality, defect or error in the notice if it is not a material one.[93] On the determination of an appeal the magistrates' court must give directions including, where appropriate, the quashing of the notice or a variation of its terms in favour of the appellant. Either the appellant or the local planning authority may appeal against the magistrates' decision to the Crown Court.[94]

---

[90] 1990 Act, s.215(1) [65(1)/71].
[91] *Ibid.* s.217(1) [105(1)/71].
[92] *Ibid.* s.217(3) [105(3)/71].
[93] *Ibid.* s.217(4) [105(4)/71].
[94] *Ibid.* s.218 [106/71].

3.48. Finality of the decision

An abatement notice cannot be questioned in any proceedings whatsoever, except by appeal under the above provisions.[95] And if any person appeals against an abatement notice under section 217, neither he nor any other person can claim in any subsequent proceedings (relating to the enforcement of the notice) that the notice was not duly served on the person who appealed.[96]

3.49. Penalty for non-compliance with notice

In addition to a liability to pay the expenses of the local authority if they enter and take the steps required by the notice, there is a criminal liability for non-compliance. If the steps required by the notice have not been taken after the expiry of the period specified therein the person served will in each case be guilty of an offence and liable on summary conviction to a fine not exceeding £400[97] and thereafter £40 per day.[98]

The validity of service of the abatement notice can no longer be contested if an appeal is brought; but a person who held an interest in the land before the notice was served on the owner and occupier and who has neither been served with the notice nor appealed may still contend that it has not been duly served.

---

[95] 1990 Act, s.285(3) [243(3)/71].
[96] *Ibid.* s.208(10) [110(2)/71].
[97] *Ibid.* s.216(2) [104(2)/71].
[98] *Ibid.* s.216(6) [104(7)/71], and see Housing and Planning Act 1986.

CHAPTER 4

DETERMINATION OF RIGHTS

A. Section 64 Determination

4.1. Scope of provision

Under section 64 of the 1990 Act [53/71] a person who proposes to carry out any operations on land or to make any change in the use of land may seek a determination whether development is involved and if so, whether an application for planning permission is required.[1]

It is important to ensure that an appeal under section 64 is not used in a case for which it is not strictly appropriate. As interpreted by the courts and by the Secretary of State, section 64 is not an all-purpose means for finding out whether planning permission is required in any case (however useful such a provision would be).[2] The following restrictions on its ambit should be noted:

(1) It is only available to an applicant who *proposes* to carry out the operation or change of use in question. This has the consequence that an appeal will not be entertained if, on the one hand, the works were started or the use instituted before the date of the application, or, on the other, the applicant has no specific proposal to carry out the works or change of use and is merely seeking to establish his "use-rights."

(2) The section cannot be used to establish the validity or scope of an existing permission.[3]

(3) It cannot be used to confirm the existence of "established use rights." This should be done by an application for an established use certificate under sections 191 to 194 [94/71] (see below).[4]

In view of the awkward limitations on the use of section 64, consideration should always be given, as an alternative to an appeal, to an application for a declaration to the High Court. This is, in general, a more flexible and comprehensive procedure, which is available even in those cases to which sections 64 and 191 to 194 apply,[5] and in other cases is probably the only procedure.

---

[1] The procedure has been extended to Crown land: 1990 Act, Pt. XIII.

[2] The Carnwath Report, *Enforcing Planning Control* 1989 (HMSO) recommends that sections 53 and 94–95 (now ss.64 and 191–196) (see para. 4.6 *et seq.*) be repealed and replaced by a single procedure whereby the authority could issue a certificate that any specified use or operation (whether or not instituted before the application) can be carried on without planning permission.

[3] *Edgewarebury Park Investments* v. *Minister of Housing and Local Government* [1963] 2 Q.B. 408.

[4] *Moran* v. *Secretary of State for the Environment and Mid-Sussex District Council* [1988] J.P.L. 24.

[5] *Pyx Granite Co.* v. *Minister of Housing and Local Government* [1960] A.C. 260; [1960] J.P.L. 400.

4.2. Right of appeal

An appeal from a section 64 [53/71] determination is, as to procedure, almost indistinguishable from an appeal from a refusal or conditional grant of permission (see Chapter 2, *ante*) and the provisions of sections 77 to 79 [35–37/71] on applied (section 64(3) [53(2)/71]). Indeed, an application to determine whether the proposed operations or change of use constitute development and, if so, whether a planning permission is required may be made as part of an application for planning permission[6] and the appeals may be heard together. There is no special form for the notice of appeal and a simple letter will suffice.

4.3. Preparation of case

It should be borne in mind that the decision will turn on legal or factual issues rather than issues of planning policy, and therefore the considerations affecting the appeal will be somewhat different from those applying to planning appeals.[7]

It is essential that the inspector should have a clear and detailed description of both the existing use and the proposed use (or of the existing and proposed buildings). These should be illustrated by plans which enable the changes to be precisely located and identified.

If there is likely to be a factual dispute as to the nature of the existing use, corroborative witnesses should be called, or, if they are not available to give oral evidence, their statements should be prepared in the form of statutory declarations.

It goes without saying that, before the evidence is prepared in detail, careful thought needs to be given to the legal basis for the claim that permission is not needed, so that the evidence can be closely related to the legal argument. It is often helpful if the legal argument is submitted in writing. The inspector will be grateful for copies of any legal authorities relied on.

4.4. Appeal to the High Court

By virtue of section 290 of the 1990 Act [247/71] an appeal to the High Court may be made on a point of law against the Secretary of State's decision on a section 64 appeal [53/71], *i.e.,* an appeal against a determination whether a proposed use or operation constitutes development. The person who applied for the decision or the local planning authority may make the appeal. The application for a determination may have been made as part of an application for planning permission and in that case only the part which relates to the section 64 application can be appealed from under this procedure.

4.5. Procedure on a section 290 appeal

Section 290 [247/71] itself provides for appealing or for requiring the Secretary of State to state a case for the opinion of the High Court. In

---

[6] 1990 Act, s.64(1) [53(1)/71].

[7] For examples of decisions on section 64 appeals, see Selected Enforcement and Allied Appeals, (published by DOE in October 1974 and updated by Circ. 109/77).

either case the procedure is to be "according as rules of court may provide." Order 94, rule 12(2) of the Rules of the Supreme Court makes no provision for stating a case, so that that procedure is not open. The appeal is brought by originating motion which must be served within 28 days of the decision appealed against being notified to the appellant. The notice of motion must be served on the Secretary of State and the local planning authority or the appellant (according to which party appeals). The appeal is heard by a single Judge of the Queen's Bench Division. The court, if satisfied that the decision was wrong in law, remits the matter to the Secretary of State for his determination.

B. Established Use Certificate

4.6. Certification of established use

Under section 191 of the 1990 Act [94/71], a use of land is established if:

(a) it was begun before the beginning of 1964 without planning permission in that behalf and has continued since the end of 1963; or

(b) it was begun before the beginning of 1964 under a planning permission in that behalf granted subject to conditions or limitations, which either have never been complied with or have not been complied with since the end of 1963; or

(c) it was begun after the end of 1963 as the result of a change of use not requiring planning permission and there has been, since the end of 1963, no change of use requiring planning permission.

Section 192(1) to (3) [94(2)/71] provides that where a person having an interest in land claims that a particular use of it has become established, he may apply to the local planning authority for a certificate to that effect. However, no such application may be made in respect of the use of land as a single dwellinghouse or of any use not subsisting at the time of the application. Section 192(4) of the 1990 Act [94(7)/71] provides that an established use certificate shall, as respects any matters stated therein, be conclusive for the purposes of an appeal to the Secretary of State against an enforcement notice served in respect of any land to which the certificate relates. This rule applies only where the notice is served after the date of the application on which the certificate was granted.

In this connection attention is drawn to paragraph 21 of Circular 109/77[8] where it is pointed out that a material change of use requiring planning permission which takes place after the date of the application for an established use will in practical terms nullify the effect of the certificate as conclusive for the purposes of an appeal against an

---

[8] Circ. 109/77, *Enforcement of Planning Control—Established Use Certificates.*

enforcement notice; the fact that the use is referred to in the certificate will in no way imply that it is a use of land which can lawfully be resumed once there has been a change.[9]

Under section 194(1) and (2) of the 1990 Act [94(3)/71] an established use certificate may be granted (a) either for the whole of the land specified in the application or part of it,[10] or (b) in the case of an application specifying two or more uses, either for all those uses or for some one or more of them. The local planning authority is under a duty, if and so far as they are satisfied that the applicant's claim is made out, to grant an established use certificate accordingly and if and so far as they are not so satisfied to refuse the application.[11]

It is an offence under section 193(6) and (7) [94(8)/71] if any person, for the purpose of procuring a particular decision on an application (whether by himself or another) for an established use certificate or an appeal arising out of such an application:

(a) knowingly or recklessly makes a statement which is false in a material particular; or

(b) with intent to deceive, produces, furnishes, sends or otherwise makes use of any document which is false in a material particular; or

(c) with intent to deceive, withholds any material information.

4.7. Appeals against refusal of established use certificate

When an application for an established use certificate is refused or refused in part (or where there is a deemed refusal by reason of failure to decide the application within the stipulated time of eight weeks) the applicant may appeal to the Secretary of State.[12] Notice of appeal must be given in writing within six months, though the Secretary of State may extend the time for an appeal. The following documents should be supplied:

(a) the application;

(b) all relevant plans, drawings, statements and particulars submitted to them (including the certificate which accompanied the application);

(c) the notice of the decision, if any;

(d) all other relevant documents and correspondence with the local planning authority;

A new section 66 [27/71] certificate should accompany the appeal.

If either party desires it the Secretary of State must cause a hearing before an inspector to be held.[13] Generally a local inquiry is ordered.

---

[9] See *LTSS Paint and Supply Services* v. *Hackney London Borough Council* [1976] 1 Q.B. 663.

[10] *Bristol City Council* v. *Secretary of State for the Environment* [1986] J.P.L. 840.

[11] 1990 Act, s.194(1) [94(4)/71].

[12] *Ibid.* s.195(1)–(3) [95(2)/71]; G.D.O., art. 29.

[13] *Ibid.* s.196(1) [95(4)/71].

The Enforcement Inquiries Procedure Rules 1981 apply. (See Appendix D.)

4.8. Powers of the Secretary of State on appeal
There are four courses which the Secretary of State may take:

(1) He may dismiss the appeal if satisfied that the authority's refusal is well founded.[14]

(2) He may grant the established use certificate.[15]

(3) He may modify the certificate granted by the authority.[16]

(4) He may himself grant a planning permission for any use of land in respect of which no certificate is granted.[17]

4.9. Description of use
Guidance as to the Secretary of State's approach to appeals relating to established use certificates will be found in Circular 109/77. One particular point which often causes difficulty should be noted. The Secretary of State takes the view that the application should relate to a *particular* use (for example, "garment manufacture") and not to a class of use (for example, "business use"). Once the particular use has been certified as established, any rights there may be to change the use to another use within the same use class are a matter for separate consideration under the Use Classes Order and, if necessary, for a section 64 application [53/71].

4.10. Evidence of fact
Evidence for the appeal will generally be factual and needs to be as carefully prepared as for any court proceedings. Contemporary documentary evidence (for example, valuation lists, invoices, accounts, *etc.*) are of special importance. If witnesses cannot attend at the inquiry, their evidence should be submitted in the form of statutory declarations if at all possible. Letters can be received, but do not carry the same weight. Evidence at the inquiry is usually on oath. It must always be remembered that the onus lies on the appellant to prove that the use began before 1964, and any other essential facts.

4.11. Planning evidence
Since the Secretary of State has power to grant planning permission, even if he refuses an established use certificate, consideration should also be given to whether to call planning evidence (as in the case of a planning appeal). There is no obligation to do so, and in many cases it will be a waste of time and expense since the prospects of obtaining permission will be negligible.

---

[14] 1990 Act, s.195(3) [95(2)(*b*)/71].
[15] *Ibid.* s.195(2) [95(2)(*a*)/71].
[16] *Ibid.*
[17] *Ibid.* s.196(5) [95(3)/71].

4.12. Application to the High Court

By virtue of section 288 of the 1990 Act [245/71], the Secretary of State's decision on an established use certificate appeal may be challenged in the High Court in the same way and on the same grounds as the Secretary of State's decision on an appeal against refusal of planning permission (see paragraph 2.45, *ante*). If the decision related both to an established use certificate appeal and to an enforcement appeal, the application to the High Court can be consolidated with an appeal against the enforcement notice (see paragraph 5.19, *post*).

CHAPTER 5

ENFORCEMENT APPEALS

A. BREACHES OF PLANNING CONTROL

5.1. General This Chapter sets out the current law and procedure on enforcement. However, it should be noted that in 1989 the Carnwath Report, *Enforcing Planning Control*[1] recommended a number of changes which have not yet been implemented but changes are likely in the near future.

5.2. Introductory

Section 172(1) of the 1990 Act[2] [87(1)/71] enables the local planning authority to deal with breaches of planning control by means of an enforcement notice, provided the breach has occurred since the end of 1963. An enforcement notice may be issued only where the authority "consider it expedient to do so having regard to the provisions of the development plan and any other material considerations." This means that an enforcement notice should not be the automatic response to any breach of planning control but should be used only where some worthwhile planning objective would be achieved by remedying the breach.[3] Once the notice takes effect it is enforceable by criminal penalties.[4] The Secretary of State has a supplementary power to serve an enforcement notice after consultation with the local planning authority and the same procedures will apply to such a notice.[5]

5.3. Breach of planning control

Before a notice is issued it must appear to the authority that there has been a breach of planning control. A breach of planning control may consist either of the carrying out of development without planning permission or a failure to comply with any conditions or limitations subject to which planning permission was granted.[6] The enforcement notice should make clear which of these two categories of breach is alleged and should give adequate particulars of the alleged breach.[7]

---

[1] HMSO, February 1989.
[2] References are to the provisions of the 1971 Act as substituted by the Local Government and Planning (Amendment) Act 1981 as consolidated by the 1990 Planning Act.
[3] See Circ. 22/80, *Development Control—Policy and Practice*, paras. 15 and 16; Circ. 20/85, *Town and Country Planning Act 1971: Enforcement Appeals and Advertisement Appeals*, Appendix 1, paras. 6 and 7 and PPG1, *General Policy and Principles*, para. 30.
[4] 1990 Act, s.179 [89/71].
[5] *Ibid.* s.182 [276(5A), (5B)/71]; also see the Listed Buildings Act 1990, s.46.
[6] *Ibid.* s.172(3) [87(3)/71].
[7] See *Eldon Garages* v. *Kingston-upon-Hull Corporation* [1974] 1 W.L.R. 276, and 1990 Act, s.173(1) [87(6)/71].

5.4. Period within which enforcement notice may be served

In respect of certain kinds of breach, an enforcement notice may be issued only within four years from the date of the breach:

(a) the carrying out without planning permission of building engineering, mining,[8] or other operations in, on, over or under land; or

(b) the failure to comply with any condition or limitation which relates to the carrying out of such operations and subject to which planning permission was granted for the development of that land[9]; or

(c) the making without planning permission of a change of use of any building to use as a single dwellinghouse; or

(d) the failure to comply with a condition which prohibits or has the effect of preventing a change of use of a building to use as a single dwellinghouse.[10]

In other cases there is no time limit for enforcement action other than the general requirement that the breach must have occurred since the end of 1963.

5.5. Service

A copy of the enforcement notice must be served on all owners and occupiers of the land to which it relates and on any other person with an interest in the land, if his interest is in the opinion of the authority materially affected by the notice. Service must be effected not later than 28 days after the issue of the notice and at least 28 days before the date on which the notice is to take effect.[11] Authorities should send with the notice (i) a copy of the standard appeal form; (ii) a duplicate enforcement notice to be sent to the Secretary of State if an appeal is made; (iii) a copy of the Department's explanatory booklet on enforcement appeals.[12]

5.6. Contents of enforcement notice

The enforcement notice must specify the steps which are to be taken to deal with the breach. Model forms are given in Circular 38/81.[13] The requirements may include demolition or alteration of buildings or works, discontinuance of any use of land and the carrying out of buildings or other operations, so far as necessary to restore the land to

---

[8] For the application of the four-year limit to mining operations see *David (Thomas) (Porthcawl)* v. *Penybont Rural District Council* [1972] 1 W.L.R. 1526; affirming [1972] W.L.R. 354 and Town and Country Planning (Minerals) Regulations 1971 (as amended) (S.I. 1971, No. 756), reg. 4.

[9] *Peacock Homes* v. *Secretary of State for the Environment* [1984] J.P.L. 729.

[10] 1990 Act, s.172(4) [87(4)/71].

[11] *Ibid.* s.172(6) [87(5)/71].

[12] Circ. 20/85, Appendix 1, para. 9.

[13] Circ. 38/81, *Planning and Enforcement Appeals.*

its condition before the development took place or to secure compliance with the conditions or limitations subject to which planning permission was granted.[14] They may also include a requirement to take steps to make the development comply with the terms of a previous planning permission or to remove or alleviate any injury to amenity caused by the development.[15] In the case of development by tipping of waste or refuse the notice may require contouring work to be carried out by specifying the required alterations to the gradients.[16] The required steps must be specified in the notice, as well as the period or periods within which each step is required to be carried out.[17] Further requirements for the notice are specified in the Enforcement Notices Regulations.[18] Of particular importance is the requirement that the notice should state the reasons why the authority consider it expedient to serve it. The mere fact that there is a breach of planning control will not be sufficient (see paragraph 5.1, *ante*). The notice should also specify, whether by a plan or otherwise, the precise boundaries of the land to which it relates and that it should include details of the appeal procedures.

5.7. Date when notice takes effect

The enforcement notice must specify a date, at least 28 days after service, on which it is to take effect.[19] The main importance of the date is that it constitutes the time limit for appeals against the notice (see below) or for withdrawal of the notice by the authority. If an appeal is made by anyone, the notice is suspended generally and only takes effect when the appeal is withdrawn or finally determined.[20] "Final determination" refers to the decision of the Secretary of State or inspector which may be appealed under section 289 [246/71]. The notice will, therefore, not take effect until the determination of any subsequent appeal to the Courts.[21]

5.8. Right of appeal

Section 88 gives a right of appeal against an enforcement notice to any person who has an interest in the land, whether or not he has been served with a copy of the notice. The Town and Country Planning Act 1984 extends the right to anyone who is in occupation of the land under a licence in writing at the date of both the notice and the appeal.[22] In this context it should be noted that, once the notice takes effect, it is binding on everyone—not merely on those who received copies of it. Subsequently, the validity of the notice cannot normally

---

[14] 1990 Act, s.173(4) [87(10)/71].

[15] *Ibid.* s.173(3) [87(9)/71].

[16] *Ibid.* s.173(6) [87(11)/71].

[17] *Ibid.* s.173(2), (5) [87(7), (8)/71].

[18] Regs. 3, 4.

[19] 1990 Act, s.172(6) and (5) [87(5), (13)/71].

[20] *Ibid.* s.175(4) [88(10)/71].

[21] See *R.* v. *Kuxhaus* [1988] Q.B. 631; [1988] J.P.L. 545.

[22] 1990 Act, s.174(1), (6) [4(2)/84], and see also the Listed Buildings Act 1990, s.39.

be questioned in any legal proceedings on any ground which could have formed the basis of an appeal under section 88. The only exception is in the case of a person who satisfies the following three conditions, that is a person who, (i) has held an interest in the land since before the notice was served, (ii) did not receive a copy of it, and (iii) satisfies the court that he did not know and could not reasonably have been expected to know of its issue and that his interests have been substantially prejudiced by the failure to serve him.[23] Accordingly, anyone who has an interest in the land and has reason to question it must take the opportunity offered by the right of appeal under section 174 [88/71]. Where it is alleged that the enforcement notice is a nullity because of some fundamental formal defect, the appropriate remedy is judicial review.[24] However, if this course is adopted it may be advisable at the same time to make an appeal without prejudice, since the time limit is likely to have lapsed before the application for judicial review is heard.

5.9. Grounds of appeal

The grounds upon which an appeal may be made are set out in section 174(2) [88(2)/71] as follows:

(a) that planning permission ought to be granted for the development to which the notice relates or, as the case may be, that a condition or limitation alleged in the enforcement notice not to have been complied with ought to be discharged;

(b) that the matters alleged in the notice do not constitute a breach of planning control;

(c) that the breach of planning control alleged in the notice has not taken place;

(d) in the case of a notice which may be issued only within the period of four years from the date of the breach of planning control to which the notice relates, that that period had elapsed at the date when the notice was issued;

(e) in the case of a notice not falling within paragraph (d), that the breach of planning control alleged by the notice occurred before the beginning of 1964;

(f) that copies of the enforcement notice were not served as required by section 172(6) [87(5)/71];

(g) that the steps required by the notice to be taken exceed what is necessary to remedy any breach of planning control or to achieve a purpose specified in section 173(4) [87(10)/71];

(h) that the period specified in the notice as the period within which any step is to be taken falls short of what should reasonably be allowed.

---

[23] 1990 Act, s.285(3) [243(1)/71].
[24] *Rhymney Valley District Council* v. *Secretary of State for Wales and Isaac* [1985] J.P.L. 27.

The letters identifying the various grounds should be noted as they are often used as shorthand by inspectors and others. The grounds fall into distinct categories. Grounds (b) to (e) constitute substantive legal objections to the allegations in the notice. Ground (f) is a procedural objection relating to service, which is of limited importance in practice in view of the Secretary of State's power to disregard the defect if no substantial prejudice has resulted.[25] Ground (a) assumes that the allegations are soundly based in fact and law but enables the planning merits of the infringing works or activities to be raised in their defence. Grounds (g) and (h) do not go to the substance of the notice but are in effect requests for amendments of detail. It is usual for a number of different grounds to be put forward in the appeal.

5.10. Notice of appeal

The appeal is made by notice in writing to the Secretary of State. Although it is not a statutory requirement, it is advisable to use the form of notice issued by the Department, which should be supplied with the enforcement notice. The notice of appeal should include not only an indication of the statutory grounds relied on, but also a brief statement of the facts on which the appellant proposes to rely in support of each ground.[26] All that is necessary is sufficient factual material under each ground to enable the authority to know the general lines of the case it has to meet. A notice which does not contain this information will not be invalid. However, the Secretary of State may require the information to be supplied within 28 days and, if that requirement is not complied with, he may dismiss the appeal without a hearing[27] or deal only with those grounds which are adequately pleaded.[28] The Secretary of State's practice when information is not supplied is as follows:

> "For all enforcement and listed building enforcement appeals which are delayed because the appellant provides insufficient information and the department's requests for further information are ignored, the Secretary of State will invoke his new powers, in regulation 5 of the Enforcement Notices and Appeals Regulations,[29] to require time limits to be observed. If an appellant fails to provide the required information in response to a request for it, the Secretary of State will formally require him to provide it within a period of 28 days. If this requirement does not produce a satisfactory response, the department will issue a warning letter, one week before the 28 day period is due to expire, to the effect that the Secretary of State may proceed to dismiss the appeal (or determine it only on those grounds of appeal for which he has sufficient information), unless the

---

[25] 1990 Act, s.176(5) [88A(3)/71].
[26] Enforcement Notices Regulations, reg. 5.
[27] 1990 Act, s.177 [88(B)/71].
[28] *Ibid.* s.184(8) [88(9)/71].
[29] S.I. 1981 No. 1742.

appellant can show that there are extenuating circumstances genuinely preventing him from providing the required information. If this warning letter fails to produce a satisfactory response within one week, the Secretary of State will proceed at once to consider, in the light of all the information and representations then available to him, whether to dismiss the appeal in accordance with section 88(6)(a) or 97(5)(a) of the 1971 Act; or to determine it, as in section 88(9) or 97(8), without regard to those grounds of appeal which have not been properly and adequately supported by a statement of facts. When an appeal is dismissed under section 88(6)(a) or 97(5)(a), the Secretary of State will not have considered the deemed planning application and any fee already paid by the appellant will be refunded by the department."[30]

The appeal must be made before the date specified in the notice as the date on which it is to take efect. This is interpreted as requiring that the notice should actually reach the Department before that date.[31] There is no power to extend the time for appeal.

5.11. Fees
Since the appeal involves a deemed planning application, a fee is payable when the notice of appeal is lodged, but is returnable if the appeal succeeds because the local planning authority failed to comply with the procedural requirements imposed on authorities by the Secretary of State.[32] The fee is payable to the Secretary of State and will be requested by him on receipt of the appeal.[33] Where there is more than one appellant, each will be required to pay a fee.

5.12. Appeal procedure
The form of procedure will depend on whether either the appellant or the authority has requested an opportunity to be heard. The Secretary of State must give such an opportunity if it is requested by either party.[34] In deciding whether to ask for a hearing, the appellant will be guided by similar considerations to those on a planning appeal (see paragraph 2.11, *ante*). However, in an enforcement appeal it is more likely that there will be disputed issues of fact (for example, as to whether a use began before 1964). In such cases the arguments in favour of an oral hearing, with an opportunity for cross-examination, are likely to be much stronger.

In practice, if a hearing is requested the Secretary of State will order a local inquiry to be held at which members of the public can appear

---

[30] Circ. 38/81, para. 35. Ss. 88(6)(a) and 97(5)(a) are now Planning Act 1990, s.176(3)(a) and Listed Buildings Act 1990, s.41(3)(a) respectively, while ss.88(9) and 97(8) are now Planning Act 1990, s.174(5) and Listed Buildings Act 1990, s.39 respectively.
[31] *Lenlyn Ltd.* v. *Secretary of State* (1984) 40 P. & C.R. 129.
[32] Town and Country Planning (Fees for Applications and Deemed Applications) Regulations 1989, reg. 10(8).
[33] *Ibid.* reg. 8(4).
[34] 1990 Act, s.175(3) [88(7)/71].

and make representations. If a local inquiry is not held, the authority is required to give prescribed information about the notice and the appeal to, and to invite comments from, occupiers of property in the locality and any others who in the opinion of the authority are affected.[35]

If an inquiry is held, the procedure is governed by the Enforcement Inquiries Procedure Rules which are printed as Appendix D.3 to this work. In general these follow the lines of the Inquiries Procedure Rules for planning appeals (see paragraphs 2.28–2.45, *ante*). The main difference is that there is no requirement for statements of case to be served or statements of evidence to be produced prior to the inquiry. As in the case of planning appeals (see paragraphs 2.38 *et seq.*, *ante*) nearly all enforcement notice appeals are now decided by inspectors rather than by the Secretary of State.[36] However, the same inquiries procedure rules apply and the procedure is substantially the same, whoever is to make the decision. Applications for costs are dealt with on the same principles as for planning appeals.[37] Unlike planning appeals, however, there is power to award costs on written representations appeals as well as on local inquiries.[38]

5.13. The authority's case

Once an appeal has been made, the authority are under a duty to serve on the Secretary of State and the appellant a statement of the submissions which they propose to put forward. If there is to be a local inquiry, this statement must be served not later than 28 days before the inquiry (unless a shorter time is agreed in writing with the Secretary of State and the appellant). If no inquiry is held, the statement must be served within 28 days of the Secretary of State's notice requiring it.[39] The statement must include a summary of the authority's response to each ground of appeal and a statement whether the authority would be prepared to grant planning permission for the development alleged in the enforcement notice, and, if so, on what conditions.[40] The authority must also, if so required by the Secretary of State, send to him not later than 14 days after being notified by him of the appeal, a copy of the enforcement notice and a list of the names and addresses of the persons on whom copies were served.[41]

Appellants should bear in mind that, if the authority fails to comply with these requirements, the Secretary of State has power to allow the appeal without further hearing and to quash the enforcement notice.[42]

---

[35] Enforcement Notices Regulations, reg. 7.
[36] Town and Country Planning (Determination of Appeals by Appointed Persons) (Prescribed Classes) Regulations (S.I. 1981 No. 804), reg. 3.
[37] See Circ. 2/87, *Awards of Costs Incurred in Planning and Compulsory Purchase Order Proceedings*.
[38] 1990 Act, s.175(7) [110(1)/71] and see [1980] J.P.L. 710, 765.
[39] See Circ. 38/81, para. 39.
[40] Enforcement Notices Regulations, reg. 6.
[41] *Ibid.* reg. 8.
[42] 1990 Act, s.176(3) [88(6)/71].

It remains to be seen how rigorously this power will be used in practice. In any event, if the authority's statement is not adequate, the appellant may of course request further particulars and, if necessary, ask for further time to deal with them.

5.14. Preparation of appellant's case

An enforcement notice appeal is generally a hybrid affair involving, on the one hand, issues of fact and law related to the contention that the development is permitted or is immune from enforcement action and, on the other, issues of policy or planning judgement related to the contention that planning permission should in any event be granted. The factual case should be prepared in the same way as for an established use certificate appeal (see paragraph 4.10, *ante*). In order to avoid unnecessary expense in ascertaining facts it is often useful for information to be exchanged with the authority before the inquiry. In particular, the expense of calling witnesses can sometimes be avoided by exchanging statutory declarations in advance. The planning case should be prepared in the same way as for an ordinary planning appeal and the considerations discussed above apply (see paragraphs 2.21 *et seq.*). It is to be noted that, even where ground (a) is not relied on, the appeal constitutes a deemed planning application for permission for the development to which it relates.[43] The planning merits will, therefore, be considered in any event.

If new grounds of appeal or facts are brought forward at a late stage or even at the inquiry, the local planning authority may be justified in seeking an adjournment of the inquiry and it is possible that costs would be awarded against the appellant in respect of any adjournment made necessary.

It should be noted that the onus of proof in enforcement appeals rests with the appellant.[44] The proper test is the civil standard of proof on the balance of probabilities.[45] In an enforcement appeal, as in a section 36 appeal, the appellant opens the case with the local planning authority coming second and a final right of reply for the appellant.

5.15. Secretary of State's powers on appeal

Under section 176(2) [88A(2)/71] the Secretary of State has power on an appeal to correct any informality, defect or error in the enforcement notice or give directions for varying its terms, if he is satisfied that the correction or variation can be made without injustice to the appellant or to the local planning authority.[46] This provision, in effect, puts into statutory form the wide interpretation given to the corresponding powers under the previous legislation.[47] It will generally

---

[43] 1990 Act, s.177 [88B(3)/71].

[44] See *Nelsovil* v. *Minister of Housing and Local Government* [1962] 1 W.L.R. 404.

[45] See *Thrasyvoulou* v. *Secretary of State for Environment and Hackney London Borough Council* [1984] J.P.L. 732.

[46] See *R.* v. *London Borough of Tower Hamlets, ex p. Ahern (London)* [1989] J.P.L. 757.

[47] See *e.g. Hammersmith London Borough Council* v. *Secretary of State for the Environment* (1975) 30 P. & C.R. 19; *Sanders* v. *Secretary of State for the Environment and Epping Forest District Council* [1981] J.P.L. 593.

be used to overcome purely technical objections to the form of the notice or the description of the alleged breach. It may also be used for the benefit of the appellant, for example, to amend the notice so far as necessary to protect established rights (for example, in cases of intensification).[48] The appellant should ensure that the description is no wider than justified by the facts, and does not have the effect of depriving them of any rights to which they are entitled, since the scope of the notice cannot be challenged in subsequent proceedings.

Section 177 [88B/71] gives to the Secretary of State (or as the case may be the inspector) wide powers to give effect to his determination on the appeal. Apart from quashing or varying the notice, he may grant planning permission (with or without conditions) for the development to which the notice relates or part of it, or for development of part of the land to which the notice relates. Such a permission may include permission to retain or complete any buildings or works on the land or to do so without complying with a previous planning condition. Similarly, he may discharge any conditions or limitations imposed by a previous permission—either altogether or by substituting a new condition or limitation (whether more or less onerous). A planning permission granted under these powers is treated for all purposes as though it had been made on an application under Part III of the Act in the ordinary way.[49] Where the complaint is that insufficient time has been allowed for relocation the Secretary of State is more likely to vary the notice so as to extend the time for compliance than to grant a temporary permission.[50] If, during the course of the proceedings, it becomes apparent to the Secretary of State that the original appeal was made out of time, he may dismiss it altogether, and he is not precluded by his earlier acceptance of it.[51]

5.16. Determination of lawful use

The Secretary of State also has a discretionary power to make a formal determination of any purpose for which the land may lawfully be used having regard to any past use of it and any planning permission relating to it.[52] This power can be useful in clarifying the planning status of the land even if the appeal itself is unsuccessful. Planning permission is not required, following an enforcement notice, to revert to the use to which the land could lawfully have been put before the offending development.[53] However, an established use commenced in breach of planning control is not a lawful use for these purposes[54] and only the last preceding use is relevant.[55] If the appellant

---

[48] See *Mansi* v. *Elstree Rural District Council* (1964) 16 P. & C.R. 153; *Trevors Warehouses* v. *Secretary of State for the Environment* (1972) 23 P. & C.R. 215.

[49] 1990 Act, s.177(5) [88B(3)/71].

[50] See *e.g.* [1973] J.P.L. 328; and see *Moldene* v. *Secretary of State for the Environment* [1979] J.P.L. 177.

[51] *R.* v. *Melton and Belvoir Justices, ex p. Tynan* (1977) 33 P. & C.R. 214; [1977] J.P.L. 368.

[52] 1990 Act, s.177(1)(c) [88B(1)(c)/71].

[53] *Ibid.* s.57(4) [23(9)/71].

[54] *LTSS Print and Supply Services* v. *Hackney London Borough Council* [1976] Q.B. 663.

[55] *Young* v. *Secretary of State for the Environment* [1983] 2 A.C. 662; [1983] J.P.L. 667.

is going to seek such a determination it is advisable for him to give advance notice to the Secretary of State and the local planning authority, and it is essential for him to come armed with adequate evidence to support the determination which he is seeking. Otherwise the Secretary of State is likely to refuse to make a determination.

5.17. Appeals to the High Court

Section 289 of the 1990 Act [246/71] provides for the appellant, the local planning authority or any other person with an interest in the land to appeal to the High Court against the Secretary of State's decision on an enforcement appeal. This is also the appropriate procedure where the Secretary of State rejects the appeal because of a defect in the notice.[56]

An appeal under this section is made to a single Judge of the Queen's Bench Division by originating motion, under the Rules of the Supreme Court.[57] A short affidavit exhibiting the decision, the inspector's report (if any) and any other essential documents will usually be sufficient. The notice and the affidavit should be served on the Secretary of State and the other party (local authority or appellant). The notice must be served and the appeal entered within 28 days of the date of the decision (although the Court has power to extend this period, it is unlikely to do so without special reasons).[58]

It should be noted that an appeal against the Secretary of State's decision may only be made on a point of law and not on any question of fact or planning judgement.[59]

In recent years the courts have been much less willing than formerly to quash enforcement notice decisions on technical points.[60]

5.18. Other methods of challenge

Section 288 [245/71] provides that generally the validity of an enforcement notice cannot be questioned except in proceedings under section 289 [246/71]. Thus, once an enforcement notice in respect of a use has been served, an action for a declaration to establish the lawfulness of the use will be struck out.[61] Similarly, on a prosecution for breach of an enforcement notice, the court cannot normally go into matters which could have been raised on appeal to the Secretary of State under sections 174 and 175 [88/71] (see paragraph 5.9, *supra*). However, it may be possible to obtain an adjournment of an enforcement notice prosecution pending determination of an appeal.[62]

---

[56] *Horsham District Council* v. *Fisher* [1977] J.P.L. 178.

[57] R.S.C., Ords. 55, 94, r. 12.

[58] R.S.C., Ord. 55, r. 4(2) and see *Ringroad Investments and Courtburn* v. *Secretary of State for the Environment* (1979) 40 P. & C.R.; 99 [1979] J.P.L. 770.

[59] 1990 Act, s.289(1) [246(1)/71].

[60] *Miller-Mead* v. *Minister of Housing and Local Government* [1963] 2 Q.B. 196.

[61] *Square Meals Frozen Foods* v. *Dunstable Corporation* [1974] 1 W.L.R. 59.

[62] *R.* v. *Polly Newland* [1987] J.P.L. 851.

B. STOP NOTICES

5.19. Stop notices

The stop notice procedure[63] normally applies when an enforcement notice has been served requiring a breach of planning control to be remedied and the authority consider it expedient to prevent, before the expiry of the period allowed for compliance with the notice, the carrying out of any activity which is or is included in, a matter alleged by the notice to constitute the breach. They may serve a fresh notice (known as a stop notice) before the date when the enforcement notice takes effect. This notice must refer to and have annexed to it a copy of the enforcement notice and be expressed to prohibit any person on whom the stop notice is served from carrying out any activity which is, or is included in, a matter alleged in the enforcement notice to constitute a breach of planning control. Departmental advice on the use of the stop notice procedure is given in Circular 4/87[64] (Welsh Office 7/87). There is no reason why a stop notice and enforcement notice cannot be served simultaneously.[64a]

5.20. Exclusions

Certain activities cannot be prevented by a stop notice. They are, (i) the use of a building as a dwellinghouse; (ii) the use of land as a site for a caravan occupied as a sole or main residence; (iii) the taking of any steps which the enforcement notice requires to be taken to remedy the breach of planning control; and (iv) any activity which commenced more than 12 months previously (even if it commenced under a temporary permission which expired less than 12 months before)[65] and which is not, or is not incidental to, building, engineering, mining or other operations or the deposit of refuse or waste materials.[66]

5.21. Effect of stop notice

The stop notice does not take effect (and so cannot be contravened) until the date specified being a date not earlier than three nor later than 28 days from the day on which it is first served on any person.[67] A stop notice ceases to have effect when (i) the enforcement notice is withdrawn or quashed; or (ii) the period allowed for compliance with the enforcement notice expires; or (iii) notice of the withdrawal of the stop notice is first served under subsection (6); or (iv) if, and to the extent that, the activities prohibited by it cease, on a variation of the enforcement notice, to be included in the matters alleged by the enforcement notice to constitute a breach of planning control.[68]

---

[63] 1990 Act, ss.183, 184 [90/71].

[64] Circ. 4/87; *section 90 of the 1971 Act: Provisions and Procedures for Stop Notices.*

[64a] *R.* v. *Pettigrew, The Times,* May 31, 1990.

[65] *Scott Markets* v. *Waltham Forest London Borough Council* (1979) 38 P. & C.R. 597; [1979] J.P.L. 392.

[66] 1990 Act, s.183(3)–(5) [90(2)/71].

[67] *Ibid.* s.184(2), (3) [90(3)/71].

[68] *Ibid.* s.184(4), (5) [90(4)/71].

It is an offence to contravene or cause or permit the contravention of a stop notice.[69] There is no right of appeal against a stop notice.

Certain compensation rights exist[70] if the stop notice or the enforcement notice is withdrawn or the appeal against the enforcement notice succeeds on any of the grounds other than those mentioned in paragraph (a) of section 174(2) of the 1990 Act [88(2)/71]. The compensation provisions are summarised in an annex to Circular 4/87.

5.22. Challenge of stop notice

There is no right of appeal against a stop notice. The only statutory remedy for improper exercise of the power is the right to compensation. However, if the stop notice can be shown to be defective in law (for example, because it was served more than 12 months after the use began) it could be challenged by proceedings for judicial review.[71] A legal defect can also be raised by way of defence to a prosecution.[72] Otherwise, the merits can only be considered at the enforcement notice appeal. If necessary the Department can be asked to expedite the appeal.

C. ENFORCEMENT OF LISTED BUILDING CONTROL

5.23. Listed building enforcement notices

Under section 38 of the Listed Buildings Act 1990 [96/71], where it appears to the local planning authority that any works have been or are being executed to a listed building in their area and are such as to involve a contravention of sections 7 or 9(1), (2) of the Listed Buildings Act 1990 [55(1), (4)/71], then they may, if they consider it expedient to do so having regard to the effect of the works on the character of the building as one of special architectural or historic interest, issue a listed building enforcement notice. The notice must specify the alleged contravention, the steps which the authority require to be taken and the period within which they are to be taken. The notice may either specify steps for restoring the building to its former state[73] or, if the authority consider that such restoration would not be reasonably practicable or would be undesirable, such further works as the authority consider necessary for alleviating the effect of the works carried out without listed building consent.[74] This power cannot be used to secure an improvement as compared to the state of the building before the unauthorised works.[75] If the contravention is the breach of the terms and conditions of a listed building consent, the notice will specify steps for bringing the building to the state in which it

---

[69] 1990 Act, s.187(1), (2) [90(7)/71].

[70] *Ibid.* s.186 [177/71].

[71] R.S.C., Ord. 53.

[72] *R.* v. *Jenner* [1983] 2 All E.R. 46; [1983] J.P.L. 547.

[73] Planning (Listed Buildings and Conservation Areas) Act 1990, s.38(2)(a) [96(1)(b)(i)/71].

[74] *Ibid.* s.38(2)(b) [96(1)(b)(ii)/71].

[75] *Bath City Council* v. *Secretary of State for the Environment* [1983] J.P.L. 737.

would have been if the terms and conditions had been complied with.[76] A copy of the notice must be served, not later than 28 days after the date of issue and not later than 28 days before the date on which it is to take effect, on the owner and occupier of the building and on any other person with an interest in the building which in the opinion of the authority is materially affected.[77]

5.24. Appeal in respect of listed building enforcement notice

The procedure for such appeals is laid down in section 39 of the Listed Buildings Act 1990 [97/71] and generally follows that for enforcement notices. The grounds of appeal are as follows:

(a) that the building is not of special architectural or historic interest;

(b) that the matters alleged to constitute a contravention of sections 7, 8 and 9 of the Listed Buildings Act 1990 [55/71] do not involve such a contravention;

(c) that the contravention of that section alleged in the notice has not taken place;

(d) that the works were urgently necessary in the interests of safety or health or for the preservation of the building;

(e) that listed building consent ought to be granted for the works, or that any relevant condition of such consent which has been granted ought to be discharged, or different conditions substituted;

(f) that copies of the notice were not served as required by section 38(4) of the Listed Buildings Act 1990 [96(3)/71];

(g) except in relation to such a requirement as is mentioned in section 38(2)(b) or (c) of the Listed Buildings Act 1990 [96(1)(b)(ii), (iii)/71], the requirements of the notice exceed what is necessary for restoring the building to its condition before the works were carried out;

(h) that the period specified in the notice as the period within which any step required thereby is to be taken falls short of what should reasonably be allowed;

(i) that the steps required by the notice for the purpose of restoring the character of the building to its former state would not serve that purpose;

(j) that steps required to be taken by virtue of section 38(2)(b) of the Act exceed what is necessary to alleviate the effect of the works executed to the building;

---

[76] Planning (Listed Buildings and Conservation Areas) Act 1990, s.38(2)(c) [96(1)(b)(iii)/71].
[77] *Ibid.* s.38(4) [96(3)/71].

(k) that steps required to be taken by virtue of section 38(2)(*c*) of the Act exceed what is necessary to bring the building to the state in which it would have been if the terms and conditions of the listed building consent had been complied with.

5.25. Appeal procedure

The requirements of the Enforcement Notices Regulations as to the content of the enforcement notice and of the notice of appeal and as to the authority's statement of case (see paragraphs 5.5, 5.9, 5.11, *supra*) apply equally to listed building enforcement notices.[78] Similarly each party has a right to be heard by a person appointed by the Secretary of State, and the Enforcement Inquiries Procedure Rules (Appendix D.3, *post*) apply to an inquiry or hearing so held. The preparation of material for the inquiry and the inquiry itself will follow the line of an enforcement notice inquiry. Where the issues relate to the importance of the building or the effect of the works on its character, evidence will be needed similar to that required for a listed building consent appeal (see paragraph 3.31, *ante*). The Secretary of State's powers to give effect to his determination of the appeal[79] correspond to those on an enforcement notice appeal (see paragraph 5.14, *supra*). They include the power to amend the notice, to grant listed building consent for the works or part of them, to discharge or substitute conditions, and to make appropriate amendments to the statutory lists of buildings of special architectural or historic interest. His decision on the appeal may be challenged on a point of law in the High Court in the same way as a decision on an enforcement notice appeal.

5.26. Injunctive Relief

The procedures for issuing enforcement notices and stop notices, it can be appreciated from the above, may be time-consuming. As an alternative the local planning authority may apply to the Court for an injunction to obtain the immediate cessation of the development where it is considered to be "expedient for the promotion or protection of the interests of the inhabitants of their area."[80] However, the Courts will usually expect that other procedures have been pursued before an application for an injunction is made.[81]

---

[78] Enforcement Notices Regulations, reg. 2.

[79] Planning (Listed Buildings and Conservation Areas) Act 1990, s.41 [97A/71].

[80] Local Government Act 1972, s.222. *Westminster City Council* v. *Jones* [1981] J.P.L. 750.

[81] See *London Borough of Southwark* v. *Frow (M.L.)* [1989] J.P.L. 645, for an example of an exceptional case in which no enforcement or stop notice was issued.

CHAPTER 6

PURCHASE NOTICES

A. Section 137, Purchase Notice on Refusal or Conditional Grant of Planning Permission

6.1. Nature of procedure

The purchase notice procedure is a means by which an owner, who claims that his land is incapable of reasonably beneficial use following an adverse planning decision, can force an authority to purchase it. Once it takes effect, the notice operates in the same way as a notice to treat served by the authority under a compulsory purchase order.

6.2. When purchase notice may be served

If permission to develop any land is refused or is granted subject to conditons, either by the local planning authority or by the Secretary of State, a purchase notice may be served by the owner requiring the council of the London borough or county district in which the land is situate to purchase his interest in that land.[1] A purchase notice once accepted or confirmed cannot be withdrawn. A purchase notice must be based upon contentions on the part of the owner of the land: (a) that the land has become incapable of reasonably beneficial use in its existing state; and (b), in a case where permission has been granted subject to conditions, that the land cannot be rendered capable of reasonably beneficial use by the carrying out of the permitted development in accordance with those conditions; and (c), in any case, that the land cannot be rendered capable of reasonably beneficial use by the carrying out of any other development for which permission has been or is deemed to be granted (under Part III of the Act) or for which the local planning authority or the Secretary of State have undertaken to grant permission. Comprehensive advice on practice and procedure relating to purchase notices is given in Circular 13/83[2] (Welsh Office 22/83).

6.3. What is a "reasonably beneficial use"?

The question to be considered is whether the land in its existing state and with its existing permissions (including any undertakings to grant permission and taking into account operations and uses for which planning permission is not required) is incapable of reasonably beneficial use.[3]

The general approach is given as follows in Circular 13/83:

---

[1] 1990 Act, s.137 [180(1)/71].

[2] Circ. 13/83, *Purchase Notices.*

[3] See *R.* v. *Minister of Housing and Local Government, ex p. Chichester Rural District Council* [1960] 1 W.L.R. 587, 11 P. & C.R. 295; *R.* v. *Minister of Housing and Local Government, ex p. Rank Organisation* [1958] 1 W.L.R. 1093, 10 P. & C.R. 9.

"13. In considering what capacity for use the land has, relevant factors are the physical state of the land, its size, shape and surroundings, and the general pattern of land uses in the area; a use of relatively low value may be regarded as reasonably beneficial if such a use is common for similar land in the vicinity. It may sometimes be possible for an area of land to be rendered capable of reasonably beneficial use by being used in conjunction with neighbouring or adjoining land, provided that a sufficient interest in that land is held by the server of the notice, or by a prospective owner of the purchase notice land. Use by a prospective owner cannot be taken into account unless there is a reasonably firm indication that there is in fact a prospective owner of the purchase notice site. (In this paragraph the word "owner" is used to include a person who has a tenancy of the land or some other interest which is sufficient to enable him to use the land.) Profit may be a useful comparison in certain circumstances, but the absence of profit (however calculated) is not necessarily material: the concept of reasonably beneficial use is not synonymous with profit."

The following points arising from the Circular are also important in considering evidence:

"16. The Secretary of State considers that, in seeking to satisfy himself whether conditions (a) to (c) in section 180(1) of the 1971 Act have been fulfilled, he may take into account, among other things, whether there is a a reasonable prospect of the server's selling or letting the land for any purpose, were its availability to be made known locally. He would normally expect to see some evidence to show that the server has attempted to dispose of his interest in the land before he could be satisfied that the land had become incapable of reasonably beneficial use.
17. Where an owner of land claims that his land has become incapable of reasonably beneficial use, he is regarded as making that claim in respect of the whole of the land in question. Therefore, if a part of the land is found to be capable of reasonably beneficial use, it follows that the server of the notice has not substantiated his claim. Consequently, the Secretary of State cannot be satisfied that the condition specified in section 180(1)(a) has been fulfilled in respect of the whole of the land."

The use must be one which is beneficial to the owner or prospective owner of the land: the fact that the use benefits the community at large is not sufficient.[4] One important factor may be whether it gives an economic return;[5] but this will not be conclusive, for example where the land is held by the owner for recreational or amenity purposes.

The causes of the land becoming incapable of beneficial use are not material, unless they involved a breach of planning control or listed

---

[4] *Adams & Wade* v. *Minister of Housing and Local Government* (1965) 18 P. & C.R. 60.
[5] See, *e.g.* appeal decision at [1988] J.P.L. 53.

building control still capable of enforcement.[6] Thus, the person who has served a purchase notice does not have to prove that the refusal of planning permission is the direct or only cause.

For the purpose of section 137(3)(c) [180(1)(c)/71] only permission granted (or deemed to be granted) and undertakings given before the service of the purchase notice may be taken into account. To be effective an undertaking must be in unequivocal language and so worded as to be binding on the local planning authority or the Secretary of State as an undertaking which the owner of the land can rely and act upon: a promise "to give favourable consideration" to an application for permission is not a binding undertaking.[7]

6.4. Why serve a purchase notice?

In considering whether to serve a purchase notice careful thought should be given to the likely consequences, particularly compensation. In normal circumstances, the fact that the land is "incapable of reasonably beneficial use" will have the corollary that its value and accordingly the likely compensation will be minimal. The owner may be better advised to keep the land and wait for policies to change. A purchase notice is, however, a valuable weapon in three particular cases. The first is where the owner has some particular reason for wanting to get the land off his hands (for example, occupier's liability). The second is where the land has potentially valuable rights under Schedule 3 to the 1990 Act [Sched. 8/71] which can only be taken into account if the land is acquired by an authority. For example, if a building is destroyed and permission to rebuild is refused, the right to rebuild will be assumed in assessing compensation.[8] A purchase notice may be the only way in which this value can be realised. The third is when the property is blighted by a public proposal, for example for a road. In assessing compensation, the effects of the "scheme" on values will normally be disregarded.

6.5. The refusal of planning permission

Before a purchase notice can be served there must be an actual refusal of planning permission or a conditional consent. The failure of the local planning authority to issue a decision within the stipulated period of eight weeks is not sufficient to justify the service of a purchase notice. In such a case the only remedy is to appeal to the Secretary of State under section 78 [37/71] and if he refuses planning permission, a purchase notice can then be served.[9]

6.6. Who can serve a purchase notice?

The notice can only be served by the owner of the land. By virtue of section 336 [290/71], "owner" means a person who is entitled to

---

[6] Circ. 13/83, para. 18: and *Balco Transport Services* v. *Secretary of State for the Environment (No. 2)* [1985] 3 All E.R. 689; [1986] J.P.L. 123, qualifying *Purbeck District Council* v. *Secretary of State for the Environment* (1983) 46 P. & C.R. 1; [1982] J.P.L. 640.

[7] *Ibid.* para. 15.

[8] Land Compensation Act 1961, s.15 and 1990 Act, Sched. 3, para. 1 [Sched. 8, para. 1/71].

[9] See Circ. 13/83, para. 2.

receive the rack rent of the land or, where the land is not let at a rack rent, would be so entitled if it were so let.

6.7. Form and service of purchase notice

A purchase notice must be in writing and be served on the council of the district in which the land is situated. In Greater London, the purchase notices relating to land in the City should be served on the Common Council and those relating to other land on the appropriate London Borough Council. It may be served either by delivering it at the offices of the council addressed to the clerk or by sending it by pre-paid post. The notice must be served within 12 months from the date of the decision in respect of which the notice is given.[10] The Secretary of State has power to extend this period if an application is made to him in a particular case, and is normally prepared to grant a short extension where the service of the notice is held up for good reasons (for example, negotiations with the local planning authority).[11] An extension may also be needed when the purchase notice follows a refusal on appeal, since the Secretary of State's decision is treated as dating from the original decision of the authority (if any).[12] Local authorities have no power to extend the period. A model form of purchase notice is contained in Appendix I to Circular No. 13/83.

6.8. The area of the land to be purchased

The purchase notice may only require the purchase of the land which was the subject of the planning decision.[13] If the purchase notice relates either to a greater or to a lesser area of land it will generally be invalid. If, however, permission is granted for part of the land and refused for the remainder, the Secretary of State takes the view that a valid notice may be served in respect of that remainder. If the application for planning permission relates to land in different owner-ships, the owners of the different parcels may combine to serve a purchase notice relating to their separate interests, if the notice as served relates to the whole of the land covered by the planning decision.[14]

Under section 142 [184/71], the Secretary of State may refuse to confirm a purchase notice relating to land for which planning permis-sion is refused or granted subject to conditions and which consists in whole or in part of land which has a restricted use by virtue of a previous planning permisison. The section treats land as having a restricted use if it is part of a larger area for which a permission has been granted and either (a) the permission contained a condition that the land in question should remain undeveloped or be preserved or laid out as amenity land, or (b) the application contemplated that the

---

[10] General Regulations, reg. 14(2).

[11] Circ. 13/83, para. 4.

[12] 1990 Act, s.336(5) [290(4)/71]; see Circ. 13/83, para. 37.

[13] See *Plymouth Corporation* v. *Secretary of State for the Environment* [1972] 1 W.L.R. 1347.

[14] Circ. 13/83, paras. 7, 9.

land in question should be outside the development or should be preserved as amenity land. The Secretary of State may refuse to confirm the purchase notice if it appears to him that the land having a restricted use by virtue of the previous planning permission ought, in accordance with that permission, to remain undeveloped or preserved or laid out as amenity land in relation to the remainder of the larger area for which the previous planning permission was granted.

6.9. Acquiring authority

The notice must require the council on which the notice is served to acquire the owner's interest in the land. Although another authority may be substituted as acquiring authority (see paragraph 6.13, *post*) this should be dealt with by agreement between the authorities concerned[15] or by the decision of the Secretary of State.[16]

6.10. Counter-notice—(a) accepting purchase notice

The authority on which the purchase notice is served must, before the end of three months beginning with the date of service of the purchase notice, serve on the owner a counter-notice.[17] If they are satisfied that the requirements of section 137 [180/71] are met and that the purchase is valid they must state that they or another local authority, or statutory undertakers have agreed to comply with the notice.[18] On service of a counter-notice by the authority accepting the purchase, they are deemed to be authorised to acquire the interest of the owner compulsorily and to have served a notice to treat[19] which cannot be withdrawn.[20] Reference to the Secretary of State is not necessary. If another local authority or a statutory undertaker is willing to comply with the purchase notice (if, for example, permission to develop the land was refused because it was required for the purposes of such other authority or undertaker, and it is specified in the counter-notice as willing to comply with the notice) the notice to treat will be deemed to be served by them.[21]

Circular 13/83 describes the procedure for transmission of the purchase notice to the Secretary of State.

> "27. It is important that a Council who have decided to transmit a purchase notice should quickly send the Secretary of State the information and documents he requires to deal with the notice. He cannot begin consideration of a notice without copies of the purchase notice, any accompanying plan, the counter-notice, the planning application with plans, and the decision on which the purchase notice was based; and, if necessary, a plan to enable

---

[15] 1990 Act, s.139(1)(*b*) [181(1)(*b*)/71].
[16] *Ibid.* ss.140(2), 141(4) [182(2), 183(4)/71].
[17] *Ibid.* 139(1) [181(1)/71].
[18] *Ibid.* s.139(1)(*a*), (*b*) [181(1)(*a*), (*b*)/71].
[19] *Ibid.* s.139(3) [181(2)/71].
[20] *Ibid.* s.167 [208/71].
[21] *Ibid.* s.139(3) [181(2)/71].

him to identify the subject site in its surroundings. These documents should, if possible, accompany the transmission of the notice; but transmission of the notice should not be delayed because all the information cannot be provided at the same time. Any information not immediately available should be sent as soon as possible afterwards. It must be remembered that failure to supply all the relevant particulars within a reasonable time could lead to deemed confirmation of the notice if, as a result of delay, the Secretary of State is unable to complete his action within the statutory time limit.

28. Additional particulars and documents are also required as follows:

(i) copies of any planning permissions relevant to the provisions of section 184 of the 1971 Act, and accompanying plans;

(ii) copies of any orders made under section 45 or 51 of the Act (or under Part II of Schedule II to the 1971 Act) and accompanying plans;

(iii) particulars of the location, acreage, present condition of the land to which the notice relates and the nature of the surrounding land;

(iv) particulars of any permission or undertaking relevant to section 180(1)(c) or section 190(1)(c) of the 1971 Act;

(v) statements whether the land, or any part of it, falls within an area which is:

(a) defined in a development plan as an area of comprehensive development, or included in an action area local plan;

(b) the subject of a compulsory purchase order; or

(c) the subject of a direction (made under the Town and Country Planning (General Interior Development) Order 1946, or any of the Town and Country Planning General Development Orders) which restricts permitted development, or restricts the grant of planning permission;

(vi) the nature of the local planning authority's intentions for the land, and the probable timing of any development involved.

Copies of the documents submitted to the Secretary of State should be sent to both the server of the notice and the county council. The Secretary of State should be told that this has been done."

6.11. Counter-notice—(b) refusing to purchase

Alternatively, the authority may state in the counter-notice that for reasons specified therein they are not willing to purchase the land and that no other local authority or statutory undertakers have been found who would agree to comply with it in their place. In that event they must also state that, before serving the counter-notice on the landowner, they transmitted a copy of both the purchase notice and the counter-notice to the Secretary of State together with a statement of their reasons.[22]

---

[22] 1990 Act, s.139(1)(c) [181(1)(c)/71].

Again, the counter-notice must be served before the end of three months beginning with the date of service of the purchase notice.

6.12. Statement of reasons for refusal to purchase

It has already been mentioned that a local authority refusing to purchase must state reasons. It may base its refusal to purchase either on a contention that the requirements of paragraphs (*a*), (*b*) and (*c*) of section 137(3) [180(1)/71] are not complied with or on other grounds to be specified by them. The Act does not expressly limit those other grounds, but obviously such grounds must take into account, and are in effect governed by, the possible courses of action open to the Secretary of State on transmission of the notice to him, which are limited (see paragraph 6.13, *post*).

The statement of reasons should be full and clear, and it is to the convenience of all concerned if it is sufficiently explicit to serve as the statement of the authority's case for the purpose of any subsequent hearing ordered by the Secretary of State under section 140(3), (4) [182(3)/71]. The person who served the purchase notice should not, for example, merely be told that the authority do not consider that his land has become incapable of reasonably beneficial use in its existing state: he should be given, as fully as possible, the authority's reasons for coming to that conclusion.

Similarly, if the authority consider that the Secretary of State should adopt one of the courses of action open to him in lieu of confirmation of the notice (for example, that he should grant permission) they should state why they regard it as desirable, or should specify the probable ultimate use of the land which would justify the substitution of another local authority or statutory undertakers as acquiring authority.[23]

6.13. Actions which may be taken by the Secretary of State

The Secretary of State may take one of the following actions:

1. If the Secretary of State is satisfied that the requirements of paragraphs (*a*), (*b*), and (*c*) of section 137(3) [180(1)/71] are fulfilled, he should confirm the notice.[24]

2. In lieu of confirming the notice he may:
    (a) grant the permission asked for by the application which gave rise to the purchase notice, or revoke or amend conditions that were imposed;[25] or
    (b) direct that permission be granted for any other development which would render the land or any part of the land capable of reasonably beneficial use;[26] or
    (c) having regard to the probable ultimate use of the land substitute as acquiring authority another local authority

---

[23] See Circ. 13/83, para. 26.
[24] 1990 Act, s.141(1) [183(1)/71].
[25] *Ibid*. s.141(2) [183(2)/71].
[26] *Ibid*. s.141(3) [183(3)/71].

or statutory undertakers for the council on whom the notice was served.[27]

3. If the Secretary of State is not satisfied that the conditions laid down in or referred to by section 141 [183/71] are fulfilled he may neither confirm the notice nor put into operation any of the courses alternative to confirmation. He may also refuse to confirm the purchase notice under the special circumstances of "restricted use" with which section 142 [184/71] deals (see paragraph 6.8, *supra*).

6.14. The Secretary of State's notice of his proposed action

When a purchase notice is transmitted to the Secretary of State by the local authority he must, whatever his decision thereon may be, give notice of this proposed action (a) to the person by whom the purchase notice was served; (b) to the council on whom the notice was served; (c) to the local planning authority for the area in which the land is situated; and (d) if the Secretary of State proposes to substitute any other local authority or statutory undertakers for the council on whom the purchase notice was served, to that other local authority or those statutory undertakers.[28]

6.15. The hearing

If within the period prescribed by the notice, which must not be less than 28 days from its service, any person, authority or undertakers on whom that notice is served so require, the Secretary of State must afford an opportunity of appearing before a person appointed by the Secretary of State for the purpose.[29] The Secretary of State may use his power under section 320 [282/71] to cause a local inquiry to be held. If as a result of the hearing it appears to him to be expedient, the Secretary of State may take a different course of action from that which he originally proposed in his section 140(2) notice [182(2)/71].[30]

In practice it is normal for an inquiry to be held, rather than a hearing, with the result that the provisions of the Local Government Act 1972, section 250 (subpoenas, orders for costs etc.) apply (see paragraph 2.49). The Inquiries Procedure Rules do not apply, but in practice the ordinary procedure is followed.[31] There seems to be no established rule as to who begins. Normally, it would seem logical for the server of the purchase notice to begin, since he has to establish that the statutory requirements are fulfilled (even though it may be the authority which has called for the hearing).

6.16. Preparation of case

The purchase notice hearing is unusual in the sense that the Secretary of State has already given a preliminary indication of his

---

[27] 1990 Act, s.141(4) [183(4)/71].
[28] *Ibid.* s.140(2) [182(2)/71].
[29] *Ibid.* s.140(3), (4) [182(3)/71].
[30] *Ibid.* s.140(5) [182(4)/71].
[31] See Circ. 13/83, paras. 35–36.

view. This is invaluable in defining the principal issues. In addition the authority should produce a pre-inquiry statement setting out their submissions.[32] This should indicate the degree to which they are accepting, adding to or challenging any matters in the Secretary of State's statements. In particular they should indicate whether they will contend that the land could be put to a reasonably beneficial use if the Secretary of State were to grant some permission, and, if so, what. The server's case will need to deal not only with the existing state of the land and its value (in particular, in comparison with similar land in the area) but also with the planning objections to any uses proposed by the authority. Often in these cases the ordinary roles are reversed, with the authority contending that planning permission should be granted for some use, the owner arguing that it should not; the evidence will need to be prepared accordingly.

Preparation of proofs, documents, etc., follows the lines of a planning appeal (see paragraph 2.39, *ante*).

6.17. Deemed confirmation of purchase notice

If, within the period of six months from the end of the period (three months) given to the council for serving its counter-notice or from the date of transmission of the purchase notice to the Secretary of State, whichever is the earlier, the Secretary of State has neither confirmed the notice nor taken any other action (such as, for example, directing that planning permission should be granted for other development) nor notified the owner that he does not propose to confirm the notice, the notice is deemed to be confirmed.[33] That time period does not run if an appeal has been made.

6.18. Further proceedings

There is no prescribed procedure for challenging the decision in the High Court. However, in an appropriate case an application for judicial review would be available.[34] It is to be noted that the Secretary of State has no power to enforce a purchase notice once confirmed. Compensation will be settled by the Lands Tribunal in case of dispute and, if the authority fails to complete the purchase, an action for specific performance would be appropriate (as in the case of compulsory purchase).

B. LISTED BUILDING PURCHASE NOTICE

6.19. Nature and procedure

Under section 32 of the Listed Buildings Act 1990 [190(1)/71], an owner may serve a listed building purchase notice where listed building consent is refused or granted conditionally or is revoked or modified.

---

[32] Circ. 13/83, para. 36.

[33] 1990 Act, s.143(2) [186(2)/71].

[34] An appeal under ss.78, 174, 175, 195, 196 of the 1990 Act, ss.20, 21, 22 or 39 of the Listed Buildings Act [36, 88, 95, 97, Sched. 11, paras. 8 or 9/71].

The grounds upon which a listed building purchase notice may be served are similar to those on which a section 137 purchase notice [180/71] may be served.

The main differences between the provisions governing listed building purchase notices and those contained in sections 137 to 144 of the 1990 Act [180–187/71] are as follows:

(i) section 32(2) of the Listed Buildings Act 1990 [190(3)/71] enables certain land, in addition to the relevant listed building, to be included in a listed building purchase notice;

(ii) (a) section 33 of the Listed Buildings Act [Sched. 19, para. 2(1)/71] enables the Secretary of State to confirm a listed building purchase notice only in respect of part of the land to which it relates, if he is satisfied that the relevant conditions are fulfilled only in respect of part of the land; and

(b) section 33 [para. 2(2)/71] also requires him not to confirm a listed building purchase notice unless he is satisfied that the notice comprises such land as is in his opinion required for preserving the building or its amenities or for affording access to it, or for its proper control or management.

So far as evidence is concerned, the advice of Circular 13/83 should be noted:

"19. When considering whether a listed building has reasonably beneficial use, a pertinent factor to be taken into account may be the estimated cost of any renovations believed to be necessary. It is therefore helpful if estimated figures for such renovations, and an indication of the likely return on the relevant expenditure can be provided, although they will not, by themselves, be considered conclusive."

CHAPTER 7

COMMISSION FOR LOCAL ADMINISTRATION

A. THE LOCAL OMBUDSMAN

7.1. Introduction

In addition to the statutory remedies under the Act and judicial review the Local Ombudsman may provide a remedy in some cases when maladministration has occurred. The powers of the Local Ombudsman are set out in the Local Government Act 1974 and exercise of those powers is reviewable by the courts. A large proportion of the complaints made to the Local Ombudsman are in the planning field. In some cases a cash payment may be a more satisfactory solution than a successful application for judicial review, the end result of which may be that the matter is reconsidered in the proper manner and the same decision reached. In any event an application to the courts may be costly.

7.2. Procedure

The procedure for making a complaint is as follows:

(a) Fill in a form of complaint which can be obtained from the Commission for Local Administration, 21 Queen Anne's Gate, London, SW1H 9BU.

(b) The form must be signed by the applicant and if possible by a councillor.

(c) The Local Ombudsman cannot normally consider a complaint unless it is sent through a councillor. However, if the councillor refuses to send the complaint on or fails to do so in reasonable time, it can be sent direct to the Local Ombudsman with the name of the councillor attached.

(d) The Local Ombudsman cannot investigate *inter alia*:
　(i) a complaint about something that happened before April 1, 1984;
　(ii) a complaint about which there has been an appeal/court proceedings. If there has been no appeal/court proceedings, although such remedy existed, the Local Ombudsman may investigate if satisfied that it is not reasonable to expect the complainant to resort or have resorted to it[1];
　(iii) a complaint affecting all/most of the inhabitants of a Council's area, for instance a complaint that the Council have wasted public money;

---

[1] 1974 Act, s.26(6).

(iv) a complaint made later than 12 months from the day upon which the person aggrieved first had notice of the matter alleged although this period may be extended where justice so requires.[2]

(e) The Local Ombudsman investigates the complaints and makes a report. The report will say whether the Local Ombudsman finds that injustice has or has not been caused by maladministration by the council.

(f) The council must consider the report and tell the Local Ombudsman what action they propose to take. Councils may make a money payment or take other action to put matters right.

(g) Generally, councils do remedy the grievance where the Local Ombudsman has found injustice; however, the Local Ombudsman cannot force a council to act.[3]

---

[2] Local Government Act 1974, s.26(4).

[3] The Local Government and Housing Act 1989 ss. 26 and 28 contain a number of amendments designed to improve the problem of effective redress for injustice resulting from maladministration, *inter alia:*

a) authorities will be required to notify the Local Ombudsman of the action taken or proposed to be taken within three months from the date of the adverse report;

b) a decision to take no action must be made by a full meeting of the authority;

c) if the Local Ombudsman is dissatisfied with the authority's actions with regard to a further report, he will be able to require the authority to publish a statement in an agreed form in two editions of a local newspaper; and in default of doing so, the publication of a statement by the Local Ombudsman at the authority's expense.

The Annual Report of the Commission for Local Administration in England for 1988/89 shows an increase of 44 per cent. over the previous year in the number of complaints received by Local Ombudsmen. A large proportion of the complaints made are in the planning field. Examples of cases dealt with by the Local Commission will be found in the Commission's Annual Reports obtainable from the offices of the Commission at 21 Queen Anne's Gate, London, SW1H 9BU and in the Journal of Planning and Environmental Law.

CHAPTER 8

PLANNING AGREEMENTS

A. INTRODUCTORY

8.1 Background

Those who advise on planning matters will be only too aware that one of the most controversial issues in recent years has been the use of planning agreements in conjunction with what has become generally and loosely known as planning gain.[1]

A working knowledge of the statutory provisions which underpin these agreements is essential both because their negotiation may well lead to the resolution of disputes in the course of the appeal process, or, even better, lead to the satisfactory grant of permission without recourse to the necessity of an appeal, and because it would be a pyrrhic victory to negotiate a successful planning agreement and obtain the grant of planning permission only to see the permission quashed as a result of proceedings for judicial review.

Before considering the particular statutory provisions it is as well to remember that this area of law, like most of the planning legislation, must be considered against a background of 40 years of evolving political and social attitudes.

The days when the purposes of law were to be seen as maintaining and protecting private property rights are long since gone. The State now regularly intervenes.

The pendulum has swung between attitudes of "direction" of the political left and "laissez faire" of the political right currently manifesting itself in the form of "deregulation."

Taxes such as Capital Gains, Betterment Levy, Development Land Tax, for example, focus attention on how the value of the land can leap by the grant of planning permission and how the State can desire to recoup a portion of this gain. However, land values can also increase as a result of local authorities providing infrastructure such as roads, sewers, schools and other facilities.

Historically, authorities have raised the money for such services through rates, central government grants and loans. At the same time as government sought to recoup a portion of gain arising from an increase in land values so local authorities began to seek contributions from developers towards these items of infrastructure, physical and social, and, in some cases, a proportion of the gain itself.[2]

---

[1] See Circ. 22/83, *Town and Country Planning Act 1971. Planning Gain. Obligations and Benefits which Extend Beyond the Development for which Planning Permission has been sought.* Articles by Grant [1975] J.P.L. 501; [1978] J.P.L. 8; Jowell [1977] J.P.L. 414; Tucker [1978] J.P.L. 806; Loughlin [1978] J.P.L.; Suddards [1979] J.P.L. 661; Hawke [1980] J.P.L. 386; Heap and Ward [1981] J.P.L. 557; Ward [1982] J.P.L. 74; Jowell and Grant [1983] J.P.L. 427.

[2] *Planning Gain Community Benefit or Commercial Bribe*—A discussion document by Debenham Tewson & Chinnocks, November 1988; *Planning Gain: An overview Royal Town Planning Institute*—S. Byrne, June 1989.

Accordingly, while Circular 22/80, *Development Control—Policy and Practice*, enshrines the proposition that a developer is entitled to a grant of planning permission unless there are clear-cut reasons to the contrary, a body of legislation has encouraged some in local government to believe that since the State grants permission, the State is entitled to a proportion of any gain which accrues as a result. These two propositions have often led to conflict and muddle.

Now, although the use of planning agreements with all the attendant controversy has rapidly increased in the last 15 years or so, statutory planning agreements themselves are not new creatures. They date from the Housing Town Planning Act of 1909 and the Town and Country Planning Act 1932. Until 1947, no ministerial consent was needed to enter into such agreements. But, concern over the possible misuse of agreements led to the statutory requirement of ministerial approval imposed by the 1947 Town and Country Planning Act.

The necessity for consent lasted until 1969 when the requirement was abolished by the Town and Country Planning Act 1968 as part of the general move to devolve power to the local authorities themselves.

Professor Jowell's research[3] has shown that from 1947 to 1969 the vast majority of agreements did, in fact, receive ministerial approval and those few that were rejected failed not on policy objections but because of technical legal objections. By today's standard, the numbers of agreements do not seem large. Jowell's figures given for the years 1964 to 1968 show that in 1964 only 55 were submitted to the Minister for approval and in 1967 there were 159.

At the same time, as planning authorities have sought to use planning agreements for their own purposes, so landowners and developers have recognised their advantages. It is not hard to see why: with well in excess of half a million planning applications being submitted each year and the number of planning appeals rising from 16,192 in 1984 to 28,659 in 1988/9[4] the planning process can take a long time for an application to be determined. The median time for an appeal decision by the Secretary of State in 1988/9 was 62 weeks and in the case of a decision by an inspector (and 98 per cent. of all cases are decided by inspectors) 37 weeks.[5] This of course is only a statistical average and some take much longer.

Since the timing of any development project may be critical in terms of the economic cycle and the provision of funding and obtaining an ultimate consumer in the form of purchaser or tenant, it is self evident that the combination of the time it takes for an appeal to be determined, the costs involved in processing the appeal and the uncertainty of its outcome,[6] all encourage a developer to negotiate a permission with the local planning authority.

---

[3] [1977] J.P.L. 414.

[4] Chief Planning Inspector's Report, April 1988 to March 1989 H.M.S.O.

[5] Chief Planning Inspector's Report.

[6] In the period 1988 to March 1989 appeals decided by the Secretary of State were as to 39.2 per cent. successful and for those decided by Inspectors 36.7 per cent.—Chief Planning Inspector's Report.

Three principal statutory provisions are usually the basis for planning agreements either alone or in combination. They are section 106 of the Town and Country Planning Act 1990 [52/71] which is primarily negative in nature, section 33 of the Local Government (Miscellaneous Provisions) Act 1982 which is its positive counterpart and section 111 of the Local Government Act 1972, a general enabling section. The first two provisions bind successors in title to the covenantor but the third does not.

B. SECTION 106 OF THE TOWN AND COUNTRY PLANNING ACT 1990

8.2 The scope of the section

Section 106(1) and (2) [52(1)/71] provides that a local planning authority may enter into an agreement with any person interested in land in their area "for the purposes of restricting or regulating the development or use of the land." The agreement can be permanent or for a period of time and can contain "incidental and consequential provisions (including provisions of a financial character) as appear to the local planning authority to be necessary or expedient for the purposes of the agreement."

Section 106(3) [52(2)/71] provides that the local planning authority may enforce the agreement against successors in title to the person "interested in land" as if the local planning authority "were possessed of adjacent land and as if the agreement had been expressed to be made for the benefit of such land."

Accordingly, not only are the original parties bound by the provisions of the agreement by privity of contract but successors are bound. There has been much argument and debate about the scope of the provisions of section 106. For example, does "agreement" mean contract or something less than that? If a contract, must the authority provide consideration? Are all the provisions of the agreement binding on successors in title or just those "restricting or regulating the development or use of the land?"

What does the expression "interested in land," mean? Is it a legal interest or will a contractual right be sufficient.[7]

From a practical point of view, the first of these points is dealt with by providing for the agreement to be entered into by deed. Alternatively, a nominal consideration is sometimes provided but on no account should consideration be expressed to be the grant of the permission itself.

As to the second, the better view is that narrow interpretations of the section should be ignored and that broadly speaking, if the principal or primary purpose of the agreement is the restriction or regulation of development of land or its use then ancillary positive covenants should all be capable of being enforced against successors in

---

[7] *Jones* v. *Secretary of State for Wales* (1974) 28 P. & C. R. 280; *Pennine Raceway* v. *Kirklees Metropolitan Borough Council* 1983 Q.B. 382; [1982] J.P.L. 780.

title without having to show a specific benefit to immediately adjoining land belonging to those seeking to enforce the covenants.

In respect of the third point, from a practical point of view, a local planning authority will wish to investigate the title of the covenantor. Nothing short of a legal estate, whether freehold or leasehold, will usually be sufficient and in the case of a leasehold interest the authority will be aware that a leaseholder will only be able to bind that estate and that if the lease comes to an end, whether by effluxion of time, surrender or forfeiture, the covenants will cease to bind the land. Depending upon the term of years granted by the lease, therefore, the freeholder may be required to join in. The planning authority will also need to obtain the consent of any mortgagee. A prospective purchaser will have no power to bind the land by virtue merely of his contract or option to purchase. Accordingly, where, for example, the land acquisition is dependent upon obtaining planning permission which may not be forthcoming unless a section 106 agreement is entered into, then provisions must be inserted in the contract or option requiring the vendor to enter into such an agreement.

Two further points occur in relation to the scope of the provisions of section 106. First, subsection (4) [52(3)/71] provides that nothing in the section shall be construed as restricting the exercise of powers in relation to land the subject of any agreement "so long as those powers are exercised in accordance with the provisions of the development plan or in accordance with any directions which may have been given by the Secretary of State as to the provisions to be included in such a plan." This seems to indicate an exception to the general rule that an authority cannot fetter its future exercise of statutory powers by authorising an authority to do so save in the case of powers exercisable in accordance with a development plan. However, any proposal for fettering an authority's power in a section 106 agreement which it has a public duty to perform must be treated with the utmost caution and from a practical point of view, cannot safely be relied upon.[8]

Secondly, because section 106 is expressed in very broad terms the use of agreements under the section has grown to cover matters not capable of being imposed by way of planning conditions. The statutory power to impose conditions is also expressed in very broad terms but, over the years, the courts have imposed limitations on the exercise of their powers.[9]

Until recently the generally accepted view was that the courts would not imply the tests applicable to conditions to a section 106 agreement. The principal reason was that the provisions of the section are additional to the general provisions of planning control. A land owner can either agree to sign a contract or not whereas a condition is imposed unilaterally by the local planning authority. The provisions of each enabling section are quite different and have quite different

---

[8] *Windsor and Maidenhead Royal Borough Council* v. *Brandrose Investments* [1983] 1 W.L.R. 509; affirming [1981] 1 W.L.R. 1083.

[9] *Newbury District Council* v. *Secretary of State for the Environment* [1981] A.C. 578, and see DOE Circ. 1/85, *The Use of Conditions in Planning Permissions*.

purposes. Nevertheless, in recent years there has been some indication that the courts may assume that some of the tests for conditions are applicable to the provisions of a section 106 agreement.[10] However, it seems the better view is that a section 106 agreement can achieve objects which a planning condition cannot and that if the agreement is entered into for a planning purpose and not for an ulterior purpose, and that the terms are not so unreasonable that no reasonable planning authority could have imposed them, the agreement will not be overturned.[11]

8.3 Crown land

Section 299 of the 1990 Act [1/T.&C.P.A. 1984] enables planning permission to be obtained for the development of Crown land prior to its disposal but there is no provision enabling the Crown to enter into a section 106 agreement. Problems have therefore arisen where a local planning authority is not prepared to grant permission unless an agreement is signed. The Government have therefore proposed[12] to amend section 299 of the 1990 Act so as to enable Government Departments to enter into such agreements.

8.4 Remedies

As far as remedies are concerned, it should be noted that breach of the provisions of a section 106 agreement gives rise to a claim for damages and the planning authority may seek an injunction. The legality of the agreement can of course be questioned in any defence to proceedings. However, there is the question whether or not section 106 agreements can be challenged by third parties as their *locus standi* is uncertain. They are also often handicapped by a lack of information concerning the agreement, because whilst it is registrable as a local land charge[13] and can be noted on the charges register of registered land at the Land Registry, there is no requirement that the terms of an agreement be entered in the public register maintained by the local planning authority under section 74 of the 1990 Act [31/71].

8.5 Variation, modification and discharge

It should always be remembered that the provisions of any section 106 agreement will ordinarily bind the land either for the period stated in the agreement or, if no period is stated, in perpetuity.[14] It is for this reason that any attempt by an authority to insert in the agreement the conditions to be attached to the permission should be resisted since

---

[10] *Bradford Metropolitan City Council* v. *Secretary of State for the Environment and Maclean Homes* (1987) 53 P. & C. R. 55; *R.* v. *Gillingham Borough Council, ex p. Parham (F.)* [1988] J.P.L., 336; *R.* v. *Westminster City Council, ex p. Monahan* [1989] 3 W.L.R. 408.

[11] *R.* v. *Wealdon District Council, Federated Homes, ex p. Charles Church South East* [1989] J.P.L. 837.

[12] DOE Consultation Paper, July 11, 1989, *Planning Agreements.*

[13] Local Land Charges Act 1975, s.1(1)(*b*).

[14] *Abbey Homesteads (Developments) Application* (1987) 53 P. & C. R. 1.

whilst there is a procedure for applying for the discharge of conditions[15] there is at present no similar procedure for the provisions of a section 106 agreement. The Government have, however, proposed[16] legislation to enable a party to an agreement to apply to the local planning authority for the agreement (or part of it) to be discharged on the ground that its planning purpose has ended or is no longer relevant.

There is proposed a right of appeal to the Secretary of State against the refusal of such an application.

It is of course always open to the parties to vary the agreement or insert provisions to allow for relaxation if further permissions are granted whether by the local planning authority or by the Secretary of State. Local planning authorities are usually most resistant to any such suggestion.

A land owner can also seek to modify the restrictive (not positive) provisions of the agreement under section 84 of the Law of Property Act 1925 (as amended).[17]

It will be recalled that the provisions of section 84 (as amended by the Law of Property Act 1969, section 28) gives power to the Lands Tribunal to discharge or modify wholly or partially a restriction if it is satisfied:

(a) that by reason of changes in the character of property or the neighbourhood or other circumstances of the case which the Lands Tribunal may deem material, the restriction ought to be deemed obsolete; or

(aa) that in a case falling within subsection (1A) below the continued existence thereof would impede some reasonable user of the land for public or private purposes or, as the case may be, would unless modified so impede such user; or

(b) that the person of full age and capacity for the time being or from time to time entitled to the benefit of the restriction, whether in respect of estates in fee simple or any lesser estates or interests in the property to which the benefit of the restriction is annexed, have agreed either expressly or by implication, by their acts or omissions, to the same being discharged or modified; or

(c) that the proposed discharge or modifications will not injure the persons entitled to the benefit of the restriction.

Subsection (1A) authorises the Tribunal to discharge or modify a restriction on ground (b) above in any case where the Tribunal is satisfied that the restriction, in impeding some reasonable user of the land,

either:
(a) does not secure to persons entitled to the benefit of it any practical benefits of substantial value or advantage to them; or

---

[15] 1990 Act, s.72(1)(a) [30(1)(a)/71].
[16] DOE Consultation Paper, July 11, 1989, *Planning Agreements*.
[17] *Beecham Group's Application* [1981] J.P.L. 55.

(b) is contrary to the public interest;
and that money will be an adequate compensation for loss or disadvantage (if any) which any such person will suffer from the discharge or modification.

Subsection (1B) provides that in determining whether the restriction ought to be discharged or modified, the Tribunal:

shall take into account the development plan and any declared or ascertainable pattern for the grant or refusal of planning permission in the relevant areas, as well as the period at which, and the context in which, the restriction was created or imposed, and any other material circumstances.

No one should regard this course as any other than a most difficult series of hurdles to overcome.[18] The provisions of section 84 were drafted in the context of private not public law and it is not easy to show obsolescence or deal with issues of land "benefited" when considering the provisions of section 106 agreements. To demonstrate that the planning authority will not be injured in its capacity as custodian of the public interest if the modification is allowed will be difficult, even where the authority has granted permission, and money will usually not be adequate compensation.[19]

8.6 Generally
A developer cannot be required to enter into an agreement by means of a planning condition and agreements are usually executed and handed over to a local planning authority conditional upon the subsequent grant of planning permission.

The agreement should never be completed on the basis of provisions coming into effect before the grant of planning permission and conditions should be inserted to ensure that the agreement is conditional upon the grant of permission and also conditional upon the implementation of the planning permission. From a developer's point of view, the agreement should contain provisions for a variation of the terms, where appropriate, if a further permission is granted whether by the local authority or on appeal.

The agreement should provide that if the permission in respect of which the agreement is entered into is modified, revoked or expires then the agreement automatically comes to an end. There should be a provision for cancelling the registration of the agreement as a land charge or at the Land Registry once the provisions of the agreement are spent.

Where acts and events are to take place pursuant to the terms of the agreement, there should be provision for certification by the local authority that the covenants have been complied with.

---

[18] *Abbey Homesteads (Developments) Application* (1986) 53 P. & C. R. 1.
[19] *Re Houdret and Co. Application* (1989) 58 P. & C.R. 310; *Re Jones and White & Co. Application* (1989) 58 P. & C.R. 512; *Re Quartleys' Application* (1989) 58 P. & C.R. 518.

8.7 The use of an agreement on appeal

In the case of a planning appeal the local planning authority may, while maintaining a root and branch objection to the proposal, nevertheless agree with the appellant that if the Secretary of State were minded to grant permission on appeal then a section 106 agreement should be executed. In those circumstances, the Secretary of State may be told that an agreement has been executed in escrow which will come into effect if permission is granted.

The Secretary of State himself has no power to enter into an agreement or to require a local planning authority to do so.

He also has no power to determine on appeal any disagreement over the terms of a section 106 agreement. It is, however, a factor which he may take into account on a planning appeal and he may indicate to the parties that if an agreement were entered into then permission would be forthcoming.

In the case of an authority which refuses to agree terms for a section 106 agreement, even on a without prejudice basis, an appellant will sometimes unilaterally hand over one part of an agreement duly executed by himself so that the Secretary of State may know that the appellant is prepared to be bound by the terms of the agreement. Alternatively, counsel may give an undertaking that the owner will do so.[20] But this is not an ideal state of affairs.

In order to deal with difficulties which have arisen the Government have proposed[21] legislation to enable a developer to give a unilateral undertaking binding on him and his successors in title "to carry out certain works or do whatever the undertaking may specify." The advantage of such an undertaking is that it would overcome the difficulty of an authority refusing to negotiate. In considering any application or appeal, the authority or the Secretary of State would be required to have regard to the terms of any undertaking offered. The power to discharge the whole or part of a section 106 agreement would equally apply to these new undertakings.

8.8 Local Government (Miscellaneous Provisions) Act 1982, section 33

In the post-war years, local authorities, faced with the limitations of section 106 agreements, where positive obligations must be ancillary to the main restrictive purpose of the agreement, sought powers to achieve a statutory counterpart for positive covenants which would bind successors in title. To this end, private Acts of Parliament were sought and, by 1973, 40 authorities had obtained enabling Acts.

In 1972 a Government Committee[22] suggested legislation which would require developers to contribute towards the cost of services provided by public authorities in connection with the development of land. This suggestion was embodied in section 126 of the Housing Act 1974 which allowed, for the first time, agreements containing as a

[20] *Augier* v. *Secretary of State for the Environment* (1978) 38 P. & C. R. 120.
[21] DOE Consultation Paper, July 11, 1989, *Planning Agreements*.
[22] *Local Authority/Private Enterprise Schemes*, HMSO 1972 and see *Widening the choice: the next step in Housing*, HMSO 1973.

principle objective positive covenants to bind successors in title. That section has now been replaced by section 33 of the Local Government (Miscellaneous Provisions) Act 1982.

The section provides that covenants can be entered into by a person with an interest in land to carry out works or to do any other thing on or in relation to that land. They must be contained in an agreement made under seal. The agreement must be executed:

(a) for the purpose of securing the carrying out of works on or facilitating the development or regulating the use of land in the council's area in which the person entering into the covenant has an interest; or

(b) for the purpose of facilitating the development or regulating the use of land outside the council's area in which the covenantor has an interest[23]; or

(c) for some other purpose which is connected with land in or outside the council's area in which the person entering into the covenant has an interest.[24]

It should be noted that the covenant must be contained in an instrument under seal. As a result the argument as to whether consideration is needed is avoided.

The power extends to land outside the authority's own area but only in respect of facilitating the development or regulating the use of land and not for securing the carrying out of works on the land which is only available in respect of land within the authority's area.

In the event of default, the council after giving 21 days notice of their intention so to do[25] can, in addition to other methods of enforcement, enter onto the land and carry out the works "or do any other thing on or in relation to that land" and recover the costs and expenses of exercising their powers.

The notice must be served on those having an interest in the land and against whom the covenant is enforceable and if requested the council must supply a copy of the covenant in question free of charge[26]

8.9 Section 111 of the Local Government Act 1972

This section gives local authorities power:

"to do anything (whether or not involving expenditure, borrowing or lending money or the acquisition or disposal of any property or rights) which is calculated to facilitate or is conducive or incidental to the discharge of their functions."

The section would, for instance, enable agreements to be made for the payment of money or the transfer of assets to a local authority where

---

[23] Circ. 22/83 gives as an example an agreement to use some of the land as a car park to serve the development on the remainder.

[24] Circ. 22/83 gives as an example an obligation to carry out certain demolition or other works or to pay towards the cost of such works if carried out by the council.

[25] Local Government (Miscellaneous Provisions) Act 1982, s.33(3).

[26] *Ibid.* s.33(4), (5).

this will facilitate the discharge of the functions of the authority. The section does not empower the local authority to require such a transfer; the transfer must be made by agreement.[27]

Any covenant entered into under this section does not bind successors in title but would enable the payment of a lump sum of money to provide infrastructure or community facilities.

As indicated, this section is often to be found used in conjunction with section 106 of the 1990 Act and section 33 of the Local Government (Miscellaneous Provisions) Act 1982.

8.10 Circular 22/83

The controversy concerning planning gain has been noted in paragraph 8.1. above. Following a report in 1981 from the Property Advisory Group, *Planning Gain*, the Government published Circular 22/83 to offer guidance to local authorities and others concerned.

First of all, the Circular defines planning gain as arising:

> "whenever in connection with a grant of planning permission a local authority seeks to impose on a developer an obligation to carry out works not included in the development for which permission is sought or to make some payment or confer some extraneous right or benefit in return for permitting development to take place."

In paragraph 5 the Circular states that whilst in many cases agreements may well assist towards securing the best use of land and a properly planned environment, an applicant's need for permission is "not to be treated as an opportunity to obtain some benefit or advantage or to exact a payment for the benefit of ratepayers at large."

Paragraph 6 sets out four tests of reasonableness. Is what is sought:

(1) needed to enable the development to proceed? The example given concerns works of infrastructure such as access, water supply and sewerage; or

(2) in the case of financial payments, needed to contribute to providing infrastructure in the near future; or

(3) otherwise, so directly related to the development and its subsequent use that the development ought not to be permitted without it? The examples given are car parking in or near the development or commuted car payments or the provision of reasonable amounts of open space related to the development; or

(4) designed in the case of mixed development to secure an acceptable balance of uses.

No example is given but, presumably, the requirement to provide a housing component in a mixed use development may be a case in point.

---

[27] See Circ. 22/83, Appendix A, para. 4.

Even if one or other of these tests is passed, there are two further requirements set out in paragraph 7.

First is the extent of what is required "fairly and reasonably related in scale and kind to the proposed development." Infrastructure can be charged for but only to the extent it is needed by the actual development proposal.

Secondly, is the charge reasonable in the sense that it is right to ask the developer to pay for it rather than providing funding by national or local taxation or by other means? Here, the example is a request to provide a new road or an improvement to an existing road which is not wholly or substantially required as a result of the development.

The Circular indicates (paragraphs 10 and 11) that a developer should not be required to dedicate open space or walkways to the public. Nor should he be asked to provide a capital endowment to maintain open space. The provision of the land itself should be the limit of his contribution.

The Circular states (paragraph 12) that it may be reasonable to require the demolition or refurbishment of a developer's building on adjoining or nearby land but not part of the application site. However, the building must be related to the development proposal as, for example, if the restored building provided a screen or foil for the new development or its demolition enhanced the new development.

The Circular warns that unreasonable demands which lead to appeals may, in turn, lead to an award of costs.

The Circular is, of course, purely advisory. It has no force of law. Have the guidelines made any difference? Certain evidence suggests not.[28] Some have urged the Government to provide rules for planning gain in statutory form.

The Government appear to have decided not to legislate but instead have issued a consultation paper (July 11, 1989) for a revised Circular to replace 22/83. It substantially reaffirms the earlier Circular but with minor amendments. It does, however, contain this draft advice which should certainly be borne in mind:

> "Whether or not the parties are willing to enter into other agreements unrelated to the development is a matter for the parties concerned; but local authorities should take care to ensure that the presence or absence of such arrangements or extraneous benefits does not influence their decision on the planning application. Authorities should bear in mind that their decision may be challenged in the Courts if it is suspected of having been improperly influenced in this way."[29]

Additionally, developers offering planning gain agreements should be equally aware of the risk challenge by third parties to of any permis-

---

[28] *Planning Gain Community Benefit or Commercial Bribe*—A discussion document by Debenham Tewson & Chinnocks, November 1988; *Planning Gain: An overview Royal Town Planning Institute*, S. Byrne, June 1989.

[29] DOE Consultation Paper, July 11, 1989, *Planning Agreements*.

sion issued in connection, and contemporaneously, with any such agreement.

The principal risk is that the local planning authority may in considering the provisions of the agreement have regard to a matter which is not a material consideration for the purposes of section 71 of the 1990 Act [29/71]. For a consideration to be material it must serve a planning purpose relating to the character of the use of the land.[30] It must also fairly and reasonably relate to the development permitted.[31] A matter is not material merely because the parties wish it so.[32]

Much will depend upon the way in which the officers report the agreement to the committee and the way in which the committee reach their decision.

There seems little doubt, however, that in this area of law, controversy and hence litigation are likely to continue.

---

[30] *Westminster City Council* v. *Great Portland Estates* [1985] A.C. 661.

[31] *R.* v. *Westminster City Council, ex p. Monahan* [1989] 3 W.L.R. 408; but see *Northumberland County Council* v. *Secretary of State for the Environment and British Coal Corporation* [1989] J.P.L. 700, for a different approach.

[32] *Bradford Metropolitan Council* v. *Secretary of State For the Environment and Maclean Homes* (1987) 53 P. & C. R. 55.

CHAPTER 9

SECTION 17 CERTIFICATES

9.1 Introductory

The certificate procedure under section 17 of the Land Compensation Act 1961 provides a means whereby in certain cases the planning potential of land can be determined solely for compensation purposes. For example, if land is being compulsorily acquired for a school, compensation will be assessed on the basis of its potential on the assumption that there was no school proposal. In those circumstances it is possible that the land might have been suitable for residential development. Section 17 of the 1961 Act enables a certificate to that effect to be obtained from the local planning authority or on appeal from the Secretary of State. A positive certificate is conclusive for the purposes of the Lands Tribunal (Land Compensation Act 1961, s.14(3)). However, the converse is not true. The fact that a positive certificate has been refused by the local planning authority does not prevent the Lands Tribunal deciding that planning permission could reasonably have been expected for some valuable use, and assessing the value on that basis.[1]

9.2 When a section 17 application may be made

Under section 17 of the 1961 Act, where an interest in land is proposed to be acquired by an authority possessing compulsory purchase powers, and that land or part thereof does not consist or form part of:

(a) an area defined in the development plan as an area of comprehensive development; or

(b) an area shown in the development plan as an area allocated primarily for a use which is of a residential, commercial or industrial character, or for a range of two or more uses any of which is of such character,

then, subject to subsection (2) of the section, either of the parties directly concerned may apply to the local planning authority for a certificate under the section.

Section 17(2) provides that if in the case of an interest in land falling within subsection (1) of the section, the authority proposing to acquire it have served a notice to treat in respect thereof, or an agreement has been made for the sale thereof to that authority, and a reference has been made to the Lands Tribunal to determine the amount of the compensation payable in respect of that interest, no application for a certificate shall be made by either party after the date of that reference except either (a) with the consent in writing of the other of those parties, or (b) with the leave of the Lands Tribunal.

---

[1] For an example of this, compare *Jelson* v. *Minister of Housing and Local Government* [1970] 1 Q.B. 243, and *Jelson* v. *Blaby U.D.C.* [1977] 1 W.L.R. 1020.

9.3 Contents of application

An application under the section made by either party must be in writing, accompanied by a plan,[2] and must:

(*a*) state whether or not there are, in the applicant's opinion, any classes of development which, either immediately or at a future time, would be appropriate for the land in question if it were not proposed to be acquired by any authority possessing compulsory purchase powers and, if so, shall specify the classes of development and the time at which they would be so appropriate;

(*b*) state the applicant's grounds for holding that opinion and

(*c*) be accompanied by a statement specifying the date on which a copy of the application has been or will be served upon the other party.[3]

9.4 Form of the certificate

Where an application is made for a certificate under the section, the local planning authority must within two months,[4] but not earlier than 21 days after the date specified in the statement mentioned in section 17(3)(*c*), issue a certificate. The certificate must state the opinion of the local planning authority regarding the grant of planning permission in respect of the land in question, if it were not proposed to be acquired by any authority possessing compulsory purchase powers. Accordingly, it may state either:

(*a*) that planning permission for development of one or more classes specified in the certificate (whether specified in the application or not) would have been granted; or

(*b*) that planning permission would not have been granted for any development other than the development (if any) which is proposed to be carried out by the authority by whom the interest is proposed to be acquired.[5]

Under section 17(5), as amended, where in the opinion of the local planning authority planning permission would have been granted as mentioned in paragraph (*a*) of subsection (4), but would only have been granted subject to conditions, or at a future time, or both subject to conditions and at a future time, the certificate should specify those conditions, or that future time, or both, as the case may be, in addition to the other matters required to be contained in the certificate.

9.5 Appeal to the Secretary of State

Under section 18 of the 1961 Act, where the local planning authority have issued a certificate under section 17 of the Act or failed to do so

---

[2] Land Compensation Development Order 1974, S.I. 1974 No. 539.

[3] Land Compensation Act 1961, s.17(3), as substituted by the Local Government, Planning and Land Act 1980, Sched. 24.

[4] 1974 Order.

[5] 1961 Act, s.17(4), as substituted.

within the two-month period, either the person for the time being entitled to an interest in the land or any authority possessing compulsory purchase powers by whom that interest is proposed to be acquired may appeal to the Secretary of State against that certificate.

Section 18(2) provides that on any appeal under this section against the certificate the Secretary of State shall consider the matters to which the certificate relates as if the applications had been made to him in the first instance and shall either conform or vary the certificate or cancel it and issue a different certificate in its place, as he may consider appropriate.

The Secretary of State must allow either party an opportunity to be heard by a person appointed for the purpose. Although there are no inquiries procedure rules, in practice the procedure follows that of a section 79 appeal [36/71] (see Chapter 2, *ante*).

9.6 Preparation of case

The preparation of a section 17 certificate appeal for both parties is in practice very similar to a section 79 appeal (see Chapter 2, *ante*). The same issues, policy and technical, will need to be considered and the same kind of evidence produced. The only difference is that the inquiry proceeds in a hypothetical world in which the possibility of the appeal site being acquired compulsorily is excluded. Thus, it is not a proper ground of objection that the land is needed for some public purpose.[6] It should be noted, however, that the possibility of other land being so acquired can still be taken into account.[7] This can be important where there is limited capacity for further development in a particular area, for example because of drainage limitations. In the hypothetical section 17 world, it may be appropriate to assume that the purpose, for which the appeal site is intended, would have had to be accommodated on other land, which has been allocated in the real world for development—thus enabling the appeal site to take advantage of the capacity so released.

9.7 Factual circumstances to be considered

In some cases the physical development of the immediate area may have been considerably influenced by the decision to allocate the appeal site for a public purpose, and this surrounding development may itself have the effect of limiting the potential of the appeal site. For example, if a narrow strip has been left for a new road through a residential estate, the shape of the strip may itself preclude its most effective use for any development other than a road. In such a case, the Lands Tribunal would be able to consider what the surrounding circumstances and consequently the value of the strip, would have been if there had *never* been a proposal for a road. However, the position in a section 17 case is more restricted.[8] The factual circum-

---

[6] See *Scunthorpe B.C.* v. *Secretary of State* [1977] J.P.L. 653; *Grampian Regional Council* v. *Secretary of State for Scotland* [1984] J.P.L. 416. See also Circs. 48/59, 115/75.

[7] *cf. Margate Corporation* v. *Devotwill Investments Limited* [1970] 3 All E.R. 864.

[8] See the cases cited at n. 1, *ante*. Note that the possibility of development in conjunction with adjoining land should be taken into account: *Sutton* v. *Secretary of State for the Environment* (1984) 49 P. & C.R. 147.

stances must be taken as they were in the real world at the date of the proposal to acquire. However, as already indicated, if this restriction results in the refusal of a positive certificate, it will not prejudice the claimant's position in the Lands Tribunal (paragraph 9.1, *ante*).

The date of the proposal for these purposes is defined by section 22(4) of the 1961 Act.[9] Where the application follows a notice to treat (or deemed notice to treat)[10] the date of that notice should be taken. Otherwise it may be the date of the offer by the authority[11] or of the first notice of the compulsory purchase order.[12]

Although the factual circumstances are, as it were, frozen at the date of the proposal, changes in planning policies can be taken into account up to the date of the decision.[13]

9.8 Challenge in the High Court.

By section 21 of the 1961 Act the decision of the Secretary of State on a section 17 appeal may be challenged by a procedure analogous to that applying to a section 79 appeal (see paragraph 2.51 *et seq., ante*).

---

[9] *Jelson* v. *Minister of Housing and Local Government, supra.* In the view of the Secretary of State the position remains unaffected by the changes made by the Community Land Act 1975 (now in the Local Government, Planning and Land Act 1980, Sched. 24): [1980] J.P.L. 610; [1981] J.P.L. 141.

[10] [1974] J.P.L. 371.

[11] [1977] J.P.L. 325.

[12] [1976] J.P.L. 584.

[13] *Hitchens (Robert) Builders* v. *Secretary of State for the Environment* [1978] J.P.L. 874.

APPENDIX A: POLICY

A.1 List of Important Circulars and Planning Policy Guidance Notes.

71/73	Publicity for Planning Applications, Appeals and other Proposals for Development.
22/80	Development Control—Policy and Practice.
17/82	Development in Flood Risk Areas—Liaison Between Planning Authorities and Water Authorities.
22/83	Town and Country Planning Act 1971. Planning Gain. Obligations and Benefits which Extend Beyond the Development for which Planning Permission has been Sought.
22/84	Memorandum on Structure and Local Plans: The Town and Country Planning Act 1971: Part II (as amended by the Town and Country Planning (Amendment) Act 1972, The Local Government Act 1972, and the Local Government, Planning and Land Act 1980).
1/85	The Use of Conditions in Planning Permissions.
14/85	Development and Employment.
20/85	Town and Country Planning Act 1971: Enforcement Appeals and Advertisement Appeals.
31/85	Aesthetic Control.
2/86	Development by Small Businesses.
18/86	Planning Appeals decided by Written Representations.
2/87	Awards of Costs Incurred in Planning and Compulsory Purchase Order Proceedings.
8/87	Historic Buildings and Conservation Areas—Policy and Procedures.
13/87	Change of Use of Buildings and Other Land: Town and Country Planning (Use Classes) Order 1987.
16/87	Development Involving Agricultural Land.
27/87	Nature Conservation.
3/88	Local Government Act 1985: Unitary Development Plans.
10/88	Town and Country Planning (Inquiries Procedure) Rules 1988, Town and Country Planning Appeals (Determination by Inspectors) (Inquiries Procedure) Rules 1988.
15/88	Town and Country Planning (Assessment of Environmental Effects) Regulations.
1988/PPG1	General Policy and Principles.
1988/PPG2	Green Belts.
1988/PPG3	Land for Housing.
1988/PPG4	Industrial and Commercial Development and Small Firms.
1988/PPG5	Simplified Planning Zones.

1988/PPG6	Major Retail Development.
1988/PPG7	Rural Enterprise and Development.
1988/PPG8	Telecommunications.
1988/PPG9	Regional Guidance for the South East.
1988/PPG 10	Strategic Guidance for the West Midlands.
1988/PPG 11	Strategic Guidance for Merseyside.
1988/PPG 12	Local Plans.
1988/PPG 13	Highway Considerations in Development Control.
1990/PPG 14	Development on Unstable Land.
1990/PPG 15	Regional Planning Guidance, Structure Plans and the Content of Development Plans.
1988/MPG 1	General Considerations and the Development Plan System.
1988/MPG 2	Applications, Permissions and Conditions.
1988/MPG 3	Opencast Coal Mining.
1988/MPG 4	The Review of Mineral Working Sites.
1988/MPG 5	Minerals Planning and the General Development Order.
1989/MPG 6	Guidelines for Aggregates Provision in England and Wales.

A.2

Planning Policy Guidance 1
General Policy and Principles

(Dated January 1988, and issued jointly by the Department of the Environment and the Welsh Office)

*   *   *

The presumption in favour of development

15. The planning system fails in its function whenever it prevents, inhibits or delays development which can reasonably be permitted. There is always a presumption in favour of allowing applications for development, having regard to all material considerations, unless that development would cause demonstrable harm to interests of acknowledged importance. Except in the case of inappropriate development in the Green Belt the developer is not required to prove the case for the development he proposes to carry out; if the planning authority consider it necessary to refuse permission, the onus is on them to demonstrate clearly why the development cannot be permitted.

The Government's planning policies

16. The courts have held that the Department's statements of planning policy are material considerations which must be taken into account, where relevant, in decisions on planning applications. The policies must be publicly known. They are normally disseminated by way of Planning Policy Guidance, supplemented by White Papers, Ministerial statements and departmental Circulars etc. Such policy statements cannot make irrelevant any matter which in a particular decision is a material consideration. But where such statements discharge the proper role of a policy in indicating the weight that should be given to relevant considerations, the decision-maker must properly understand them and have regard to them. If he then elects not to follow them, he must give clear reasons for not doing so. (See Mr Justice Woolf, in *E C Gransden and Co Ltd v. SSE and Gillingham BC, (1985)*.)

The purpose of the planning system

17. The purpose of the planning system is to regulate the development and use of land *in the public interest*. It is not to protect the private interests of one person against the activities of another. While considerations of public interest may in the particular case serve to protect private interests, the material question is not whether owners and occupiers of neighbouring properties would suffer financial or other loss from a particular development, but whether the proposal would affect the locality generally and unacceptably affect amenities that ought in the public interest to be protected.

18. Any relevant views expressed by third parties, by local residents and other neighbouring occupiers of land should be taken into account in determining planning applications. Nevertheless, on its own, local opposition to a proposal is not a ground for the refusal of planning permission unless that opposition is founded upon valid planning reasons which are supported by substantial evidence. While the substance of local opposition must be considered, the duty is to decide each case on its planning merits.

19. The system is concerned with land-use planning matters, *i.e.*, those relating directly to the physical development and use of land, and not to other matters (which in consequence of other duties and powers may well be in those contexts the proper concern of authorities which are local planning authorities). This principle applies to the content of development plans, to decisions in individual cases and to the imposition of planning conditions.

20. Decisions in individual cases should be based on planning grounds only and must be reasonable. The 'other material considerations' of section 29(1) of the 1971 Act can cover a wide field: 'In principle . . . consideration which relates to the use and development of land is capable of being a planning consideration,' (Cooke J, in *Stringer v. Ministry of Housing and Local Government (1971)*). They must however, be genuine planning considerations, ie, they must be related to the purpose of planning legislation, which is to regulate the development and use of land.

21. It follows that planning authorities should, in refusing planning permission, give reasons (as they are required to do by article 7 of the General Development Order) which are complete, precise, clear, specific and relevant to the application. Where a decision is considered at a planning inquiry and the local planning authority cannot show that they had reasonable planning grounds for the decision, costs incurred in the appeal proceedings may be awarded against them.

22. Moreover, planning legislation should not normally be used to secure objects achievable under other legislation. For example, planning permission for a betting office should not be refused on moral grounds or because it is considered that there are sufficient such offices in the area already. The Gambling Acts provide for licensing of betting offices, *inter alia*, on the basis of the demand from place to place.

23. More generally, it is not the function of the planning system to interfere with or inhibit competition between users and investors in land, or to regulate the overall provision and character of space for particular uses for other than land-use planning reasons. Where development is acceptable in land-use terms, it is up to landowners, developers and tenants to decide whether to proceed with it. If, however, the applicant can demonstrate that there is a weighty national or local need for a particular type of development in that location, that consideration may be sufficient to outweigh important planning objections which might be a sufficient basis for refusal in the absence of the demonstrated need for the development. The existence of alternative sites which might be suitable for a particular development is not normally a reason for refusing planning permission if the development is acceptable in planning terms.

*   *   *

Aesthetic control

27. Matters of detailed design have long been an unnecessary source of contention and delay in the planning system. Aesthetics is an extremely subjective matter. Planning authorities should not impose their tastes on developers simply because they believe them to be superior. Developers should not be compelled to conform to the fashion of the moment at the expense of individuality, originality or traditional styles. Nor should they be asked to adopt designs which are unpopular with their customers or clients.

28. Nevertheless control of external appearance can be important, especially for instance in environmentally sensitive areas such as National Parks, Areas of Outstanding Natural Beauty, conservation areas and areas where the quality of the environment is of a particularly high standard. Local planning authorities should reject obviously poor designs which are out of scale or character with their surroundings. They should confine concern to those aspects of design which are significant for the aesthetic quality of the area. Only exceptionally should they control design details if the sensitive character of the area or the particular building justifies it. Even where such detailed control is exercised it should not be over-fastidious in such matters as, for example, the precise shade of colour of bricks. Authorities should be closely guided in such matters by their professionally qualified advisers. This is especially important where a building has been designed by an architect for a particular site. Design guides may have a useful role to play provided that they are used as guidance and not as detailed rules.

29. Control of external appearance should only be exercised where there is fully justified reason for doing so. Where there are no reasonable objections to the external appearance proposed by the applicant and a refusal of permission is based simply on a preference for a different external appearance, there may be grounds for an award of costs in an inquiry appeal.

Enforcement and discontinuance

30. It is clearly undersiable that development should be carried out in advance of any necessary planning permission being obtained. However the power to issue an enforcement notice alleging that there has been a breach of planning control is discretionary. It may only be used if the authority "consider it expedient to do so having regard to the provisions of the development plan and to any other material considerations". This discretionary power should be used, in regard to either operational development or material changes of use, only where planning reasons clearly warrant such action, and there is no alternative to enforcement proceedings. Where the activity involved is one

which would not give rise to insuperable planning objections if it were carried out somewhere else, then the planning authority should do all it can to help in finding suitable alternative premises before initiating enforcement action.

31. Analogous considerations apply, but with even more force, to opposed orders to discontinue authorised or established uses of land. Given that existing rights are at issue, such an action should be taken only if there appears to be an overriding justification on planning grounds. Special considerations apply to the use of land and buildings by small businesses (see PPG4).

*   *   *

A.3
Circular No. 2/87
Awards of Costs Incurred in Planning and Compulsory Purchase Order Proceedings

(Dated February 17, 1987, and issued by the Department of the Environment and the Welsh Office; Circular No. 5/87 of that office)

*   *   *

Awards against planning authorities

Unreasonable refusal of planning permission

7. A planning authority should not prevent, inhibit or delay development which could reasonably be permitted. In accordance with the advice given in Circular 22/80 (WO 40/80) a planning authority should refuse planning permission only where this serves a sound and clear planning purpose and the economic effects have been taken into account. As stated in Circular 14/85 (WO 38/85) "There is . . . always a presumption in favour of allowing applications for development, having regard to all material considerations, unless that development would cause demonstrable harm to interests of acknowledged importance." Reasons for refusal should be complete, precise, specific and relevant to the application. In any appeal proceedings authorities will be expected to produce evidence to substantiate their reasons for refusal. If they cannot do so, costs may be awarded against them. Indeed, this is the ground on which costs are most commonly awarded against a planning authority. In a case of this nature, each of the reasons given for refusal will be examined to see whether there is evidence to show that the relevant advice given in Departmental circulars and relevant judicial authority were properly taken into account, and that the application was considered on its merits in the light of these and other material considerations. Where one reason for refusal cannot be supported in this way but evidence has been produced to substantiate other reasons for refusal, a partial award may be made in respect of the costs of opposing that reason. While planning authorities are not bound to follow advice from their officers, or from statutory bodies such as Water Authorities or the Health and Safety Executive, or from other Government Departments, they will be expected to show that they had reasonable planning grounds for a decision taken against such advice and that they were able to produce evidence to support those grounds. If they fail to do so costs may be awarded against them.

Examples of unreasonable refusal

8. Section 29(1) of the 1971 Act requires a local planning authority, when considering a planning application, to "have regard to the provisions of the development plan, so far as material to the applications, and to any other material considerations." The courts have held that the requirement to "have regard" to the provisions of the development plan does not require the authority to adhere slavishly to its provisions. Circular 14/85 (WO 38/85) points out that development plan policies may be out of date and not well related to today's conditions, and in particular that such plans cannot be expected to anticipate every need or opportunity for economic development that may arise. A refusal of planning permission which is based solely on development plan provisions may in some circumstances be regarded as unreasonable, for example where it is clear that no proper consideration has been given to the merits of the application before the planning authority, or the development plan was clearly out of date and changed circumstances or other material considerations were not taken into account.

9. Planning authorities are expected to take into account the views of local residents when determining a planning application. Nevertheless, on its own, local opposition to a proposal is not a reasonable ground for the refusal of a planning application unless that opposition is founded upon valid planning reasons which are supported by substantial evidence. While the planning authority will need to consider the substance of any local opposition to the proposal their duty is to decide a case on its planning merits. They are unlikely to be considered to have acted reasonably in refusing an application if no

material departure from statutory plans or policies is involved and there are no other planning reasons why permission should be refused.

10. The local planning authority should consider on its merits any planning application which is put before them. Where there are no reasonable planning objections to the development as proposed by the applicant, a refusal of permission based mainly on the local planning authority's preference for a change in some aspect of external appearance, or the imposition of detailed requirements relating to changes in the design or choice of materials, will normally be regarded as unreasonable. Circulars 22/80 and 31/85 (WO 40/80 and 69/85) emphasise that planning powers to control the detailed design of buildings should not be used to impose the planning authority's tastes simply because they believe them to be superior; they also give guidance on the circumstances in which detailed control of external appearance may be warranted - notably in conservation areas. Even where, exceptionally, design control is exercised, it should not be used over-fastidiously in such matters as, for example, the precise colour of brickwork or pointing. Where there are other legitimate objections to the proposal, a partial award of costs may be justified if design considerations have also been given, without very good reasons, as a ground for refusal of planning permission.

11. A planning authority is likely to be regarded as having acted unreasonably in refusing an application if an earlier appeal against the refusal of a similar application in respect of the site has been dismissed but it is clear from the decision on that appeal that no objection would be seen to a revised application in this form. Similarly a planning authority will be at risk of costs in refusing an application where it must have been obvious from official statements of policy or judicial authority that an appeal was virtually certain to succeed. They may be held to have acted unreasonably if they fail to take into consideration reported judicial authority, or well-publicised appeal decisions relevant to their reasons for refusal of which they should have been aware, or if they ignore the statements of policy set out in Government White Papers, Department Circulars and Development Control Policy Notes, or in Parliamentary statements of which they should have been aware. Circular 22/83 (WO 46/83), for example, made it clear that the Secretary of State will consider sympathetically an application for costs where proceedings have arisen because of what he considers to be an unreasonable obligation in terms of planning gain imposed by a planning authority in connection with a grant of planning permission.

12. A planning authority may also be considered to have behaved unreasonably where they cannot show good reason - such as a material changes in planning circumstances - for failing to renew an extant or a recently expired planning permission as advised at paragraph 48 of the Annex to Circular 1/85. Such a permission is a material factor which must be taken into account when a planning authority consider a subsequent application for the same development. However, subject to the guidance in Circular 1/72 (WO 3/82) it will not normally be considered unreasonable for a planning authority to refuse to renew an extant or recently expired planning permission to extract minerals where a condition of that permission stipulated a date by which operations must cease.

Conditions

13. Circular 1/85 gives detailed guidance on the use of conditions: it makes it plain that they should be imposed only when they are both necessary and reasonable, as well as enforceable, precise, and relevant both in planning terms and to the proposed development. The imposition of conditions which clearly fail to meet these criteria may lead to an award of costs against the planning authority. The advice at paragraph 10 of Circular 1/85 should also be noted, that where a problem posed by a development could be solved by imposing a necessary and reasonable planning condition an agreement under section 52 of the 1971 Act should not be sought.

Unreasonable issue of enforcement notice

14. Decisions to award costs in relation to enforcement appeals are based on the same principles as for planning appeals. A planning authority will therefore be expected to exercise care to ensure that an enforcement notice takes full account of relevant case law and of planning policy and advice stated in Circulars. Moreover, in enforcement cases the Secretary of State will need to consider whether the planning authority had reasonable grounds for concluding that there had been a breach of planning control and

also the adequacy of their stated reasons (as required by Regulation 3 of Town and Country Planning (Enforcement Notices and Appeals) Regulations 1981) when enforcement action was considered expedient in the particular circumstances. For example, it will generally be regarded as unreasonable for a planning authority to have issued an enforcement notice when their sole reason for doing so is the absence of a valid planning permission for the particular development enforced against and it is concluded on appeal that there is no significant planning objection to the alleged breach of control.

The handling of the planning application/enforcement notice

15. If a planning authority fail to determine an application within the statutory period, or any extended period to which the applicant agrees, the applicant may appeal to the Secretary of State. Circular 22/80 (WO 40/80) advises that if a decision will be unavoidably delayed the applicant ought to be given a proper explanation, including information about consultations with other bodies and some indication as to when a decision is likely to be given. In any appeal under section 37 of the 1971 Act planning authorities will be expected to show that they had specific and adequate reasons for not reaching a decision. If they fail to do so, an award of costs may be made against them.

16. If the planning authority have refused a requested from the appellant to discuss the planning application, or the possibility of granting planning permission (including a conditional permission) for the development alleged in the enforcement notice, or have refused to provide information which they could be reasonably expected to provide, an award of costs may be made if the appeal might otherwise have been avoided.

17. A planning authority will be expected to have sought further details of an application if they are unclear about the applicant's intentions from the details supplied; a planning authority who have not sought these further details may be regarded as having acted unreasonably in refusing planning permission on the grounds that insufficient details have been supplied. Similarly, before issuing an enforcement notice, a planning authority should undertake reasonable investigation to establish whether or not there has been a breach of planning control by, for example, making inquiries of the owner and the occupier of the premises, and consulting their own records for information about any previous planning consent. Failure to undertake reasonable investigation of this nature may provide grounds for an award of costs if it results in an appeal to the Secretary of State which might otherwise have been avoided.

Procedures relating to the handling of the appeal

18. Costs may also be awarded in cases where, although the proceedings could not reasonably have been avoided, they have been conducted in an unreasonable manner which has caused the appellant to incur unnecessary expense. Examples are where the planning authority introduce a reason for refusal at a late stage in the proceedings, or drop a reason for refusal or withdraw an enforcement notice in the course of the proceedings, or where the planning authority's refusal to co-operate in settling agreed facts or supplying relevant information has unnecessarily prolonged the proceedings.

19. If an appellant has been seriously prejudiced by a planning authority's failure to comply with procedural requirements, the Inspector may adjourn the inquiry. An example is where the planning authority bring forward submissions on matters not included in their pre-inquiry statement when it is too late to postpone the start of the inquiry. In these circumstances, an award of costs may be made relating to the extra expense arising from the adjournment.

Awards against appellants

Unreasonable appeal

20. The right of appeal is a statutory right, but it should be exercised in a reasonable manner. Where there has been a recent appeal in respect of the same site and the same or a very similar development proposal, and the Secretary of State or his Inspector has made it plain that the development should not be allowed, an appellant who persists with a further appeal despite the previous decision may be at risk of having costs awarded against him if circumstances have not materially changed in the meantime. An appeal may also be considered unreasonable when it must have been obvious from official

statements of policy or judicial authority that the appeal had no reasonable prospect of success - for instance, an appeal relating to a major development which is in conflict with Green Belt policy. In such cases the planning authority will strengthen their case for an award of costs if they can show that they drew the appellant's attention to the relevant facts, and to the possible consequences of persisting with an appeal.

Procedures relating to the handling of the appeal

21. An appellant is expected to comply with the normal procedural requirements of inquiries. For instance, failing to provide an adequate pre-inquiry statement when required to do so, or introducing a new ground of appeal when it is too late to postpone the start of the inquiry, may be unreasonable behaviour. This could result in costs being awarded against the appellant if the behaviour caused unnecessary expense to the planning authority or another party by, for example, causing an adjournment or causing witnesses to be present unnecessarily at the inquiry. Costs may also be awarded against an appellant who is wilfully unco-operative, for example, by refusing to explain the grounds of appeal, or by refusing to discuss the appeal, if the planning authority are thereby put to unnecessary expense.

22. Deliberately unco-operative behaviour by any appellant, whether or not professionally represented, may be grounds for an award of costs. But where technical issues of precedent or procedure arise, in judging whether behaviour is unreasonable the Secretary of State will take into account the extent to which an appellant obtained professional advice. Where the planning authority drew the appellant's attention to relevant facts (see paragraph 20 above) the Secretary of State will take that into account too.

Withdrawal/failure to pursue an appeal

23. When appeals are to be dealt with by way of inquiry it is the Department's practice, when fixing the date, to indicate to appellants that if subsequently they decide to withdraw their appeal they should do so in good time to enable the inquiry to be cancelled and all parties notified. Appellants are asked to notify (or confirm) the withdrawal ot the Department in writing. If an appellant does not give the Department such notification of withdrawal in sufficient time for planning authority and all the other parties and their witnesses to be contacted and those parties are present when the inquiry is opened, an award may be made covering the costs of attendance of the planning authority and of any other principal party, as well as any third parties who have notified the appellant of their intention to be present. A warning to the planning authority of an intention to withdraw will not be sufficient: until the Department has been formally notified in writing of withdrawal, the appeal is still before the Secretary of State for determination and the planning authority and other parties will need to attend.

*   *   *

A.4

Circular No. 22/83
Town and Country Planning Act 1971
Planning Gain
Obligations and Benefits which extend beyond the Development
for which Planning Permission has been sought

(Dated August 25, 1983, issued jointly by the Department of the Environment and the Welsh Office; Circular No. 46/83 of that office)

* * *

General Policy

4. It is a matter of law as well as of good administration that planning applications should be considered on their merits having regard to the provisions of the development plan and any other material consideration and that they should be refused only when this serves a clear planning purpose and the economic effects have been taken into account. (More detailed advice is given in DOE Circular 22/80 (WO Circular 40/80). By the same token, the question of imposing a condition or obligation—whether negative or positive in character—should only arise where it is considered that it would not be reasonable to grant a permission in the terms sought which is not subject to such condition or obligation. A wholly unacceptable development should not of course be permitted just because of extraneous benefits offered by the developer.

5. If a planning application is considered in this light it may be reasonable, depending on the circumstances, either to impose conditions on the grant of planning permission, or (where the authority's purpose cannot be achieved by means of a condition) to seek an agreement with the developer which would be associated with any permission granted. Such agreements may well assist towards securing the best use of land and a properly planned environment. But this does not mean that an authority is entitled to treat an applicant's need for permission as an opportunity to obtain some extraneous benefit or advantage or as an opportunity to exact a payment for the benefit of ratepayers at large. Nor should the preparation of such an agreement be permitted to delay unduly the decision on the application.

6. The test of the reasonableness of imposing such obligations on developers depends substantially on whether what is required:

(1) is needed to enable the development to go ahead, eg provision of adequate access, water supply and sewerage and sewage disposal facilities (advice on the provision of infrastructure is given in Annex A to DOE Circular 22/80 (WO Circular 40/80) and on land drainage in DOE Circular 17/82 (WO Circular 15/82); or

(2) in the case of financial payments, will contribute to meeting the cost of providing such facilities in the near future; or

(3) is otherwise so directly related to the proposed development and to the use of the land after its completion, that the development ought not to be permitted without it, eg the provision, whether by the developer or by the authority at the developer's expense, of car-parking in or near the development or of reasonable amounts of open space related to the development; or

(4) is designed in the case of mixed development to secure an acceptable balance of uses.

Appendix B illustrates the application of these general principles to the provision of car parking.

7. If what is required or sought passes one of the tests set out in the preceding paragraph, a further test has to be applied. This is whether the *extent* of what is required or sought is fairly and reasonably related in case and kind to the proposed development. Thus while the developer may reasonably be expected to pay for or contribute to the cost of infrastructure which would not have been necessary but for his development, and while some public benefit may eventually accrue from this, his payments should be directly related in scale and kind to the benefit which the proposed development will derive from the facilities to be provided.

8. There is also a final test, namely whether what the developer is being asked to provide or help to finance represents in itself a reasonable charge on the developer as

distinct from being financed by national or local taxation or other means—*e.g.* as a charge on those using the facility provided. The essential principle to apply is that the facility to be provided or financed should be directly related to the development in question or the use of the land after development. It would not normally be reasonable, for example, to seek a contribution to road construction or improvement in the immediate vicinity of the proposed development unless the need for this arises wholly and substantially from the new development.

*   *   *

APPENDIX B: DEPARTMENTAL GUIDANCE ON PRACTICE AND PROCEDURE

B.1   Written Representations—Procedural Steps

(Circular 11/87: Annex A)

APPELLANT	DEPARTMENT	LPA	THIRD PARTIES
			(including public bodies)

Submits statement of case (the appeal form and any necessary documents) to Department and at the same time sends duplicate form to LPA.

Receives Appeal. Notifies LPA and appellant of starting date by return, citing the appeal reference, appellant and appeal site.

Receives Appeal Form; accepts procedure, notifies interested persons and bodies of appeal within 5 working days of starting date.

Receive notification of appeal. Submit any additional comments direct to the Department within 28 days of the starting date.

Receives questionnaire from LPA. Where this forms their statement, sends any relevant observations within 17 days of date of questionnaire to Department and LPA. Otherwise awaits LPA statement.

Receives questionnaire. Notifies parties of target period for site visit (4/5 wks time if questionnaire is statement) 6/7 wks time where additional statement is made.

Submits completed questionnaire to appellant and Department together with supporting documents within 14 days of starting date and indicates whether this forms their statement.

Receives statement of case, sends any relevant observations within 17 days of date of statement to Department and LPA

Receives statement

Submits statement of case to appellant and Department within 28 days of starting date

Receives third party comments, copies to LPA and appellant

Final cut off date for further comments—7 days from the date of the response of the appellant to the LPA's questionnaire (where that forms their statement) or to the LPA's statement. (38 or 52 days respectively from the starting date).

Site Visit arranged; decision letter issued (or report sent to Department) within 14* days of the site visit.

* 7 days target to be attained when Information Technology Strategy Implemented

142

B.2   Written Representations—Notification of Appeal to Third Parties.

(Circular 11/87: Annex B)

Dear Sir/Madam

TOWN AND COUNTRY PLANNING ACT 1971 (as amended)

LAND AT ....

....

PROPOSED DEVELOPMENT ....

....

Application reference ....

DOE/WO Appeal Reference ....

Appeal starting Date ....

Appellant's name ....

I am writing to let you know that an appeal has been made to the Secretary of State in respect of the above site.

The appeal follows the/refusal of planning permission/failure to determine a planning application within the time allowed/imposition of conditions on a grant of planning permission by this Council.

The appeal is to be decided on the basis of an exchange of written statements by the parties and a site visit by an Inspector.

Any comments already made following the original application for planning permission (unless they are expressly confidential) will be forwarded to the Department and copied to the appellant and will be taken into account by the Inspector in deciding the appeal. Should you wish to withdraw or modify your earlier comments in any way, or request a copy of the appeal decision letter, you should write direct to the Department of the Environment, Room ...., Tollgate House, Houlton Street, Bristol BS2 9DJ/Welsh Office, Cathays Park, Cardiff, CF1 3NQ, within 28 days of the appeal starting date (above) quoting the appeal reference number.

B.3 Timetabling Provisions for Main Pre-Inquiry Stages (with pre-inquiry meeting)

(Circular 10/88: Annex 4)

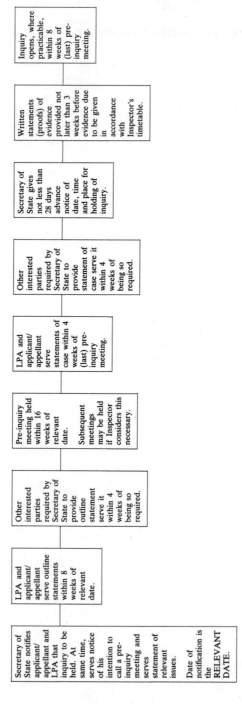

Secretary of State notifies applicant/appellant and LPA that inquiry to be held. At same time, serves notice of his intention to call a pre-inquiry meeting and serves statement of relevant issues.

Date of notification is the RELEVANT DATE.

LPA and applicant/appellant serve outline statements within 8 weeks of relevant date.

Other interested parties required by Secretary of State to provide outline statement serve it within 4 weeks of being so required.

Pre-inquiry meeting held within 16 weeks of relevant date.

Subsequent meetings may be held if Inspector considers this necessary.

LPA and applicant/appellant serve statements of case within 4 weeks of (last) pre-inquiry meeting.

Other interested parties required by Secretary of State to provide statement of case serve it within 4 weeks of being so required.

Secretary of State gives not less than 28 days advance notice of date, time and place for holding of inquiry.

Written statements (proofs) of evidence provided not later than 3 weeks before evidence due to be given in accordance with Inspector's timetable.

Inquiry opens, where practicable, within 8 weeks of (last) pre-inquiry meeting.

B.4   Timetabling Provisions for Main Pre-Inquiry Stages
(excluding cases where Secretary of State applies rule 5 of
S.I. 1988 No. 944 by calling a pre-inquiry meeting)

(Circular 10/88: Annex 3)

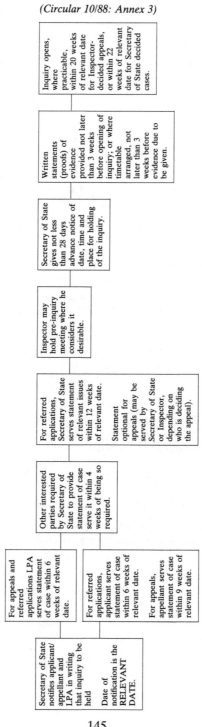

The flowchart reads, from bottom to top:

Secretary of State notifies applicant/appellant and LPA in writing that inquiry to be held

Date of notification is the RELEVANT DATE.

For appeals and referred applications LPA serves statement of case within 6 weeks of relevant date.

For referred applications, applicant serves statement of case within 6 weeks of relevant date.

For appeals, appellant serves statement of case within 9 weeks of relevant date.

Other interested parties required by Secretary of State to provide statement of case serve it within 4 weeks of being so required.

For referred applications, Secretary of State serves statement of relevant issues within 12 weeks of relevant date.

Statement optional for appeals (may be served by Secretary of State or Inspector, depending on who is deciding the appeal).

Inspector may hold pre-inquiry meeting where he considers it desirable.

Secretary of State gives not less than 28 days advance notice of date, time and place for holding of the inquiry.

Written statements (proofs) of evidence provided not later than 3 weeks before opening of inquiry; or where timetable arranged, not later than 3 weeks before evidence due to be given.

Inquiry opens, where practicable, within 20 weeks of relevant date for Inspector-decided appeals, or within 22 weeks of relevant date for Secretary of State decided cases.

145

B.5　Extract from Chief Planning Inspector's Report
for 1986/87

(Circular 10/88: Annex 5)

Pre-Inquiry Meetings

1.　Over the last few years it has become customary for the Inspectorate to arrange pre-inquiry meetings prior to inquiries which are expected to last several weeks, either because highly technical evidence is likely to be submitted or because the inquiry is to deal with several proposals involving more than one applicant or appellant.

2.　In holding such meetings the Inspector's objective is to encourage the parties to prepare for the inquiry so that, at the inquiry, time will not be wasted or taken up with matters which are not relevant nor in dispute.

3.　In so far as inquiry time is saved, the parties benefit directly; they are also likely to benefit indirectly where the Inspector's task of preparing a decision letter or report is made easier.

4.　Among the matters which may be discussed and resolved at pre-inquiry meetings are the following:—

Procedure at inquiry

Normal sitting hours;

Estimates of duration of the cases (including examination in chief, cross examination and re-examination) to be provided to allow a programme to be prepared prior to the inquiry;

Order of presentation of cases—for example, whether parts of the evidence should be dealt with on a topic basis, what the Inspector will be looking for in opening and closing submissions;

Facilities available at venue;

Evidence

Identification of issues and of areas of uncertainty about which the Inspector will need clarification prior to or at the inquiry;

Nature of the evidence to be submitted;

Scope for professional witnesses to agree statements of factual material in advance (including site description, planning history) and to narrow areas in dispute;

Agreement in respect of preparation and exchange of proofs including format (with summary and with technical material as appendices), presentation (with only the summary needing to be read in examination in chief), and timing of exchange of proofs in advance of the inquiry or of being submitted;

Listing and numbering of documents, plans etc."

Note: Consideration is also being given to the scope for making pre-inquiry arrangements of these kinds without necessarily bringing the parties together for a meeting.

B.6   Preparing for Major Planning Inquiries in England and Wales

Circular 10/88: Annex 1

A Code of Practice

1. This code of practice relates to procedures leading up to major inquiries held under the Planning Acts in England and Wales. The purpose of the code is to enable the Inspector to structure the inquiry in such a way as to ensure that the proceedings run smoothly, speedily and efficiently, and to help participants to concentrate on the real issues that have to be resolved. This is in the interests of all parties to the inquiry.

2. The code is based on experience gained at a number of past inquiries, and takes as its legal basis the provisions of te recently promulgated inquiries procedure rules in so far as they apply to inquiries where the Secretary of State has decided to apply the alternative pre-inquiry procedures appropriate to a major inquiry. At the same time, the code also includes administrative arrangements which are not set out formally in the Rules but which are intended to be helpful to all participants during the pre-inquiry stages of a major planning case. Because of procedural differences, the code will not be applied to inquiries in Scotland, nor to inquiries into an Order proposed by a Minister (though elements of the code could usefully be applied to such Orders where relevant-as they could be to inquiries into major proposals held under other legislation).

3. The code is intended for application in cases where the development proposal is of major public interest because of its national or regional implications, or the extent or complexity of the environmental, safety, technical or scientific issues involved, and where for these reasons there are a number of third parties involved as well as the applicant and the local planning authority.

4. Experience suggests that some of these third parties are likely to wish to be represented formally at the inquiry, and to play a major part in the proceedings, for example by calling witnesses and by cross-examination of witnesses called by other parties, particularly the promoters of the scheme. Other third parties may simply wish to have the opportunity to express their concern about the scheme, without playing a major part in the remainder of the inquiry.

5. The code seeks to help the Inspector and the parties prepare for the inquiry by:
   (a) identifying in advance those who intend to participate in the inquiry and the extent to which they wish to do so, making them known to one another, and enabling them to dispose of their time and resources to best advantage;
   (b) getting advance presentation of information and views to help participants to concentrate their inquiry statements on the key issues;
   (c) where possible, getting certain facts generally agreed between the parties; and
   (d) enabling the inquiry arrangements and procedures to be properly planned for the benefit of all concerned.

First steps

6. It will be for the Department to decide whether or not the special rule provisions relating to major inquiries and the code should be applied to any particular inquiry. This decision will be taken as soon as possible after the calling in of the application under the provision of section 35 of the Town and Country Planning Act 1971 or the submission of the planned appeal to the Secretary of State. It is likely to be applied only to a few very big inquiries, and when it is applied, a separate inquiry secretariat will be set up.

7. Once a decision has been taken to apply the code, the applicant and local planning authority will be notified and sent a copy of the code, together with a written statement of the matters which appear to the Secretary of State to be likely to be relevant to his consideration of the application or appeal. (This statement may be supplemented at a later stage if necessary.)

8. The local planning authority will, in addition, be sent a standard registration form for use by interested parties who wish to participate in the inquiry. This form will request the following information:
   (a) the name, address and telephone number of the person or organisation registering;
   (b) the name, address and telephone number of any agent, or, in the case of an

147

organisation, of the contact person;

(c) whether or not the person or organisation registering has an interest in any property that will be affected by the proposal;

(d) whether or not the person or organisation registering is likely to want to be represented formally and to play a major part in the inquiry, *e.g.*, by calling witnesses and/or cross-examining other parties and their witnesses;

(e) if not, whether or not the person or organisation registering will wish to give oral evidence at the inquiry or will wish only to submit representations in writing.

9. The Department will notify the local planning authority of those persons or organisations who are known to it at that stage to have a right to appear at the inquiry or to have an interest in the proposal. The local planning authority will be asked:

(a) to send a copy of the code, the Secretary of State's statement of relevant issues and the standard registration form to all those interested persons notified to them by the Department; to any section 29(3) parties; and to any other person or organisation known to them to have an interest in the proposal;

(b) to publish, in the local press, the formal notification of the application of the code; the application of the special rule provisions relating to major inquiries; the Secretary of State's statement of relevant issues; and a request that anyone interested in participating in the inquiry should obtain from the local authority a copy of the code and the registration form.

The local planning authority will be asked to confirm to the Department that the steps at (a) and (b) have been undertaken and to forward a copy of the press notice.

10. The registration forms will include the address of the inquiry secretariat or other nominated persons to whom they should be returned and the date by which this should be done. This will normally be within 21 days of the publication of the formal notification in the local press.

11. The inquiry secretariat will liaise with the local planning authority to ensure that the authority has sufficient copies of the code, the registration form and the statement of relevant issues to distribute as necessary.

Register of participants

12. The inquiry secretariat will prepare a register of participants fro the information contained in the registration forms. The register will be in 3 parts. Part 1 will contain details of all those who have indicated that they wish to play a major part in the proceedings (referred to subsequently as "major participants"). Part 2 will contain details of those who have indicated that they wish to give oral evidence without playing a major part in the remainder of the proceedings. Part 3 will contain details of those who wish to submit representations in writing without taking part in the inquiry itself. A copy of the register will be sent to the applicant, the local planning authority and other major participants, and arrangements will also be made for copies to be available for public inspection. Additions or deletions or transfers between one part of the register and another can be made at any time, and these will be notified in the same way.

13. The Inspector will normally allow all those included in Part 1 of the register to appear at the inquiry, regardless of their legal entitlement to do so. Those included in Part 2 of the register will also normally be allowed to appear, provided that their evidence is relevant, and does not merely duplicate evidence already given by others. Those not included in Part 1 or Part 2 of the register with no legal entitlement to appear at the inquiry will be allowed to appear at the discretion of the Inspector.

14. It is the major participants who are likely to derive most benefit from formal pre-inquiry procedures. They will be sent a copy of the code, and will be expected to comply with its provisions on such matters as the pre-inquiry exchange of documents, and, provided they do so, they will in turn receive copies of documents circulated by other participants, which are relevant to their interests. They will also receive individual notification of arrangements for pre-inquiry meetings.

15. While other participants will be much less affected by the provisions of the code, its use is not intended in any way to diminish their opportunity to make representations or the importance of their contribution to the inquiry proceedings. The information obtained will help the Inspector to plan the inquiry in the most effective manner, and to prepare a timetable for it, and this will be to the benefit of everyone. The register will also enable all those with an interest in the inquiry to discover who is taking part, and this will provide an opportunity for those with similar points of view to get together and to consider combining their representations.

Preliminary notification of the inquiry arrangements

16. As soon as possible after the publication of the formal notification of the application of the code in the local press, the Department will notify the applicant, the local planning authority, any interested government department and all those who are known to have a right to appear at the inquiry and who wish to do so of:

(a) the name of the Inspector appointed to hold the inquiry;

(b) the name of any assessors (where required, and if known at this stage);

(c) the arrangements for the first pre-inquiry meeting;

(d) the target date for the commencement of the inquiry.

The local planning authority will be asked to publish this information in the local press, and it will also be sent to other major participants as they register.

Outline statement

17. In accordance with the provisions of rule 5 of the statutory Rules, the inquiry secretariat will ask the local planning authority and the applicant to provide, not later than 8 weeks after the Secretary of State's notification that any inquiry is to be held, a written outline statement. Other major participants may also be asked to serve such a statement. If so they will be required by the inquiries rules to provide it within 4 weeks of being asked to do so. These statements should contain the general lines of the case which they intend to put forward and explain its relationship to the matters identified by the Secretary of State as likely to be relevant. They should include an estimate of how long the presentation of the case is likely to take; information about witnesses likely to be called and an indication of which other witness the participants would like to cross-examine; and a list of any special studies which have been taken into account or are being prepared. Major participants will normally be sent a copy of statements relevant to their interests unless the statements are very lengthy or the number of participants included is too great to allow this to be done. In any event, arrangements will be made for copies of all statements to be available for public inspection. In addition, all participants remain free to submit other written statements to the Inspector at any time: such statements will be made available for public inspection and circulated as appropriate.

18. The outline statements have two functions. First, they provide advance warning of arguments which the various participants are proposing to deploy at the inquiry. It should be possible to identify from these statements the issues that are likely to feature most prominently at the inquiry. Secondly, the outline statements provide the information that the Inspector requires to structure and programme the inquiry. In the light of what is said in them the Inspector may wish to invite participants who appear to hold the same or similar views to consider collaborating to present a single case at the inquiry. The outline statements will also help the Inspector to see whether there are any relevant issues which are in danger of not being properly covered at the inquiry, and to consider how to remedy any deficiencies, for example by inviting persons who have expert knowledge of the matter concerned to take part in the inquiry.

19. The Inspector will seek to identify from the statements those areas where facts appear to be capable of agreement between main parties, such as description of the proposal, the site and surroundings, or facts and methodologies relating to environment effects. He will do this as soon as possible after the receipt of the outline statements. A statement of generally agreed facts and matters still in dispute which are relevant to the inquiry will then be deposited and circulated in the same way as the written statements. When participants agree to work together to prepare an agreed statement of facts (see paragraph 21(d) below), the statement will be circulated as soon as possible after agreement has been reached.

The pre-inquiry and programme meeting

20. The purpose of the pre-inquiry meeting is to help the Inspector and the participants to prepare for the inquiry proper, and so enable the proceedings to be conducted as efficiently and speedily as possible. It will be a public meeting, presided over by the Inspector, and more than one meeting may be held where the Inspector considers this to be desirable.

21. The matters to be considered at the pre-inquiry meeting will include:

(a) any necessary clarification of the Departmental statement of relevant matters;

(b) identification of any material required by the Inspector and not already covered by statements, and consideration of how this is to be provided, including the progress of any special studies being undertaken, and the need for additional participants;

(c) responses to any invitation from the Inspector to participants to consider collaboration;

(d) arrangements for preparation of generally agreed statements of facts including arrangements for any informal meetings that may be required to assist in preparing such statements;

(e) a review of the timetable for the work to be done before the inquiry opens, including the submissions of any further statements;

(f) the role of any assessors.

22. Procedural matters will also be considered at the pre-inquiry meetings and a separate meeting (the programme meeting) may be held for this purpose. The matters to be considered will include:

(a) details of the venue and proposed dates and times of sittings including any provision for evening sessions or for sessions away from the main venue;

(b) programming the inquiry including the order of appearances and whether a topic by topic programme is to be adopted;

(c) accommodation and facilities at the inquiry (*e.g.*, copying, transcripts, telephones, public address system and facilities for the media);

(d) secretariat arrangements;

(e) procedural matters including consideration of the form of opening and closing statements, the need for and use of daily summaries, and whether proofs of evidence (or parts of them) can be taken as read:

(f) arrangements for the submission, circulation and inspection of documents, including the listing of documents already submitted;

(g) agreement on the units of measurement, nomeenclature, acronyms, etc, to be used at the inquiry.

23. The secretariat will send a note of conclusions reached at any pre-inquiry meeting to major participants, and arrangements will be made for copies to be made available for public inspection. In addition the applicant, the local planning authority, persons included in Parts 1 and 2 of the register and any persons not included in those parts of the register who have a right to appear at the inquiry will be given notice in writing of the date, time and place for the holding of the inquiry.

Informal meetings

24. Either before or during the inquiry the Inspector may wish to arrange for informal meetings to be held to see whether agreed statements of facts can be prepared on particular issues (eg, statistical methodology) to help participants with similar views to consider the possibility of collaboration, or for similar purposes. It would *not* be the function of the meeting to hear evidence on matters which should appropriately be discussed at the inquiry itself. The Inspector will indicate the purpose of such meetings, and designate a chairman who will normally be either the Inspector himself or one of his assessors. In the case of technical evidence, the chairman should ai to produce a report which will identify matters which are agreed, the matters in dispute, and the factors or assumptions which had led to the differences of view. Wherever possible copies of the report will be sent to major participants who have an interest in the issue concerned at least two weeks before evidence on that issue is due to be given.

Written statement of case

25. The applicant and local planning authority will, and other major participants may, be required to provide a written statement containing full particulars of the submissions which they propose to put forward, together with a list of any documents (including maps and plans) which they intend to refer to, or put in evidence, at the inquiry. If such a statement is required it will need to be provided not later than four weeks after the last pre-inquiry meeting.

Statement of evidence

26. If a person entitled to appear at the inquiry proposes to give, or call upon a witness to give, evidence at the inquiry by reading a written statement of that evidence, he will be required by the statutory rules to provide the Inspector with a copy of the statement of evidence not later than three weeks before the date when the participant is due to give

evidence. The Inspector may require the participant to prepare a summary of that statement and to read the summary, rather than the full statement, as evidence. The full statement may be tendered in evidence where the person who served it so wishes and the person reading the summary may be cross-examined on the contents of the full statement.

Introduction of new evidence

27. If a participant giving oral evidence at the inquiry introduces into his submissions any matters not covered by his pre-inquiry statements, the Inspector may agree to a request from another participant to adjourn the inquiry to allow time for the consideration of the additional material. He may also agree to such a request where failure to provide a statement by the required date has prejudiced presentation of another participant's case. The Inspector may consider making a recommendation for an award of costs against a person who unreasonably causes such an adjournment.

B.7   Planning Appeals-Code of Practice for Hearings

(Circular 10/88: Annex 2)

1. Appeals to the Secretary of State under section 36 of the Town and Country Planning Act 1971 are, in general, transferred for determination by a person appointed by him ("the Inspector"). The appellant and the local planning authority have the right to appear before and be heard by the Inspector before he reaches his decision on such an appeal. In practice the Secretary of State will almost always provide for an appellant or local planning authority to be heard by way of a local inquiry if either of them wish. However, he may, in appropriate cases, offer them the alternative of a hearing. It is important that, in agreeing the the appeal should be determined following a hearing, both the appellant and the local planning authority understand and accept that whereas a local inquiry is subject to statutory rules of procedure,* a hearing will be conducted in accordance with the non-statutory procedure set out in this code of practice. Both procedures are, of course, designed to embody the rules of natural justice.

2. This code contains the procedure which the appellant and the local planning authority will be invited to follow where a hearing has been agreed to. This procedure is intended to save the parties time and money and to allow for the Inspector to lead a discussion about the matters at issue. The aim is to give everybody, including interested third parties, a fair hearing and to provide the Inspector with all the information necessary for his decision, but in a more relaxed and less formal atmosphere than at a local inquiry.

3. A hearing will not be appropriate if many members of the public are likely to be present; if the appeal raises complicated matters of policy; if there are likely to be substantial legal issues raised; or if there is a likelihood that formal cross-examination will be needed to test the opposing cases.

4. It will be for the Secretary of State to decide whether a hearing would be an appropriate means of considering an appeal. When notification is received that either the appellant or the local planning authority wish to exercise their right to be heard, the Department will consider whether the case would be suitable for a hearing. If it is, both parties will be offered - normally within 5 working days of receipt of the notification - the choice between a local inquiry and a hearing. A hearing will be held if both parties agree to it; otherwise a local inquiry will be held. Each party should, within 7 working days of the date a hearing is offered to them, inform the Department whether or not the hearing procedure is accepted. They should bear in mind that where a hearing is held there is no entitlement to make an application for an award of costs, neither may they seek the issue of any form of summons to compel any person to attend a hearing.

5. The aim will be to arrange the hearing within 12 weeks from the date the parties agree to a hearing. Not less than 28 days' notice of the arrangements for the hearing will be given. The local planning authority will send details of the arrangements to all those, other than the appellant, with an interest in the land and to all who wrote to them about the proposed development at the applicant stage. They will also give such other publicity to the hearing as they think advisable. Those notified of the arrangements for the hearing will be sent a copy of this code, and will be told by the local planning authority where and when they can inspect copies of the pre-hearing statements and any other associated documents. they will also be advised that they may, at the discretion of the Inspector, participate in the discussion at the hearing.

6. An important element of this procedure is that the Inspector must be fully aware of the issues involved and the arguments likely to be made at the hearing, so that he can properly lead the discussion. It is therefore essential that at least 3 weeks before the hearing, and in any event no later than 6 weeks from the date of agreeing to a hearing, the appellant and the local planning authority provide a written statement containing full particulars of the case they wish wish to make at the hearing, including a list of any documents they intend to refer to. The statements will be passed to the Inspector to enable him to prepare adequately for the hearing. At the same time as sending their statement to the Department, the appellant and the local planning authority should send a copy to each other. When the parties agree to a hearing after notification that an inquiry will be held, any written statement already provided for the purpose of the inquiry will instead be used for the purpose of the hearing.

7. Failure to adhere to this time-table can be fatal to the procedure. If the Inspector cannot be provided with the necessary information in sufficient time before the hearing it

may be necessary to delay or defer it, or to hold a local inquiry with procedure governed by statutory rules.

8. The arrangements for the hearing and the conduct of it will be designed to create the right atmosphere for discussion and to eliminate or reduce the formalities of the traditional local inquiry. To this end the accommodation provided for the hearing should also be informal and the Inspector and the parties should wherever possible sit round a table; a small committee room is frequently satisfactory and the more formal atmosphere of a council chamber should always be avoided.

9. If at any time before the hearing the appellant or the local planning authority decide that they no longer wish to proceed in this way, they should inform the Department forthwith and a local inquiry, with its more formal procedures, will be arranged instead. If either party comes to the view during the hearing itself that the informal procedure is inappropriate, they should explain their reasons to the Inspector who will, after seeking the views of the other party, decide whether an inquiry should be held instead. Alternatively, if it becomes apparent to the Inspector during the hearing that the procedure is inappropriate, he will close the proceedings and a local inquiry will be arranged.

10. The Inspector will conduct the hearing. After resolving any doubts about the application or plans, he will explain that the hearing will take the form of a discussion which he will lead.

11. The Inspector will then review the case as he sees it from his reading of the papers and any pre-hearing site visit that he has made. He will outline what he considers to be the main issues and indicate that matters for which he requires further explanation or clarification. This will not preclude the parties from referring to other aspects which they consider to be relevant.

12. The appellant will be asked to start the discussion. He may do this through an agent or adviser if he wishes but such representation is not essential. Written material should have been circulated and exchanged before-hand so that it is fully understood and will not normally need to be read out at the hearing. Every effort should be made by the parties to avoid introducing, at the hearing, new material or documents not previously referred to, as this may necessitate adjournment of the hearing to a later date and frustrate the objectives of the hearing procedure. If documents are made available at the hearing the Inspector will ask or allow questions on those points on which he or others taking part in the hearing require further information or clarification.

13. Those participating in the hearing will be encouraged to ask questions informally throughout the proceedings, subject only to the questions being relevant and the discussion being conducted in an orderly manner. The appellant will be given the opportunity to make any final comments before the discussion is closed.

14. It may appear to the Inspector that certain matters could be more satisfactorily resolved if he were to adjourn the hearing to the site, normally then to be concluded there. The Inspector would only do this when, having regard to all the circumstances, including weather conditions, he was also satisfied that:

    (i) the discussion could proceed satisfactorily and that no one involved would be at a disadvantage;

    (ii) all parties present at the hearing had the opportunity to attend; and

    (iii), no one participating in the hearing objected to discussion being continued on the site.

15. Unless the hearing is to be adjourned to the site, the Inspector will ask the appellant and the local planning authority at the hearing whether they wish him to visit the site in their company. If one of them expresses such a wish, the date and time of the visit will be arranged at the hearing. The appellant, landowner and representative of the local planning authority may attend the visit, as may any other person at the discretion of the Inspector with the consent of the landowner.

16. If the Inspector is to decide the appeal and thinks it appropriate he may offer to give informal advance notification of his decision. Provided that the appellant and the local planning authority agree, he will, normally within 24 hours of the hearing, write to them indicating his intention to allow (with conditions where relevant) or dismiss the appeal. This letter will not constitute the decision on the appeal and should not be acted upon. The formal decision letter, which will include a statement of the reasons for the Inspector's decision, will follow in due course and will be sent to all those that took part in the hearing.

* The Town and Country Planning Appeals (Determination by Inspectors) (Inquiries Procedure) Rules 1988 (S.I. No. 945)—which apply to appeals decided by Inspectors. In those cases where an appeal is to be decided by the Secretary of State, the relevant rules are the Town and Country Planning (Inquiries Procedure) Rules 1988 (S.I. No. 944).

B.8 Good Practice at Planning Inquiries

(Circular 10/88: Annex 6)

The following note was prepared in the spring of 1986 and issued as an appendix to the Chief Planning Inspector's Report for the period January 1985 to March 1986.

It does not therefore reflect the changes introduced by the 1988 Rules but it will be updated once experience has been gained of the new Rules.

In the meantime, the key to the new Rules operating successfully is set out in paragraph 3 of the note—willingness by the parties to disclose their case in advance to one another and to the Inspector.

Introduction

1. The task of Inspectors at planning appeals or similar inquiries is to obtain the material necessary to make an informed and reasoned decision or recommendation. To do this they hear evidence from the parties and may also seek such other additional information as they consider necessary. Inspectors must be satisfied before the inquiry ends that they understand what the subject of the inquiry is and what the relevant arguments and submissions are. They need also to ensure that the parties are satisfied that their cases have been understood and that they have had a fair hearing. While Inspectors must always act in accordance with the principles of fairness, openness and impartiality set out in the Franks Report they are also responsible for ensuring that the inquiry is run efficiently and that inquiry time is not wasted. Thus they will seek to avoid inquiry time being spent on matters which are not in dispute or where, in their view, sufficient evidence has been heard to establish a point at issue, or on matters where expert witness can reach agreement more quickly or easily prior to the inquiry.

2. The great majority of planning inquiries are completed in 1 day and there is little scope for saving time at these, but nevertheless some of the points made in the following paragraphs apply to all inquiries. There are however each year a substantial number of longer running inquiries where time could be saved at the inquiry, and this would in turn help to reduce the time required by the Inspector to prepare his report or decision letter, and hence speed up the final decision.

Preparing for the inquiry

3. Adequate preparation by the parties and by Inspectors is essential and present practice frequently does not allow this to take place. Some improvements can be achieved by changes to the Inquiries Procedure Rules, and these are under review, but what is needed is basically a willingness by the parties to disclose their case in advance to each other and to the Inspector. At present pre-inquiry statements submitted by local planning authorities and by appellants (when requested to do so) are intended to provide the other parties and the Inspector with the gist of the cases to be presented. Too often they fail to do so: they tend to be couched in very general terms and contain none of the substance of the case that will be presented at the inquiry.

4. In this respect they tend to be less satisfactory than the statements produced for informal hearings. The Code of Practice for Informal Hearings requires both parties to produce comprehensive statements 3 weeks before the informal hearing. These ensure the Inspector knows in advance what the cases are and enables him to open the hearing by identifying the issues in the appeal and summarising the main arguments on each. This practice is welcomed by the parties and is indeed one of the reasons why informal hearings are popular with parties and with Inspectors.

5. Pre-inquiry meetings are found to be useful in advance of inquiries which are expected to last more than a week or so. They provide an opportunity for the Inspector

to obtain agreement on the scope and date of submission of pre-inquiry statements, on the exchange of proofs of evidence in advance, on witnesses meeting to agree material before the inquiry starts and on inquiry programming. When such meetings have been held, it has on occasions resulted in witnesses for the appellant and local planning authority submitting an agreed statement of facts together with documents, plans and suggested planning conditions prior to or at the commencement of the inquiry. This is good practice which could with benefit adopted in those cases where pre-inquiry meetings are not held.

6. Even though many statements are at present of limited use in assisting the Inspector or the parties to prepare for the inquiry, they can on occasions serve to encourage the parties to enter into negotiation. But if the statements are served close to the 28 day limit before the inquiry the time available for negotiation is limited and the Inspectorate is often faced with last minute requests for adjournment or late cancellations. While it is clearly desirable to resolve matters without the expense and delay involved in a public inquiry, late cancellations or adjournments impose costs in the Inspectorate, and prevent other appellants having their case brought forward. Hence it is good practice for pre-inquiry statements to be exchanged as early in the appeals process of possible.

7. Inspectors have the discretion to permit additional evidence. But the last minute introduction of a material consideration intended to catch an opposing party off-guard, is not "good practice". In some circumstances it may lead to an adjournment and this in turn could result in a successful application for costs against the offending party.

At the inquiry

8. The Inquiries Procedure Rules provide for the appellant (and the applicant in section 35 call-in cases) to present their case first, and to have the last word, but this often means that more ground is covered by the appellant than is necessary. If it appears that the local planning authority's case is going to deal with only a limited number of points, it may be advantageous for that case to be heard first. Then the appellant has only to adduce evidence in response to the local planning authority's case, and any additional material requested by the Inspector.

9. There are also some inquiries where there are a number of discrete issues, each requiring complex technical evidence to be submitted and tested. In such cases it can be useful for each issue to be dealt with in turn. These cases have to be identified well in advance, pre-inquiry meetings arranged and agreement of the parties obtained to present their cases on a "topic" basis. This can result in appreciable savings in time, both at the inquiry and in preparation of the Inspector's report; the practice is strongly commended in every appropriate case.

Opening submissions

10. Short opening statements lasting no more than 20 to 30 minutes outlining the cases to be presented by witnesses are all that is required if there has been adequate exchange of information in advance. It can be very useful in multi-day inquiries if all the principal parties provide such statements on the first morning, when there tends to be maximum press and public interest, as these statements help those present to understand what the inquiry is all about.

Presentation of evidence

11. It is generally the task of the advocate to ensure that when there is more than one witness, proofs are consistent, and do not cover the same ground. At the inquiry sufficient copies should be available for the parties, if not circulated in advanced, and for members of the public present: copies of plans and photographs which are submitted should also be made available or, preferably, displayed so that they can be easily seen.

12. The major criticism of proofs is that they are too long and many could with advantage be shortened with more use made of annexes to provide the detailed

evidence, for example, extracts of policy statements, tables and statistics, historical background, *etc.* It is particularly useful when complex or technical evidence is submitted for summaries containing the salient points to be prepared and for only these to be read out in evidence. Copies of the whole proof should of course be available to the parties and the public, and the witness would be open to cross-examinatin on all evidence he has submitted.

Cross examination

13. Cross examination can be helpful to the Inspector and the inquiry in for example:
Testing the validity of the facts and assumptions on which cases are based to expose any defects,
Exploring how the application of policies would forward the objectives they are intended to achieve,
Identifying and *narrowing* the issues which are in dispute.

14. Cross examination is much less useful when it is directed to persuading a professional witness to change an opinion for example on aesthetic matters, or in attempting to establish inconsistencies in wording of policies which are not intended to be construed as statute.

15. Where Inspectors find cross examination or repetitious, they should and do indicate this; they must also ensure that the cross examination does not lead to intimidation of the witness.

16. At many inquiries however the difficulty faced by Inspectors is that of one side not having the skills or experience to probe and test the evidence of opposing witnesses. In such cases the role of the inspector has to become more inquisitorial. They need to establish what weight is to be given to evidence submitted, to assess how realistic are the assumptions and on what forecasts are based. In doing this they must be thorough, though of course always impartial, but unless they are given proofs in advance they may be at a serious disadvantage.

Re-examination

17. Re-examination should not be used to introduce new evidence, nor in general should questions be put in such a way as to suggest the desired answer.

Participation by Interested Persons and Groups

18. On occasions interested persons and groups may seek to introduce material irrelevant to the inquiry or consider that repetition will add to the strength of their case and inspectors must discourage this. In general however groups and individuals with similar cases do respond well to requests for co-operation, for example by nominating one of their number as a spokesman. This good practice is to be encouraged.

Conditions

19. Parties are now expected to submit suggested conditions which would be attached to planning permissions if granted and it is becoming more common for the parties to discuss these in advance and obtain a measure of agreement. However the opportunity should be taken at the inquiry to resolve remaining disagreements.

20. It must be emphasised that Inspectors do not take submission of suggested conditions by local authorities to indicate any weakness in their opposition to the proposed development. Inspectors have been making this point clear when opening the inquiries as there have been cases when local residents have construed the measure as a 'sell out' by the local planning authority.

Closing submissions

21. Closing submissions can be of great value particularly in multi-day inquiries when covering a multiplicity of topics and issues. Not only do they summarise the cases for the

parties as they have emerged from cross examination and re-examination but logically ordered summaries can also provide Inspectors with a framework for the report. Some advocates have been providing Inspectors with copies of summaries of the closing submissions and increasingly Inspectors will ask for these to be provided if possible.

B.9

Good Practice at Inquiries
The Submission of Documents

(Chief Inspector's Report 1988/9: Appendix E)

Introduction

1.   Experience has shown that the quality of inquiry documentation varies enormously. At its best, it can greatly assist in both the handling of public inquiries and the subsequent decision-making process. At its worst, it can be a positive bar to the efficient running of the inquiry and can make the always difficult and complex task of decision-making even more intractable and lengthy.

Purpose of Documents

2.   All parties to planning appeals and inquiries are therefore urged to make common cause to improve all aspects of future document selection, preparation and presentation. It is as well to remember the precise aims and purposes of producing inquiry documents, be they in the form of text, tables, drawings, graphs or photographs: *i.e.* to set out in a readily-identifiable and assimilable form the factual material and technical data upon which evidence is based. To be effective all documents should be carefully prepared, presented and where appropriate edited of irrelevant matters.

Presentation of Documents

3.   Documents should be autonomous and should not be bound in with Statements of Evidence which in turn should be confined to the facts and expert opinions deriving from witnesses' own professional or local knowledge as applied to individual cases. Other relevant date, such as technical publications and official guidance may be referred to but must be available as separate documents carrying an identifiable reference number. To facilitate handling and reproduction, all documents should be submitted in A4 size. Extracts from published material must indicate their precise context with full titles, chapter headings and relevant dates for verification purposes.In such cases, a copy of the original document's title or cover page might well be appropriate.

4.   Plans, maps and diagrams should be treated in every respect like documents since the distinction between them is somewhat artificial. They and other essential documents should always be made available at the inquiry in reasonably quantity. They should be of A4 size or folded to A4 size in such a way that the title box is displayed when the right hand corner of the plan is folded back.

5.   Photographs should be likewise treated and if not A4 in size should be mounted on A4 size card or placed in A4 size albums or envelopes. Panoramic photographs should similarly be mounted on a series of A4 size cards. All photographs should be individually numbered and their respective viewpoints shown on a separate OS extract plan at a suitable scale. Time and date must always be given for original photographs.

6.   Where models of development proposals or display panels have been used at inquiries, these should be photographed, preferably in colour, and copy enlargement prints submitted as documents.

Indexing of Documents

7.   It follows that the indexing of documents is of particular importance. The numbering and subsequent listing of documents can be a very lengthy and tedious process. Since they will be mostly available before the inquiry, it would be of considerable help in reducing decision times if at least the principal parties would carry out their part of the process themselves, as Statements of Evidence are being prepared.

8.   The following guidelines should be followed when indexing documents:
   (a)   core document lists, *e.g.* policy statements, development plan extracts, should be compiled and indexed by LPAs and submitted with Statements of Case;

(b)   principal parties should list all documents serially using a unique prefix;

(c)   plans, diagrams and photographs should be listed as documents and, like other documents, should also display prominently the already-notified DOE appeal or called-in application reference;

(d)   LPAs are requested to include both a copy of the Inquiry Notice and the Inquiry Attendance List as documents as well as specifically to identify the application site plan and application drawings;

(e)   bundles of correspondence can be submitted as single documents provided the individual letters are discretely numbered within a separate series.

9.   It should be remembered that Statements of Evidence are not necessarily inquiry documents and so should not be serially numbered unless the Inspector decides otherside. Statements of Evidence should rather be separately indexed.

10.   Completed lists of documents should be handed in to the Inspector just before the close of the inquiry.

APPENDIX C: PRECEDENTS

C.1   Illustrative Form of Notice of Motion

IN THE HIGH COURT OF JUSTICE   CO/—
QUEEN'S BENCH DIVISION

In the Matter of the Town and Country Planning Act 1990

In the Matter of Land at (address)

B E T W E E N :

        A.B. [plc]   *Applicant*

        and

        THE SECRETARY OF STATE FOR THE ENVIRONMENT

        [and the .... Council]

                                              Respondent[s]

TAKE NOTICE that the High Court of Justice, Queen's Bench Division, at the Royal Courts of Justice, Strand, London, WC2A 2LL, will be moved [before His Lordship Mr. Justice . . .] [at the expiration of [35] days from the service upon you of this notice or on [Mon]day, the .... day of .... 19....., at the sitting of the Court] or so soon thereafter as counsel can be heard, by counsel on behalf of A.B. [for an order or for the following relief, namely]:

1.   That the decision of the [First Respondent or his inspector to be treated as that of the First Respondent] under section 78 of [and the Ninth Schedule to] the above-mentioned Act given by letter dated .... 19..... whereby the Applicant's appeal against a decision of the [Second] Respondents dated .... 19..... refusing planning permission for (specify matters and plans for which permission was sought) was [dismissed or allowed subject to the following court directions] be quashed;

AND that the costs of and incidental to this application may be paid by the [First] Respondent, or that such other order as to costs may be made as the Court may think fit.

[AND FURTHER TAKE NOTICE that the grounds of this application are:

    (1) that the said decision is not within the powers conferred by the above-mentioned Act [or alternatively or and]
    (2) that the requirements of the [Town and Country Planning (Inquiries Procedure) Rules 1988 or Town and Country Planning Appeals (Determination by Appointed Persons) (Inquiries Procedure) Rules 1988] have not been complied with.

PARTICULARS

(1)   the said conditions [do not reasonably relate to the permitted development or affect land not in the Applicant's control], or

(2) [the First Respondent or his inspector] in dismissing the appeal [had or failed to have] regard to the following [immaterial or material] considerations namely (specify the considerations), or

(3) [the First Respondent or his inspector] acted contrary to the rules of natural justice in that [he refused to allow a proper adjournment of the Inquiry in order to permit the Applicant to consider the deal with evidence submitted by the [Second] Respondent of which no notice had been given in the said Respondent's Statement of Case or he failed to give any or any sufficient reasons for his decision or he refused to permit the Applicant to cross-examine the witness of the [Second] Respondent], or

(4) in breach of rule 16(4) of the said Rules the [First] Respondent] [differed from his inspector on the following finding of fact namely (specify finding of fact) or took into consideration [new evidence or a new issue of fact namely (specify issue of fact) and failed to notify the Applicant of his intention to do so]] and

(5) the interests of the Applicant have thereby been substantially prejudiced].

[[A copy of copies] of the affidavit[s] and the exhibit[s] thereto which are intended to be relied on in support of this application are served herewith.]

DATED the .... day of .... 19.......

[C.D. of (address), Solicitor for the above-named Applicant A.B. or A.B. whose address for service is (address), Applicant in person.]

To the Secretary of State and to .... Esq., of the .... Council

C.2 Illustrative Affidavit supporting motion to quash decision of Secretary of State or his inspector on a planning appeal

Applicant: C.D.: 1st .... 19.......

(Heading as in Notice of Motion)

I, C.D. of (address of residence of work-place and occupation or description) make oath and say as follows:

1.   I am (occupation) and am duly authorised to make this affidavit on behalf of the above named A.B. which, save as hereafter appears, I do of my own knowledge.

2.   There is now produced and shown to me marked "C.D.1" a bundle containing copies of the following documents:

The application for planning permission dated .... 19....;
The Second Respondent's Notice of Refusal thereof dated .... 19....;
The Notice of Appeal against the said decision dated .... 19....;
The Second Respondent's Statement of Submission prepared under rule 6(1) of the Inquiries Procedures Rules 1988.*

3.   There is also produced and shown to the marked "C.D.2" a copy of The first Respondent's [Inspector's] decision set out in a letter dated .... 19........ [together with his Inspector's report] referred to therein.

4.   I was present at the inquiry held at .... on .... 19........

5.   In the course of the inquiry the Second Respondent raised for the first time a highway objection to the Applicant proposed development. The details thereof are reported at paragraph [4] of the inspector's report. As appears from the Statement of Case no notice of their intention to raise this issue has been given in accordance with the Rules.

6.   On behalf of the Applicant A.B. Counsel sought an adjournment of the Inquiry so that the Appellant could call an expert witness to deal with the objection, but as appears from paragraph [9] of the inspector's report the said application was refused.

7.   The Applicant is advised that the appropriateness of the standards adopted in the Second Respondent's evidence is not accepted by all highway engineers and, in the circumstances he has been substantially prejudiced by being unable to put other evidence before the inspector.

SWORN at (address) this ....
day of .... 19...... before me
          (Signature)   (Signature of
A [Commissioner for Oaths or Solicitor or   deponent)
Officer of the Court appointed by the Judge
to take affidavits]

This affidavit is filed on behalf of the Appellant

---

* where relevant to grounds of notice of motion.

C.3   Format of Illustrative Planning Proof

1. Full name, qualifications and experience.

2. Factual background of the applications:

   The application in outline or detail
   Reasons for refusal
   Officers recommendation

3. Description of site and surrounding area.

4. Government advice including reference to relevant Circulars.

5. Development Plan Policies—Structure plan policies
   Local plan policies
   Unitary develoment plan policies
   Non-statutory policies

6. Identification of the planning issues.

7. Comments on the planning issues.

8. Consideration of any relevant appeal decisions.

9. Comments upon local planning authority/appellant's case.

10. Conclusions.

D.1   The Town and Country Planning (Inquiries Procedure) Rules 1988

(S.I. 1988 No. 944)

(Dated May 24, 1988, and made by the Lord Chancellor in exercise of the powers conferred upon him by section 11 of the Tribunals and Inquiries Act 1971, and of all other powers enabling him on that behalf.)

Citation and Commencement

1. These Rules may be sited as the Town and Country Planning (Inquiries Procedure) Rules 1988 and shall come into force on 7th July 1988.

Interpretation

2. In these Rules, unless the context otherwise requires, references to sections and Schedules, are references to sections of, and Schedules to, the Town and Country Planning Act 1971 and—

"applicant", in the case of an appeal, means the appellant;

"assessor" means a person appointed by the Secretary of State to sit with an inspector at an inquiry or re-opened inquiry to advise the inspector on such matters arising as the Secretary of State may specify;

"the Commission" means the Historic Buildings and Monuments Commission for England;

"conservation area consent" means consent required by section 277A(2);

"development order" has the meaning assigned to it by section 24;

"document" includes a photograph, map or plan;

"inquiry" means a local inquiry in relation to which these Rules apply;

"inspector" means a person appointed by the Secretary of State to hold an inquiry or a re-opened inquiry;

"land" means the land, tree or building to which an inquiry relates;

"listed building consent" has the meaning assigned to it by section 55(3A);

"local authority" has the meaning assigned to it by section 290(1);

"local planning authority" means—

    (i) in relation to a referred application, the body who would otherwise have dealt with the application;

    (ii) in relation to an appeal, the body who were responsible for dealing with the application occasioning the appeal;

"outline statement" means a written statement of the principal submissions which a person proposes to put forward at an inquiry;

"pre-inquiry meeting" means a meeting held before an inquiry to consider what may be done with a view to securing that the inquiry is conducted efficiently and expeditiously, and where two or more such meetings are held references to the conclusion of a pre-inquiry meeting are references to the conclusion of the final meeting;

"referred application" means an application of any description mentioned in rule 3(1) which is referred to the Secretary of State for determination;

"relevant date" means the date of the Secretary of State's written notice to the applicant and the local planning authority of his intention to cause an inquiry to be held, and "relevant notice" means that notice;

"the 1974 Rules" means the Town and Country Planning (Inquiries Procedure) Rules 1974;

"section 29(3) party" means—

    (a) a person whose representations the Secretary of State is required by the application of section 29(3) or by regulations under Part I of Schedule 11 to take into account in determining the referred application or appeal to which an inquiry relates; and

    (b) in the case of an appeal, a person whose representations the local planning authority were required by section 29(3) or those regulations to take into account in determining the application occasioning the appeal;

"statement of case" means a written statement which contains full particulars of the case which a person proposes to put forward at an inquiry and a list of any documents which that

person intends to refer to or put in evidence;

"tree preservation order" means an order under section 60.

Application of Rules

3.—(1) These Rules apply in relation to any local inquiry caused by the Secretary of State to be held in England or Wales before he determines:

    (a) an application in relation to planning permissiion referred to him under section 35 or an appeal to him under section 36, or under section 36 as applied by section 37;

    (b) an application for consent referred to him under a tree preservation order or an appeal to him under such an order, with the exceptions that rule 4(1) shall not apply and the references to a section 29(3) party shall be omitted;

    (c) an application in relation to listed building consent referred to him under paragraph 4 of Schedule 11 or an appeal to him under paragraph 8 of Schedule 11, or under paragraph 8 as applied by paragraph 9 of that Schedule, including an application or appeal referred or made under any of those paragraphs as applied by section 56B(2);

    (d) an application in relation to conservation area consent referred to him under paragraph 4 of Schedule 11, or under paragraph 8 of Schedule 11, or under paragraph 8 as applied by paragraph 9 of that Schedule, as those paragraphs are applied by paragraph 9 of that Schedule, as those paragraphs are applied in the case of such an application or appeal by virtue of section 277A, including an application or appeal to which section 56B(2) is applied by section 277A,

but do not apply in relation to any local inquiry by reason of the application of any provision mentioned in this paragraph by any other enactment.

(2) Where these Rules apply in relation to an appeal which at some time fell to be disposed of in accordance with the Town and Country Planning Appeals (Determination by Inspectors) (Inquiries Procedure) Rules 1988 or Rules superseded by those Rules, any step taken or thing done under those Rules which could have been done under any corresponding provision of these Rules shall have effect as if it had been taken or done under that corresponding provision.

Preliminary information to be supplied by local planning authority

4.—(1) The local planning authority shall, on receipt of a notice from the Secretary of State of his intention to cause an inquiry to be held ("the relevant notice"), forthwith inform him and the applicant in writing of the name and address of any section 29(3) party who has made representations to them; and the Secretary of State shall as soon as practicable thereafter inform the applicant and the local planning authority in writing of the name and address of any section 29(3) party who has made representations to him.

(2) This paragraph applies where:

    (a) the Secretary of State or any local authority has given to the local planning authority a direction restricting the grant of planning permission for which application was made; or

    (b) in a case relating to listed building consent, the Commission has given a direction to the local planning authority pursuant to paragraph 6(2)(b) of Schedule 11 as to how the application is to be determined; or

(c) the Secretary of State or any other Minister of the Crown or any government department or local authority has expressed in writing to the local planning authority the view that the application should not be granted either wholly or in part, or should be granted only subject to conditions, or, in the case of an application for consent under a tree preservation order, should be granted together with a direction requiring replanting; or

(d) any authority or person consulted in pursuance of a development order has made representations to the local planning authority about the application.

(3) Where paragraph (2) app[lies, the local planning authority shall forthwith after the date of the relevant notice ("the relevant date") inform the person or body concerned of the inquiry and, unless they have already done so, that person or body shall thereupon give the local planning authority a written statement of the reasons for making the direction, expressing the view or making the representations, as the case may be.

Procedure where Secretary of State causes pre-inquiry meeting to be held

5.—(1) The Secretary of State may cause a pre-inquiry meeting to be held if it appears to him desirable and where he does so the following paragraphs apply.

(2) The Secretary of State shall serve with the relevant notice a notification of his intention to cause a meeting to be held and a statement of the matters which appear to him to be likely to be relevant to his consideration of the application or appeal in question; and where another Minister of the Crown or a government department has expressed in writing to the Secretary of State a view which is mentioned in rule 4(2)(c), the Secretary of State shall set this out in his statement and shall supply a copy of the statement to the Minister or government department concerned.

(3) The local planning authority shall cause to be published in a newspaper circulating in the locality in which the land is situated a notice of the Secretary of State's intention to cause a meeting to be held and of the statement served in accordance with paragraph (2) in such form as the Secretary of State may specify.

(4) The local planning authority and the applicant shall, not later than 8 weeks after the relevant date, each serve an outline statement on the other and on the Secretary of State.

(5) Where rule 4(2) applies, the local planning authority shall:

(a) include in their outline statement the terms of—

(i) any direction given together with a statement of the reasons therefor; and

(ii) any view expressed or representation made on which they intend to rely in their submissions at the inquiry; and

(b) within the period mentioned in paragraph (4), supply a copy of their statement to the person or body concerned.

(6) The Secretary of State may in writing require any other person who has notified him of an intention or a wish to appear at the inquiry to serve, within 4 weeks of being so required, an outline statement on him, the applicant and the local planning authority.

(7) The meeting (or, where there is more than one, the first meeting) shall be held not later than 16 weeks after the relevant date.

(8) The Secretary of State shall give not less than 21 days written notice of the meeting to the local planning authority, the applicant, any person known at the date of the notice to be entitled to appear at the inquiry and any other person whose presence at the meeting seems to him to be desirable; and he may require the local planning authority to take, in relation to notification of the meeting, one or more of the steps which he may under rule 10(6) require them to take in relation to notification of the inquiry.

(9) The inspector shall preside at the meeting and shall determine the matters to be discussed and the procedure to be followed, and he may require any person present at the meeting who, in his opinion, is behaving in a disruptive manner to leave and may refuse to permit that person to return or to attend any further meeting, or may permit him to return or attend only on such conditions as he may specify.

(10) Where a pre-inquiry meeting has been held pursuant to paragraph (1), the inspector may hold a further meeting. He shall arrange for such notice to be given of a

further meeting as appears to him necessary; and paragraph (9) shall apply to such a meeting.

Service of statements of case etc.

6.—(1) The local planning authority shall, not later than—

(a) 6 weeks after the relevant date, or

(b) where a pre-inquiry meeting is held pursuant to rule 5, 4 weeks after the conclusion of that meeting,

serve a statement of case on the Secretary of State, the applicant and any section 29(3) party.

(2) Where rule 4(2) applies, the local planning authority shall, unless they have already done so in an outline statement, include in their statement of case the matters mentioned in rule 5(5)(a) and shall supply a copy of the statement to the person or body concerned.

(3) The applicant shall, not later than:

(a) in the case of a referred application where no pre-inquiry meeting is held pursuant to rule 5, 6 weeks after the relevant date, or

(b) in the case of an appeal where no such meeting is held, 9 weeks after the relevant date, or

(c) in any case where a pre-inquiry meeting is held pursuant to rule 5, 4 weeks after the conclusion of that meeting,

serve a statement of case on the Secretary of State, the local planning authority and any section 29(3) party.

(4) The Secretary of State may in writing require any other person who has notified him of an intention or a wish to appear at any inquiry to serve a statement of case, within 4 weeks of being so required, on the applicant, the local planning authority, the Secretary of State and any (or any other) section 29(3) party.

(5) The Secretary of State shall supply any person from whom he requires a statement of case in accordance with paragraph (4) with a copy of the local planning authority's and the applicant's statement of case and shall inform that person of the name and address of every person on whom his statement of case is required to be served.

(6) The Secretary of State or an inspector may require any person who has served a statement of case in accordance with this rule to provide such further information about the matters contained in the statement as he may specify.

(7) Any person serving a statement of case on the local planning authority shall serve with it a copy of any document, or of the relevant part of any document, referred to in it.

(8) Unless he has already done so, the Secretary of State, in the case of a referred application, shall, and, in the case of an appeal, may, not later than 12 weeks from the relevant date, serve a written statement of the matters referred to in that paragraph on the applicant, the local planning authority, any section 29(3) party and any person from whom he has required a statement of case.

(9) The local planning authority shall afford to any person who so requests a reasonable opportunity to inspect and, where practicable, take copies of any statement or document which, or a copy of which, has been served on them in accordance with any of the preceding paragraphs of this rule, and of any statement so served by them together with a copy of any document, or of the relevant part of any document, referred to in it; and shall specify in the statement served in acordance with paragraph (1) the time and place at which the opportunity will be afforded.

Further power of inspector to hold pre-inquiry meetings

7.—(1) Where no pre-inquiry meeting is held pursuant to rule 5, an inspector may hold one if he thinks it desirable.

(2) An inspector shall arrange for not less than 14 days written notice of a meeting he proposes to hold under paragraph (1) to be given to the applicant, the local planning authority, any person known at the date of the notice to be entitled to appear at the

inquiry and any other person whose presence at the meeting appears to him to be desirable.

(3) Rule 5(9) shall apply to a meeting held under this rule.

Inquire time-table

8. Where a pre-inquiry meeting is held pursuant to rule 5 an inspector shall, and in any other case may, arrange a time-table for the proceedings at, or at part of, an inquiry and may at any time vary the time-table.

Date and notification of inquiry

10.—(1) The date fixed by the Secretary of State for the holding of an inquiry shall be, unless he considers such a date impracticable, not later than:

 (a) 22 weeks after the relevant date; or

 (b) in a case where a pre-inquiry meeting is held pursuant to rule 5, 8 weeks after the conclusion of that meeting.

(2) Where the Secretary of State considers it impracticable to fix a date in accordance with paragraph (1), the date fixed shall be the earliest date after the end of the relevant period mentioned in that paragraph which he considers to be practicable.

(3) Unless the Secretary of State agrees a lesser period of notice with the applicant and the local planning authority, he shall give not less than 28 days written notice of the date, time and place fixed by him for the holding of an inquiry to every person entitled to appear at the inquiry.

(4) The Secretary of State may vary the date fixed for the holding of an inquiry, whether or not the date as varied is within the relevant period mentioned in paragraph (1); and

paragraph (3) shall apply to a variation of a date as it applied to the date originally fixed.

(5) The Secretary of State may also vary the time or place for the holding of an inquiry and shall give such notice of any such variation as appears to him to be reasonable.

(6) The Secretary of State may require the local planning authority to take one or more of the following steps—

 (a) to publish not less than 14 days before the date fixed for the holding of an inquiry in one or more newspapers circulating in the locality in which the land is situated such notice of the inquiry as he may direct;

 (b) to serve within such period as he may specify notice of an inquiry in such form and on such persons or classes of persons as he may specify;

 (c) to post within such period as he may specify such notice of an inquiry as he may direct in a conspicuous place near to the land.

(7) Where the land is under the control of the applicant he shall, if so required by the Secretary of State, affix firmly to the land or to some object on or near the land, in such manner as to be readily visible to and legible by members of the public, such notice of the inquiry as the Secretary of State may specify; and he shall not remove the notice, or cause or permit it to be removed, for such period before the inquiry as the Secretary of State may specify.

Appearances at inquiry

11.—(1) The persons entitled to appear at an inquiry are:

 (a) the applicant;

 (b) the local planning authority;

 (c) any of the following bodies if the land is situated in their area and they are not the local planning authority—

  (i) a county or district council;

  (ii) a National Park Committee within the meaning of paragraph 5 of Schedule 17 to the Local Government Act 1972;

(iii) a joint planning board constituted under section 1(2) or a joint planning board or special planning board reconstituted under Part I of Schedule 17 to the Local Government Act 1972;

(iv) an urban development corporation established under section 135 of the Local Government, Planning and Land Act 1980:

(d) where the land is in an area designated as a new town, the development corporation for the new town or the Commission for the New Towns as its successor;

(e) a section 29(3) party;

(f) the council of the parish or community in which the land is situated if that council made representations to the local planning authority in respect of the application in pursuance of a provision of a development order;

(g) where the application was required to be notified to the Commission under paragraph 6 of Schedule 11 (listed building consent in Greater London), the Commission;

(h) any other person who has served a statement of case in accordance with rule 6(4) or who has served an outline statement in accordance with rule 5(6).

(2) Any other person may appear at an inquiry at the discretion of the inspector.

(3) Any person entitled or permitted to appear may do so on his own behalf or be represented by counsel, solicitor or any other person.

(4) An inspector may allow one or more persons to appear for the benefit of some or all of any persons having a similar interest in the matter under inquiry.

Representatives of government departments and other authorities at inquiry

12.—(1) Where:

(a) the Secretary of State, any local authority or the Commission have given a direction such as is described in rule 4(2)(a) or (b); or

(b) the Secretary of State or any other Minister of the Crown or any government department or local authority has expressed a view such as is described in rule 4(2)(c) and the local planning authority have included the terms of the expression of view in a statement served in accordance with rule 5(4) or 6(1); or

(c) another Minister of the Crown or any government department has expressed a view such as is mentioned in rule 4(2)(c) and the Secretary of State has included its terms in a statement served in accordance with rule 5(2) or rule 6(8),

the applicant may, not later than 14 days before the date of an inquiry, apply in writing to the Secretary of State for a representative of the Secretary of State or of the other Minister, department or body concerned to be made available at the inquiry.

(2) Where an application is made in accordance with paragraph (1), the Secretary of State shall make a representative available to attend the inquiry or, as the case may be, transmit the application to the other Minister, department or body concerned, who shall make a representative available to attend the inquiry.

(3) A person attending an inquiry as a representative in pursuance of this rule shall state the reasons for the direction or expression of view in question and shall give evidence and be subject to cross-examination to the same extent as any other witness.

(4) Nothing in paragraph (3) shall require a representative of a Minister or a government department to answer any question which in the opinion of the inspector is directed to the merits of government policy.

Statements of evidence

13.—(1) A person entitled to appear at an inquiry who proposes to give, or call another person to give, evidence at the inquiry by reading a written statement shall send a copy of the statement to the inspector and shall, if so required by the inspector, supply a written summary of that evidence.

(2) The statement shall be sent to the inspector not later than 3 weeks before the date on which the person is due to give evidence in accordance with the time-table arranged persuant to rule 8 or, if there is no such time-table, 3 weeks before the date fixed for the inquiry, and the summary shall be sent within such period as may be specified by the inspector.

(3) Where the applicant or the local planning authority send a copy of a statement of evidence or a summary to an inspector in accordance with paragraph (1) they shall at the same time send a copy to the other party; and where any other party so sends such a copy statement or summary he shall at the same time send a copy to the applicant and the local planning authority.

(4) Where the inspector has required a written summary of evidence in accordance with paragraph (1), the person giving that evidence at the inquiry shall do so only by reading the written summary, unless permitted by the inspector to do otherwise.

(5) Any person required by this rule to send a copy of a statement of evidence to any other person shall send with it a copy of the whole, or the relevant part, of any documents referred to in it, unless copies of the documents or parts of documents in question have already been made available by the local planning authority pursuant to rule 6(9).

Procedure at inquiry

14.—(1) Except as otherwise provided in these Rules, the inspector shall determine the procedure at an inquiry.

(2) Unless in any particular case the inspector with the consent of the applicant otherwise determines, the applicant shall begin and shall have the right of final reply; and the other persons entitled or permitted to appear shall be heard in such order as the inspector may determine.

(3) A person entitled to appear at an inquiry shall be entitled to call evidence and the applicant, the local planning authority and a section 29(3) party shall be entitled to cross-examine persons giving evidence, but, subject to the foregoing and paragraphs (4) and (5), the calling of evidence and the cross-examination of persons giving evidence shall otherwise be at the inspector's discretion.

(4) The inspector may refuse to permit:

    (a) the giving or production of evidence;

    (b) the cross-examination of persons giving evidence; or

    (c) the presentation of any other matter,

which he considers to be irrelevant or repetitious; but where he refuses to permit the giving of oral evidence, the person wishing to give the evidence may submit to him any evidence or other matter in writing before the close of the inquiry.

(5) Where a person gives evidence at an inquiry by reading a summary of his evidence in accordance with rule 13(4), the statement of evidence referred to in rule 13(1) may be tendered in evidence, and the person whose evidence the statement contains shall then be subject to cross-examination on it to the same extent as if it were evidence he had given orally.

(6) The inspector may direct that facilities shall be afforded to any person appearing at an inquiry to take or obtain copies of documentary evidence open to public inspection.

(7) The inspector may require any person appearing or present at an inquiry who, in his opinion, is behaving in a disruptive manner to leave and may refuse to permit that person to return, or may permit him to return only on such conditions as he may specify; but any such person may submit to him any evidence or other matter in writing before the close of the inquiry.

(8) The inspector may allow any person to alter or add to a statement of case served under rule 6 so far as may be necessary for the purposes of the inquiry; but he shall (if necessary by adjourning the inquiry) give every other person entitled to appear who is appearing at the inquiry an adequate opportunity of considering any fresh matter or document.

(9) The inspector may proceed with an inquiry in the absence of any person entitled to appear at it.

(10) The inspector may take into account any written reprsentation or evidence or any other document received by him from any person before an inquiry opens or during the inquiry provided that he discloses it at the inquiry.

(11) The inspector may from time to time adjourn an inquiry and, if the date, time and place of the adjourned inquiry are announced at the inquiry before the adjournment, no further notice shall be required.

Site inspections

15.—(1) The inspector may make an unaccompanied inspection of the land before or during an inquiry without giving notice of his intention to the persons entitled to appear at the inquiry.

(2) The inspector may, during an inquiry or after its close, inspect the land in the company of the applicant, the local planning authority and any section 29(3) party; and he shall make such an inspection if so requested by the applicant or the local planning authority before or during an inquiry.

(3) In all cases where the inspector intends to make an inspection of the kind referred to in paragraph (2) he shall announce during the inquiry the date and time at which he proposes to make it.

(4) The inspector shall not be bound to defer an inspection of the kind referred to in paragraph (2) where any person mentioned in that paragraph is not present at the time appointed.

Procedure after inquiry

16.—(1) After the close of an inquiry, the inspector shall make a report in writing to the Secretary of State which shall include his conclusions and his recommendations or his reasons for not making any recommendations.

(2) Where an assessor has been appointed, he may, after the close of the inquiry, make a report in writing to the inspector in respect of the matters on which he was appointed to advise.

(3) Where an assessor makes a report in accordance with paragraph (2), the inspector shall append it to his own report and shall state in his own report how far he agrees or disagrees with the assessor's report and, where he disagrees with the assessor, his reasons for that disagreement.

(4) If, after the close of an inquiry, the Secretary of State:

(a) differs from the inspector on any matter of fact mentioned in, or appearing to him to be material to, a conclusion reached by the inspector, or

(b) takes into consideration any new evidence or new matter of fact (not being a matter of government policy),

and is for that reason disposed to disagree with a recommendation made by the inspector, he shall not come to a decision which is at variance with that recommendation without first notifying the persons entitled to appear at the inquiry who appeared at it of his disagreement and the reasons for it; and affording to them an opportunity of making written representations to him within 21 days of the date of the notification, or (if the Secretary of State has taken into consideration any new evidence or new matter of fact, not being a matter of government policy) of asking within that period for the re-opening of the inquiry.

(5) The Secretary of State may, as he thinks fit, cause an inquiry to be re-opened to afford an opportunity for persons to be heard on such matters relating to an application or appeal as
he may specify, and he shall do so if asked by the applicant or the local planning authority in the circumstances and within the period mentioned in paragraph (4); and where an inquiry is re-opened (whether by the same or a different inspector)—

(a) the Secretary of State shall send to the persons entitled to appear at the inquiry who appeared at it a written statement of the specified matters; and

(b) paragraphs (3) to (7) of rule 10 shall apply as if the references to an inquiry were references to a re-opened inquiry.

Notification of decision

17.—(1) The Secretary of State shall notify his decision on an application or appeal, and his reasons for it, in writing to all persons entitled to appear at the inquiry who did appear, and to any other person who, having appeared at the inquiry, has asked to be notified of the decision.

(2) Where a copy of the inspector's report is not sent with the notification of the decision, the notification shall be accompanied by a statement of his conclusions and of any recommendations made by him; and if a person entitled to be notified of the decision has not received a copy of that report, he shall be supplied with a copy of it on written application made to the Secretary of State within 4 weeks of the date of the decision.

(3) In this rule "report" includes any assessor's report appended to the inspector's report but does not include any other

documents so appended; but any person who had received a copy of the report may apply to the Secretary of State in writing, within 6 weeks of the date of the Secretary of State's decision, for an opportunity of inspecting any such documents and the Secretary of State shall afford him that opportunity.

Procedure following quashing of decision

18. Where a decision of the Secretary of State on an application or appeal in respect of which an inquiry has been held is quashed in proceedings before any court, the Secretary of State:

(a) shall send to the persons entitled to appear at the inquiry who appeared at it a written statement of the matters with respect to which further representations are invited for the purposes of his further consideration of the application or appeal; and

(b) shall afford to those persons the opportunity of making, within 21 days of the date of the written statement, written representations tohim in rspect of those matters or of asking for the re-opening of the inquiry; and

(c) may, as he thinks fit, cause the inquiry to be reopened (whether by the same or a different inspector) and if he does so paragraphs (3) to (7) of rule 10 shall apply as if the references to an inquiry were references to a re-opened inquiry.

Allowing further time

19. The Secretary of State may at any time in any particular case allow further time for the taking of any step which is required or enabled to be taken by virtue of these Rules, and reference in these Rules to a day by which, or a period within which, any step is required or enabled to be taken shall be construed accordingly.

Service of notices by post

20. Notices or documents required or authorised to be served or sent under any of the provisions of these Rules may be sent by post.

Revocations and savings

21. Subject to rule 22, the Town and Country Planning (Inquiries Procedure) Rules 1974 and rule 2(1) of and Schedule 1 to the Town and Country Planning (Various Inquiries) (Procedure) (Amendment) Rules 1986 are hereby revoked, except that the 1974 Rules shall continue to apply to any local inquiry or hearing held for the purpose of any application or appeal mentioned in rule 2(1)(d) of those Rules (control of advertisements).

Transitional provisions

22.—(1) The following paragraphs of this rule apply where at the date on which these Rules come into force ("the commencement date") an application or appeal mentioned in rule 3(1) of these Rules is awaiting the Secretary of State's determination.

(2) Where at the commencement date a local inquiry has been opened but the inspector has not yet reported, the 1974 Rules shall continue to regulate the procedure

until immediately before he reports, but these Rules shall apply to the making of the report and thereafter.

(3) Where at the commencement date a local inquiry has not been opened the 1974 Rules shall continue to apply until the inquiry is opened, but these Rules shall apply thereafter.

(4) The 1974 Rules shall continue to apply as respects hearings but only if the applicant or the local planning authority have before the commencement date expressed a wish to be heard.

D.2 The Town and Country Planning Appeals (Determination by Inspectors) (Inquiries Procedure) Rules 1988

(S.I. 1988 No. 945)

(Dated May 24, 1988 and made by the Lord Chancellor in exercise of the powers conferred upon him by section 11 of the Tribunals and Inquiries Action 1971, and of all other powers enabling him on that behalf.)

Citation and Commencement

1. These Rules may be cited as the Town and Country Planning Appeals (Determination by Inspectors) (Inquiries Procedure) Rules 1988 and shall come into force on 7th July 1988.

Interpretation

2. In these Rules, unless the context otherwise requires, references to sections and Schedules are references to sections of, and Schedules to, the Town and Country Planning Act 1971 and—

"assessor" means a person appointed by the Secretary of State to site with an Inspector at an inquiry or re-opened inquiry to advise the Inspector on such matters arising as the Secretary of State may specify;

"the Commission" means the Historic Buildings and Monuments Commission for England;

"conservation area consent" means consent required by section 227A(2);

"development order" has the meaning assigned to it by section 24;

"document" includes a photograph, map or plan'

"inquiry" means a local inquiry in relation to which these Rules apply;

"Inspector" means a person appointed by theSecretary of State under Schedule 9 to determine an appeal.

"the land" means the land or building to which an inquiry relate;

"listed building consent" has the meaning assigned to it by section 55(3A);

"local authority" has the meaning assigned to it by section 290(1);

"local planning authority" means the body who were responsible for dealing with the application occasioning the appeal;

"pre-inquiry meeting" means a meeting held before an inquiry to consider what may be done with a view to securing that the inquiry is conducted efficiently and expeditiously;

"relevant date" means the date of the written notice informing the appellant and the local planning authority that an inquiry is to be held, and "relevant notice" means that notice;

"the 1974 Rules" means the Town and Country Planning Appeals (Determination by Appointed Persons) (Inquiries Procedure) Rules 1974:

"section 29(3) party" means—

(a) a person whose representations the Inspector is required by the application of section 29(3) or by regulations under Part I of Schedule 11 to take into account in determining an appeal; and

(b) a person whose representations the local planning authority were required by section 29(3) or those regulations to take into account in determining the application occasioning the appeal;

"statement of case" means a written statement which contains full particulars of the case which a person proposes to put forward at an inquiry and a list of any documents which that person intends to refer to or put in evidence.

Application of Rules

3.—(1) These Rules apply in relation to any local inquiry held in England or Wales by an Inspector before he determines:

(a) an appeal to the Secretary of State in relation to planning permission under section 36 or under section 36 as applied by section 37;

(b) an appeal to the Secretary of State in relation to listed building consent under paragraph 8 of Schedule 11 or under paragraph 8 as applied by paragraph 9 of that Schedule (including an appeal under one or both of those paragraphs as applied by section 56B(2), or in relation to conservation area consent under paragraph 8 or under paragraph 8 as applied by paragraph 9, as those paragraphs are applied by virtue of section 277A, including the application by that section of section 56B(2),

but do not apply in relation to any local inquiry by reason of the application of any provision mentioned in this paragraph by any other enactment.

(2) Where these Rules apply in relation to an appeal which at some time fell to be disposed of in accordance with the Town and Country Planning (Inquiries Procedure) Rules 1988 or Rules superseded by those Rules, any step taken or thing done under those Rules which could have been done under any corresponding provision of these Rules shall have effect as if it had been taken or done under that corresponding provision.

Preliminary information to be supplied by local planning authority

4.—(1) The local planning authority shall, on receipt of a notice informing them that an inquiry is to be held ("the relevant notice") forthwith inform the Secretary of State and the appellant in writing of the name and address of any section 29(3) party who has made representations to them; and the Secretary of State shall as soon as practicable thereafter inform the appellant and the local planning authority of the name and address of any section 29(3) party who has made representations to him.

(2) This paragraph applies where:
    (a) the Secretary of State or any local authority has given to the local planning authority a direction restricting the grant of planning permission for which application was made; or
    (b) in a case relating to listed building consent, the Commission has given a direction to the local planning authority pursuant to paragraph 6(2)(b) of Schedule 11 as to how the application is to be determined; or
    (c) the Secretary of State or any other Minister of the Crown or any government department or local authority has expressed in writing to the local planning authority the view that the application should not be granted either wholly or in part, or should be granted only subject to conditions; or
    (d) any authority or person consulted in pursuance of a development order has made representations to the local planning authority about the application.

(3) Where paragraph (2) applies, the local planning authority shall forthwith after the date of the relevant notice ("the relevant date") inform the person or body concerned of the inquiry and, unless they have already done so, that person or body shall thereupon give the local planning authority a written statement of the reasons for making the direction, expressing the view or making the representations, as the case may be.

Notification of identity of Inspector

5.—(1) The local planning authority shall, not later than 6 weeks after the relevant date, serve a statement of case on the Secretary of State, the appellant and any section 29(3) party.

(2) Where the Secretary of State appoints another inspector instead of the person previously appointed and it is not practicable to notify the new appointment before the inquiry is held, the inspector holding the inquiry shall, at its commencement, announce his name and the fact of his appointment.

Service of statements of case etc.

6.—(1) The local planning authority shall, not later than 6 weeks after the relevant date, serve a statement of case on the Secretary of State, the appellant and any section 29(3) party.

(2) Where rule 4(2) applies, the local planning authority shall:
    (a) include in their statement a case the terms of—
        (i) any direction given together with a statement of the reasons therefore; and

(ii) any views expressed or representation made on which they intend to rely in their submissions at the inquiry; and

(b) within the period mentioned in paragraph (1) supply a copy of their statement to the person or body concerned.

(3) The appellant shall, not later than 9 weeks after the relevant date, serve a statement of case on the Secretary of State, the local planning authority and any section 29(3) party.

(4) The Secretary of State may in writing require any other person who has notified him of an intention or a wish to appear at an inquiry to serve a statement of case, within 4 weeks of being so required, on the appellant, the local planning authority, the Secretary of State and any (or any other) section 29(3) party.

(5) The Secretary of State shall supply any person from whom he requires a statement of case in accordance with paragraph (4) with a copy of the local planning authority's and the appellant's statement of case and shall inform that person of the name and address of every person on whom his statement of case is required to be served.

(6) The Secretary of State may require any person who has served a statement of case in accordance with this rule to provide such further information about the matters contained in the statement as he may specify.

(7) Any person serving a statement of case on the local planning authority shall serve with it a copy of any document, or of the relevant part of any document, referred to in it.

(8) The Secretary of State shall transmit any statement of case served on him in accordance with this rule to the Inspector.

(9) The local planning authority shall afford to any person who so requests a reasonable opportunity to inspect and, where practicable, take copies of any statement or document which, or a copy of which, has been served on them in accordance with any of the preceding paragraphs of this rule, and of any statements so served by them together with a copy of any document, or of the relevant part of any document, referred to in it; and shall specify in the statement served in accordance with paragraph (1) the time and place at which the opportunity will be afforded.

Statements of relevant matters and pre-inquiry meetings

7.—(1) An Inspector may, not later than 12 weeks after the relevant date, cause to be served on the appellant, the local planning authority and any section 29(3) party a written statement of the matters which appear to him to be likely to be relevant to his consideration of the appeal.

(2) An Inspector may hold a pre-inquiry meeting where he considers it desirable and shall arrange for not less than 14 days' written notice of it to be given to the appellant, the local planning authority, any section 29(3) party, any other person known to be entitled to appear at the inquiry and any other person whose presence at the meeting appears to him to be desirable.

(3) The Inspector shall preside at the pre-inquiry meeting and shall determine the matters to be discussed and the procedure to be followed, and he may require any person present at the meeting who, in his opinion, is behaving in a disruptive manner to leave and may refuse to permit that person to return or to attend any further meeting, or may permit him to return or attend only on such conditions as he may specify.

Inquiry time-table

8. An Inspector may at any time arrange a time-table for the proceedings at, or at part of, an inquiry and may at any time vary the time-table.

Notification of appointment of assessor

9. Where the Secretary of State appoints an assessor, he shall notify every person entitled to appear at the inquiry of the name of the assessor and of the matters on which he is to advise the Inspector.

Date and notification of inquiry

10.—(1) The date fixed by the Secretary of State for the holding of an inquiry shall be, unless he considers such a date impracticable, not later than 20 weeks after the relevant date; and where he considers it impracticable to fix a date in accordance with the preceding provisions of this paragraph, the date fixed shall be the earliest date after the end of the period mentioned which he considers to be practicable.

(2) Unless the Secretary of State agrees a lesser period of notice with the appellant and the local planning authority, he shall give not less than 28 days' written notice of the date, time and place for the holding of an inquiry to every person entitled to appear at the inquiry.

(3) The Secretary of State may vary the date fixed for the holding of an inquiry, whether or not the date as varied is within the period of 20 weeks mentioned in paragraph (1); and paragraph (2) shall apply to the variation of a date as it applied to the date originally fixed.

(4) The Secretary of State may also vary the time or place for the holding of an inquiry and shall give such notice of any such variation as appears to h im to be reasonable.

(5) The Secretary of State may require the local planning authority to take one or more of the following steps:

(a) to publish not less than 14 days before the date fixed for the holding of an inquiry in one or more newspapers circulating in the locality in which the land is situated such notice of the inquiry as he may direct;

(b) to serve within such period as he may specify notice of an inquiry in such form and on such persons or classes of persons as he may specify;

(c) to post within such period as he may specify such notice of an inquiry as he may direct in a conspicuous place near to the land.

(6) Where the land is under the control of the appellant he shall, if so required by the Secretary of State, affix firmly to the land or to some object on or near the land, in such manner as to be readily visible to and legible by members of the public, such notice of the inquiry as the Secretary of State may specify; and he shall not remove the notice, or cause or permit it to be removed, for such period before the inquiry as the Secretary of State may specify.

Appearances at inquiry

11.—(1) The persons entitled to appear at an inquiry are:

(a) the appellant;

(b) the local planning authority;

(c) any of the following bodies if the land is situated in their area and they are not the local planning authority—

(i) a county or district council:

(ii) a National Park Committee within the meaning of paragraph 5 of Schedule 17 to the Local Government Act 1972;

(iii) a joint planning board constituted under section 1(2) or a joint planning board or special planning board reconstituted under Part I of Schedule 17 to the Local Government Act 1972;

(iv) an urban development corporation established under section 135 of the Local Government, Planning and Land Act 1980;

(d) where the land is in an area designated as a new town, the development corporation for the new town or the Commission for the New Towns as its successor;

(e) a section 29(3) party;

(f) the council of the parish or community in which the land is situated, if that council made representations to the local planning authority in respect of the application in pursuance of a provision of a development order;

(g) where the application was required to be notified to the Commission under paragraph 6 of Schedule 11 (listed building consent in Greater London), the Commission;

(h) any other person who has served a statement of case in accordance with rule 6(4).

(2) Any other person may appear at an inquiry at the discretion of the Inspector.

(3) Any person entitled or permitted to appear may do so on his own behalf or be represented by counsel, solicitor or any other person.

(4) The Inspector may allow one or more persons to appear for the benefit of some or all of any persons having a similar interest in the matter under inquiry.

Representatives of government departments and other authorities at inquiry

12.—(1) Where:

    (a) the Secretary of State, any local authority or the Commission have given a direction such as is described in rule 4(2)(a) of (b); or

    (b) the Secretary of State or any other Minister of the Crown or any government department or local authority has expressed a view such as is described in rule 4(2)(c) and the local planning authority have included its terms in a statement served in accordance with rule 6(1),

the appellant may, not later than 14 days before the date of an inquiry, apply in writing to the Secretary of State for a representative of the Secretary of State or of the other Minister, department or body concerned to be made available at the inquiry.

(2) Where an application is made in accordance with paragraph (1), the Secretary of State shall make a representative available to attend the inquiry or, as the case may be, transmit the application to the other Minister, department of body concerned who shall make a representative available to attend the inquiry.

(3) A person attending an inquiry as a representative in pursuance of this rule shall state the reasons for the direction or expression of view in question and shall give evidence and be subject to cross-examination to the same extent as any other witness.

(4) Nothing in paragraph (3) shall require a representative of a Minister or a government department to answer any question which in the opinion of the Inspector is directed to the merits of government policy.

Inspector may act in place of Secretary of State

13. An Inspector may in place of the Secretary of State take such steps as the Secretary of State is required or enabled to take under or by virtue of rule 6(4) to (6), rule 10, rule 12(1) or (2) or rule 20.

Statements of evidence

14.—(1) A person entitled to appear at an inquiry who proposes to give, or to call another person to give, evidence at the inquiry by reading a written statement shall send a copy of the statement to the Inspector and shall, if so required by the Inspector, supply a written summary of that evidence.

(2) The statement shall be sent to the Inspector not later than 3 weeks before the date on which the person is due to give evidence in accordance with the time-table arranged pursuant to rule 8 or, if there is no such time-table, 3 weeks before the date fixed for the inquiry, and the summary shall be sent within such period as may be specified by the Inspector.

(3) Where the appellant or the local planning authority send a copy of a statement of evidence or a summary to an Inspector in accordance with paragraph (1) they shall at the same time send a copy to the other party; and where any other party so sends such a copy statement or summary he shall at the same time send a copy to the appellant and the local planning authority.

(4) Where the Inspector has required a written summary of evidence in accordance with paragraph (1), the person giving that evidence at the inquiry shall do so only by reading the written summary, unless permitted by the Inspector to do otherwise.

(5) Any person required by this rule to send a copy of a statement of evidence to any other person shall send with it a copy of the whole, or the relevant part of, any documents referred to in it, unless copies of the documents or parts of documents in question have already been made available by the local planning authority pursuant to rule 6(9).

Procedure at inquiry

15.—(1) Except as otherwise provided in these Rules, the Inspector shall determine the procedure at an inquiry.

(2) Unless in any particular case the Inspector with the consent of the appellant otherwise determines, the appellant shall begin and shall have the right of final reply;

and the other persons entitled or permitted to appear shall be heard in such order as the Inspector may determine.

(3) A person entitled to appear at an inquiry shall be entitled to call evidence and the appellant, the local planning authority and a section 29(3) party shall be entitled to cross-examine persons giving evidence, but, subject to the foregoing and paragraphs (4) and (5), the calling of evidence and the cross-examination of persons giving evidence shall otherwise be at the Inspector's discretion.

(4) The Inspector may refuse to permit:

    (a) the giving or production of evidence,

    (b) the cross-examination of person giving evidence, or

    (c) the presentation of any other matter,

which he considers to be irrelevant or repetitious; but where he refuses to permit the giving of oral evidence, the person wishing to give the evidence may submit to him any evidence or other matter in writing before the close of the inquiry.

(5) Where a person gives evidence at an inquiry by reading a summary of his evidence in accordance with rule 14(4), the statement of evidence referred to in rule 14(1) may be tendered in evidence, and the person whose evidence the statement contains shall then be subject to cross-examination on it to the same extent as if it were evidence he had given orally.

(6) The Inspector may direct that facilities shall be afforded to any person appearing at an inquiry to take or obtain copies of documentary evidence open to public inspection.

(7) The Inspector may require any person appearing or present at an inquiry who, in his opinion, is behaving in a disruptive manner to leave and may refuse to permit that person to return, or may permit him to return only on such condition as he may specify; but any such person may submit to him any evidence or other matter in writing before the close of the inquiry.

(8) The Inspector may allow any person to alter or add to a statement of case served under rule 6 so far as may be necessary for considering any of the matters under inquiry; but he shall (if necessary by adjourning the inquiry) give every other person entitled to appear who is appearing at the inquiry an adequate opportunity of considering any fresh matter or document.

(9) The Inspector may proceed with an inquiry in the absence of any person entitled to appear at it.

(10) The Inspector may take into account any written representation or evidence or any other document received by him from any person before an inquiry opens or during the inquiry provided that he discloses it at the inquiry.

(11) The Inspector may from time to time adjourn an inquiry and, if the date, time and place of the adjourned inquiry are announced before the adjournment, no further notice shall be required.

Site inspections

16.—(1) The Inspector may make an unaccompanied inspection of the land before or during an inquiry without giving notice of his intention to the persons entitled to appear at the inquiry.

(2) The Inspector may, during an inquiry or after its close, inspect the land in the company of the appellant, the local planning authority and any section 29(3) party, and he shall make such an inspection if so requested by the appellant or the local planning authority before or during an inquiry.

(3) In all cases where the Inspector intends to make an inspection of the kind referred to in paragraph (2) he shall announce during the inquiry the date and time at which he proposes to make it.

(4) The Inspector shall not be bound to defer an inspection of the kind referred to in paragraph (2) where any person mentioned in that paragraph is not present at the time appointed.

Procedure after inquiry

17.—(1) Where an assessor has been appointed, he may, after the close of the inquiry, make a report in writing to the Inspector in respect of the matters on which he was appointed to advise, and where he does so the Inspector shall state in his notification of his decision pursuant to rule 18 that such a report was made.

(2) If, after the close of an inquiry, an Inspector proposed to take into consideration any new evidence or any new matter of fact (not being a matter of government policy) which was not raised at the inquiry and which he considers to be material to his decision, he shall not come to a decision without first:

(a) notifying the persons entitled to appear at the inquiry who appeared at it of the matter in question; and

(b) affording to them an opportunity of making written representations to him with respect to it within 21 days of the date of the notification or of asking within that period for the re-opening of the inquiry.

(3) An Inspector may, as he thinks fit, cause an inquiry to be re-opened to afford an opportunity for persons to be heard on such matters relating to an appeal as he may specify, and he shall do so if asked by the appellant or the local planning authority in the circumstances and within the period mentioned in paragraph (2); and where an inquiry is re-opened:

(a) the Inspector shall send to the persons entitled to appear at the inquiry who appeared at it a written statement of the specified matters; and

(b) paragraphs (2) to (6) of rule 10 shall apply as if the references to an inquiry were references to a re-opened inquiry.

Notification of decision

18.—(1) An Inspector shall notify his decision on an appeal, and his reasons for it, in writing to all persons entitled to appear at the inquiry who did appear, and to any other person who, having appeared at the inquiry, has asked to be notified of the decision.

(2) Any person entitled to be notified of the Inspector's decision under paragraph (1) may apply to the Secretary of State in writing, within 6 weeks of the date of the decision, for an opportunity of inspecting any documents listed in the notification and any report made by an assessor and the Secretary of State shall afford him that opportunity.

Procedure following quashing of decision

19. Where a decision of an Inspector on an appeal in respect of which an inquiry has been held is quashed in proceedings before any court, the Secretary of State:

(a) shall send to the persons entitled to appear at the inquiry who appeared at it a written statement of the matters with respect to which further representations are invited for the purposes of the further consideration of the appeal; and

(b) shall afford to those persons the opportunity of making, within 21 days of the date of the written statement, written representations to him in respect of those matters or of asking for the re-opening of the inquiry; and

(c) may, as he thinks fit, direct that the inquiry be re-opened, and if he does so paragraphs (2) to (6) of rule 10 shall apply as if the references to an inquiry were references to a re-opened inquiry.

Allowing further time

20. The Secretary of State may at any tie in any particular case allow further time for the taking of any step which is required or enabled to be taken by virtue of these Rules, and references in these Rules to a day by which, or a period within which, any step is required or enabled to be taken shall be construed accordingly.

Service of notices by post

21. Notices or documents required or authorised to be served or sent under any of the provisions of these rules may be sent by post.

Revocations

22. Subject to rule 23, the Town and Country Planning Appeals (Determination by Appointed Persons) (Inquiries Procedure) Rules 1974 and rule 2(2) of and Schedule 2 to the Town and Country Planning (Various Inquiries) (Procedure) (Amendment) Rules 1986 are hereby revoked.

Transitional provisions

23.—(1) The following paragraphs of this rule apply where at the date on which these Rules come into force ("the commencement date") and appeal mentioned in rule 3(1) of these Rules is awaiting determination by an Inspector.

(2) where at the commencement date a local inquiry has been opened, the 1974 Rules shall continue to apply until its close, but these Rules shall regular the procedure thereafter (including any re-opening of the inquiry).

(3) Where at the commencement date a local inquiry has not been opened, the 1974 Rules shall continue to apply until the inquiry is opened, but these Rules shall apply thereafter.

(4) The 1974 Rules shall continue to apply as respects hearings but only if the appellant or the local planning authority have before the commencement date expressed a wish to be heard.

D.3. Town and Country Planning (Enforcement)
(Inquiries Procedure) Rules 1981

(S.I. 1981 No. 1743)

*(Dated December 3, 1981, made by the Lord Chancellor, in exercise of the powers
conferred on him by section 11 of the Tribunals and Inquiries Act 1971 and by that
section as applied by paragraph 7 of Schedule 9 to the Town and Country Planning Act
1971 and after consultation with the Council on Tribunals.)*

Citation and commencement

1.—(1) These rules may be cited as the Town and Country Planning (Enforcement)
(Inquiries Procedure) Rules 1981.

(2) These Rules shall come into operation on 11th January 1982 but shall not apply to
any appeal brought before that date.

Application of Rules

2.—(1)These Rules apply:

   (*a*) to local inquiries caused by the Secretary of State to be held for the purpose of
   appeals against enforcement notices made to him under section 88 of the
   Town and Country Planning Act 1971;

   (*b*) to local inquiries held by a person appointed by the Secretary of State for the
   purpose of appeals to the Secretary of State under section 88 of the Town and
   Country Planning Act 1971, where such appeals fall to be determined by the
   said person instead of by the Secretary of State by virtue of the powers
   contained in Schedule 9 to the Act and of regulations made thereunder;

   (*c*) to local inquiries caused by the Secretary of State to be held for the purpose of
   appeals against listed building enforcement notices made to him under section
   97 of the Town and Country Planning Act 1971;

   (*d*) to local inquiries held by a person appointed by the Secretary of State under
   Schedule 9 to the Town and Country Planning act 1971 to determine appeals
   under section 97 (listed building enforcement notices) or under that section as
   extended by section 277A (buildings in conservation areas); and

   (*e*) to local inquiries cause by the Secretary of State to be held in connection with
   the determination by him of applications or appeals under section 95 of the
   Town and Country Planning Act 1971 (established use certificates)
      (2) *[Omitted by S.I. 1986 No. 420.]*

Interpretation

3. In these Rules, unless the context otherwise requires—
   "the Act" means the Town and Country Planning Act 1971;
   "appellant" in the case of an application of the kind referred to in rule 2(1)(*d*),
      means the applicant; "appointed person" means—
   (i) in relation to an inquiry caused by the Secretary of State to be held, the
   person appointed by the Secretary of State to hold the inquiry; and
   (ii) in relation to an inquiry held by a person appointed by the Secretary of State
   for the purpose of a transferred appeal, that person;
   *"county planning authority" and "district planning authority" have the meanings
      assigned to them by section 1 of the Act;*
   "enforcement notice" has the meaning assigned to it by section 87(1) of the Act;
   "enterprise zone" and "enterprise zone authority" have the meanings assigned to
      them by Schedule 32 to the Local Government, Planning and Land Act
      1980;

"established use certificate" has the meaning assigned to it by section 94(2) of the Act;

"inquiry" means a local inquiry to which these Rules apply;

"listed building enforcement notice" has the meaning assigned to it by section 96(2) of the Act;

"the land"means the land to which the relevant enforcement notice, the relevant listed building enforcement notice or the application for an established use certificate (as the case may be) relates;

"local authority" has the meaning assigned to it by section 290(1) of the Act;

¹["local planning authority" means the body who issued the relevant enforcement notice or listed building enforcement notice or the body to whom it fell to determine the relevant application for an established use certificate;]

"National Park Committee" has the meaning assigned to it by paragraph 5 of Schedule 17 to the Local Government Act 1972;

"transferred appeal" means an appeal which falls to be determined by a person appointed by the Secretary of State pursuant to the provisions of Schedule 9 to the Act and of regulations made thereunder;

"the relevant enforcement notice" means the enforcement notice which is the subject of the appeal;

"the relevant listed building enforcement notice" means the listed building enforcement notice which is the subject of the appeal;

"urban development area" and "urban development corporation" have the meanings assigned to them by section 134 and section 135 respectively of the Local Government, Planning and Land Act 1980.

Notification of inquiry

4.—(1) A date, time and place for the holding of the inquiry shall be fixed and may be varied by the Secretary of State, who shall give not less than 42 days' notice in writing of such date, time and place to the appellant and to the local planning authority:

Provided that—

(i) with the consent of the appellant and of the local planning authority, the Secretary of State may give such lesser period of notice as shall be agreed with them, and in that event he may specify a date for service of the statements referred to in paragraphs (1), (4) and (5) of rule 6 and of the list of documents referred to in rule 6(2) later than the date therein prescribed;

(ii) where it becomes necessary or advisable to vary the time or place fixed for the inquiry, the Secretary of State shall give such notice of the variation as may appear to him to be reasonable in the circumstances.

(2) Without prejudice to the foregoing provisions of this rule, the Secretary of State may require the local planning authority to take one or more of the following steps:

(a) to publish in one or more newspapers circulating in the locality in which the land is situated such notices of the inquiry as he may direct;

(b) to serve notice of the inquiry in such form and on such persons or classes of persons as he may specify;

(c) to post such notices of the inquiry as he may direct in a conspicuous place or places near to the land;

but the requirements as to the period of notice contained in paragraph (1) of this rule shall not apply to any such notices.

(3) Where the land is under the control of the appellant, he shall, if so required by the Secretary of State, affix firmly to some object on the land, in such a manner as to be readily visible to and legible by the public, such notice of the inquiry as the Secretary of State may specify, and thereafter for such period before the inquiry as the Secretary of State may specify, the appellant shall not remove the notice, or cause or permit it to be removed.

Notification of identity of appointed person

5. In the case of a transferred appeal, the Secretary of State shall give to the appellant and to the local planning authority written notice informing them of the name of the appointed person:

Provided that, where, in exercise of his powers under paragraph 4 of Schedule 9 to the Act, the Secretary of State has appointed another person to determine the appeal in the place of a person previously appointed for that purpose and it is not practicable to give written notice of the new appointment before the inquiry is held, in lieu of the Secretary of State's giving such notice the person holding the inquiry shall, at the commencement thereof, announce his own name and the fact of his appointment.

Service of statements and inspection of documents before inquiry

6.—(1) Where either a government department or a local authority has:

    (a) in the case of an appeal of the kinds referred to in rule 2(1)(a), (b) or (c), expressed in writing—

        (i) a view as to the expediency of issuing an enforcement notice or listed building enforcement notice in respect of the land;

        (ii) an opinion on any of the terms of the relevant enforcement notice, or of the relevant listed building enforcement notice (as the case may be); or

        (iii) a view as to whether planning permission should be granted for the development to which the relevant enforcement notice relates or whether listed building consent should be granted for the works to which the relevant listed building enforcement notice relates (as the case may be); or

    (b) in the case of an application or appeal of the kinds referred to in rule 2(1)(d), expressed in writing the view that an established use certificate should not be granted on the application or that such a certificate should be granted only in respect of part of the land or only in respect of some one or more of the uses specified in the application,

and the local planning authority propose to rely on such expression of view or opinion in their submissions at the inquiry they shall, not later than 28 days before the date of the inquiry (or such later date as the Secretary of State may specify under proviso (1) to paragraph (1) of rule 4), serve on the appellant a statement to that effect, together with a copy of the expression of view or opinion in question.

(2) Where the local planning authority intend to refer to, or put in evidence, at the inquiry documents (including maps and plans), they shall serve on the appellant, not later than 28 days before the date of the inquiry (or such later date as the Secretary of State may specify under proviso (i) to paragraph (1) of rule 4), a list of such documents, together with a notice stating the times and place at which the documents may be inspected by the appellant; and the local planning authority shall afford him a reasonable opportunity to inspect and, where practicable, to take copies of the documents.

(3) The local planning authority shall afford any other person interested a reasonable opportunity to inspect and, where practicable, to take copies of any statement served under paragraph (1) of this rule, any of the documents referred to in paragraph (2) of this rule and any statement served on them under paragraph (5) of this rule.

(4) In the case of an application or appeal of the kinds referred to in rule 2(1)(d), the local planning authority shall, not later than 28 days before the inquiry (or such later date as the Secretary of State may specify under proviso (i) to paragraph (1) of rule 4):

    (a) serve on the appellant a written statement of any submission which the local planning authority propose to put forward at the inquiry; and

    (b) supply a copy of the statement to the Secretary of State;

and the authority shall afford any other person interested a reasonable opportunity to inspect and, where practicable, to take copies of the statement.

(5) In the case of any appeal or application of the kinds referred to in rule 2, the appellant shall, if so required by the Secretary of State, serve on the local planning authority and on the Secretary of State, within such time before the inquiry as the Secretary of State may specify, a written statement of the submissions which he proposes to put forward at the inquiry; and such statement shall be accompanied by a list of any documents (including maps and plans) which the appellant intends to refer to, or put in evidence, at the inquiry, and he shall, if so required by the Secretary of State, afford the local planning authority a reasonable opportunity to inspect and, where practicable, to take copies of such documents.

Appointed person acting in place of Secretary of State

7. Where the appeal is a transferred appeal, the appointed person may himself, in place of the Secretary of State, take such steps as the Secretary of State is required or enabled to take under or by virtue of rule 4, rule 9(2) or rule 10(2).

Appearances at inquiry

8.—(1) The persons entitled to appear at the inquiry are:

(a) the appellant;

(b) the local planning authority;

(c) any person on whom the Secretary of State has required notice to be served under rule 4(2)(b);

(d) a body of any of the following descriptions where the relevant land is in the area in which that body has responsibilities and it is not otherwise entitled to appear—

(i) a county council

(ii) a London borough council,

(iii) a district council,

(iv) a National Park committee,

(v) a joint or special planning board,

(vi) a new town development corporation,

(vii) an urban development corporation,

(viii) an enterprise zone authority;

(e) where the inquiry relates to a listed building enforcement notice concerning a building in Greater London and it is not otherwise entitled to appear, the Historic Buildings and Monuments Commission for England.
In this paragraph "London borough council"includes the Common Council of the City of London and "district council" includes the Council of the Isles of Scilly.

(2) Any other person may appear at the inquiry at the discretion of the appointed person.

(3) A local authority may appear by their clerk or by any other officer appointed for the purpose by the local authority, or by counsel or solicitor; and any other person may appear on his own behalf or be represented by council, solicitor or any other person.

(4)Where there are two or more persons having a similar interest in the matter under inquiry, the appointed person may allow one or more persons to appear for the benefit of some or all persons so interested.

Representatives of government departments at inquiry

9.—(1) Where the local planning authority have served on the appellant a statement of the kind referred to in paragraph (1) of rule 6 which relates to an expression of view or opinion by a government department, the appellant may, not later than 14 days before the date of the inquiry, apply in writing to the Secretary of State for a representative of the government department concerned to be made available at the inquiry.

(2) Where an application is made to the Secretary of State under the last foregoing paragraph he shall:

(a) in the case of a view or opinion expressed by his own department, make a representative of his department available to attend the inquiry; or

(b) in any other case, transmit the application to the other government department concerned, who shall make a representative of that department available to attend the inquiry.

(3) A representative of the Secretary of State's department who, in pursuance of this rule, attends an inquiry shall state the reasons for the view or opinion expressed by his department and shall give evidence and be subject to cross-examination to the same extent as any other witness.

(4) A representative of a government department other than the Secretary of State's department who, in pursuance of this rule, attends an inquiry shall be called as a witness by the local planning authority and shall state the reasons for the view expressed by his department, and shall give evidence and be subject to cross-examination to the same extent as any other witness.

(5) Nothing in either of the last two foregoing paragraphs shall require a representative of a government department to answer any question which in the opinion of the appointed person is directed to the merits of government policy, and the appointed person shall disallow any such question.

Representatives of local authorities at inquiry

10.—(1) Where the local planning authority have served on the appellant a statement of the kind referred to in paragraph (1) of rule 6 which relates to an expression of view or opinion by a local authority, the appellant may, not later than 14 days before the date of the inquiry, apply in writing to the Secretary of State for a representative of the authority concerned to be made available to attend the inquiry.

(2) Where an application is made to the Secretary of State under the last foregoing paragraph he shall transmit the application to the authority concerned, who shall make a representative of the authority available to attend the inquiry.

(3) A representative of a local authority who, in pursuance of this rule, attends an inquiry shall be called as a witness by the local planning authority and shall state the reasons for the view or opinion expressed by the authority and shall give evidence and be subject to cross-examination to the same extent as any other witness.

Procedure at inquiry

11.—(1) Except as otherwise provided in these Rules, the procedure at the inquiry shall be such as the appointed person shall in his discretion determine.

(2) Unless in any particular case the appointed person with the consent of the appellant otherwise determines, the appellant shall begin and shall have the right of final reply; and the other persons entitled or permitted to appear shall be heard in such order as the appointed person may determine.

(3) The appellant and the local planning authority shall be entitled to call evidence and cross-examine persons giving evidence, but any other person appearing at the inquiry may do so only to the extent permitted by the appointed person.

(4) The appointed person shall not require or permit the giving or production of any evidence, whether written or oral, which would be contrary to the public interest; but save as aforesaid and without prejudice to the provisions of rule 9(5) any evidence may be admitted at the discretion of the appointed person, who may direct that documents tendered in evidence may be inspected by any person entitled or permitted to appear at the inquiry and that facilities be afforded him to take or obtain copies thereof.

(5) The appointed person may allow the appellant or the local planning authority:

    (a) to alter or add to the submissions contained in any statement served under rule 6 of these Rules or under any other enactment requiring the serving of a statement before the inquiry;

    (b) to alter or add to any list of documents which accompanied any such statement,

so far as may be necessary for the purpose of determining the questions in controversy between the parties, but shall (if necessary by adjourning the inquiry) give the local planning authority or the appellant, as the case may be, an adequate opportunity of considering any such fresh submission or document; and the appointed person may make a recommendation to the Secretary of State as to the payment of any additional costs occasioned by such adjournment.

(6) If any person entitled to appear at the inquiry fails to do so, the appointed person may proceed with the inquiry at his discretion.

(7) The appointed person shall be entitled (subject to disclosure thereof at the inquiry) to take into account any written representations or statements received by him before the inquiry from any person.

(8) The appointed person may from time to time adjourn the inquiry and, if the date, time and place of the adjourned inquiry are announced before the adjournment, no further notice shall be required.

Site inspections

12.—(1) The appointed person may make an unaccompanied inspection of the land before or during the inquiry without giving notice of his intention to the persons entitled to appear at the inquiry.

(2) The appointed person may, and shall if so requested by the appellant or the local planning authority before or during the inquiry, inspect the land after the close of the inquiry and shall, in all cases where he intends to make such an inspection, announce during the inquiry the date and time at which he proposes to do so.

(3) The appellant and the local planning authority shall be entitled to accompany the appointed person on any inspection after the close of the inquiry; but the appointed person shall not be bound to defer his inspection if any person entitled to accompany is not present at the time appointed.

Report of inquiry

13. Where:

    (*a*) the appeal is not a transferred appeal; or

    (*b*) the appeal is a transferred appeal but the Secretary of State has, under paragraph 3 of Schedule 9 to the Act, directed that the appeal shall be determined by the Secretary of State,

the appointed person shall after the close of the inquiry make a report in writing to the Secretary of State which shall include the appointed person's findings of fact, his conclusions and his recommendations, if any (or his reason for not making any recommendation).

Procedure after inquiry

14.—(1) Where, in a case where a report is made to the Secretary of State by the appointed person in accordance with the requirement in rule 13, the Secretary of State:

    (*a*) differs from the appointed person on a finding of fact; or

    (*b*) after the close of the inquiry takes into consideration any new evidence (including expert opinion on a matter of fact) or any new issue of fact (not being a matter of government policy) which was not raised at the inquiry,

and by reason thereof is disposed to disagree with a recommendation made by the appointed person, he shall not come to a decision which is at variance with any such recommendation without first notifying the appellant and the local planning authority of his disagreement and the reasons for it and affording them an opportunity of making representations in writing within 21 days or (if the Secretary of State has taken into consideration any new evidence or any new issue of fact, not being a matter of government policy) of asking within 21 days for the reopening of the inquiry.

(2) If, in the case of a transferred appeal, the appointed person proposes, after the close of the inquiry, to take into consideration any new evidence (including expert opinion on a matter of fact) or any new issue of fact (not being a matter of government policy) which was not raised at the inquiry and which he considers to be material in his decision, he shall not come to a decision without first notifying the appellant and the local planning authority of the substance of the new evidence or of the new issue of fact and affording them an opportunity of making representations thereon in writing within 21 days or of asking within that time for the reopening of the inquiry.

(3) The Secretary of State or, in the case of a transferred appeal, the appointed person may, in any case if he thinks fit, cause the inquiry to be reopened, and shall cause it to be reopened if asked to do so in accordance with paragraph (1) or paragraph (2) of this rule (as the case may be); and if the inquiry is reopened, paragraphs (1) and (2) of rule 4 shall apply as they applied to the original inquiry, with the following modifications:

    (*a*) for the figure "42" in paragraph (1), there shall be substituted the figure "28";

    (*b*) in the case of a transferred appeal, for references to the Secretary of State, wherever they occur, there shall be substituted references to the appointed person.

Costs

15. Where any person makes application at the inquiry for an award of costs, the appointed person shall report in writing the proceedings on such application to the Secretary of State and draw attention to any considerations which appear to him to be relevant to the Secretary of State's decision and he may include in his report a recommendation on the matter.

Notification of decision

16.—(1) In the case of a transferred appeal, the appointed person shall (unless the Secretary of State has, under paragraph 3 of Schedule 9 to the Act, directed that the appeal shall be determined by the Secretary of State) notify his decision and his reasons therefore in writing to the appellant, to the local planning authority and to any person who, having appeared at the inquiry, has asked to be notified of the decision.

(2) In the case of an appeal which falls to be determined by the Secretary of State, the Secretary of State shall notify his decision, and his reasons therefore, in writing to the apellant, to the local planning authority and to any person who, having appeared at the inquiry, has asked to be notified of the decision.

(3) Where a decision is notified in accordance with paragraph (2) of this rule and a copy of the appointed person's report is not sent with the notification of decision, the notification shall be accompanied by a summary of the appointed person's conclusions and recommendations; and if any person entitled to be notified of the Secretary of State's decision under the said paragraph (2) has not received a copy of the appointed person's report, he shall be supplied with a copy thereof on written application made to the Secretary of State within one month from the date of his decision.

(4) For the purposes of paragraph (3) of this rule "report" does not include documents, photographs or plans appended to the appointed person's report, but any person entitled to be supplied with a copy of the report under that paragraph may apply to the Secretary of State in writing within six weeks of the notification to him of the decision or the supply to him of the report, whichever is the later, for an opportunity of inspecting such documents, photographs and plans and the Secretary of State shall afford him an opportunity accordingly.

(5) In the case of a transferred appeal, any person entitled to be notified of the decision of the appointed person under paragraph (1) of this rule may apply to the Secretary of State in writing within six weeks of the notification to him of the decision for an opportunity of inspecting any documents, photographs or plans listed in the notification and the Secretary of State shall afford him an opportunity accordingly.

Service of notices by post

17. Notices or documents required or authorised to be served or sent under the provisions of any of these Rules may be sent by post.

Application to Greater London

18. In their application to Greater London these Rules shall apply with the following modifications:

    (*a*) in rule 2—
        (i) after the definition of "the Act" there shall be added:—
            " "the Act of 1963" means the London Government Act 1963"; and
        (ii) for the definition of "local planning authority", the following definition shall be substituted:—
            " "local planning authority" means:—
            (*a*) in relation to the appeals referred to in rule 2(1)(*a*), (*b*) and (*c*), the local authority or other body who issued the relevant enforcement notice or listed building enforcement notice; or
            (*b*) in relation to the applications and appeals referred to in rule 2(1)(*d*, the Common Council of the City of London or the council of the London borough in which the land is situated, as the case may be;"

(*b*) for rule 7(1)(*c*) and (*d*) there shall be substituted the following—

"(*c*) the Greater London Council, if not the local planning authority;

  (*d*) the council of the London borough in which the land is situated, if not the local planning authority."

INDEX

References are to paragraph numbers. Lettered 'paragraphs' refer to the Appendices

191

193

196